Heath Mathematics

Walter E. Rucker

Clyde A. Dilley

D. C. Heath and Company
Lexington, Massachusetts   Toronto

About the authors

Walter E. Rucker Former Specialist in Education with the Curriculum Laboratory of the University of Illinois, has taught mathematics in public schools and is a coauthor of successful mathematics programs for elementary and junior high schools.

Clyde A. Dilley Professor, University of Toledo, Toledo, Ohio, is teaching methods courses in elementary and secondary mathematics. He has taught mathematics in public schools and is a coauthor of successful mathematics programs for elementary and junior high schools.

Illustrations Lynn Titleman and Joe Veno/Gwen Goldstein

Photography Jonathan Barkan: 48, 49, 113/Fredrik Bodin: 47, 55, 85, 231, 301/Bicycle Manufacturers Association of America, Inc.: 354, 355/Christian Delbert: 1, 263, 283/F.P.G.: 8, 9/Kevin Galvin: 207/Jonathan Goell: 6, 7, 81, 136, 137, 138, 278/Hallinan, Alpha: 344, 345/Grant Heilman: 21/Jim Holland/Stock, Boston: 78, 79/Julie O'Neil: 51, 72, 92, 100, 101, 110, 111, 174, 175, 181, 200, 201, 276, 313, 314, 317, 348, 349, 360, 361, 362, 363/Rick Rizzotto: 117, 185/Deidra Delano Stead: Cover, 17, 32, 42, 66, 143, 152, 153, 183, 196, 238, 259, 270, 297/Zimmerman, Alpha: 147/Tickets p. 352 courtesy of Globe Ticket Co.

International Standard Book Number: 0-669-03422-3

Contents

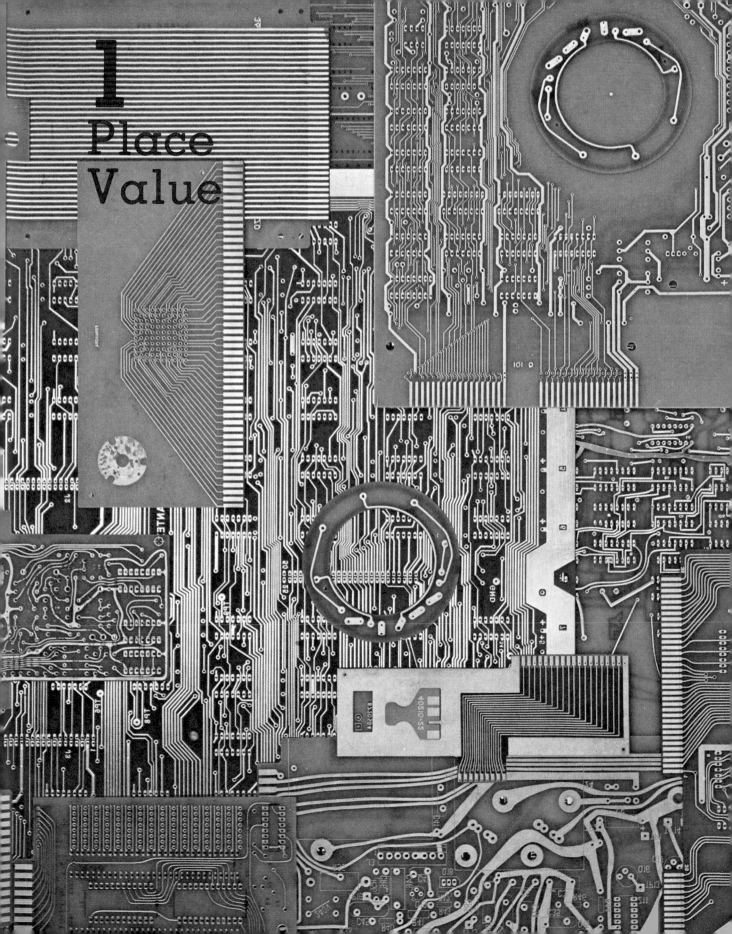

1
Place
Value

Thousands

We use these digits in our place-value system to write numerals.

Below are three ways to write about the number of small blocks.

Thousands	Hundreds	Tens	Ones
1	3	5	8

standard numeral   1358

The 1 stands for 1 thousand, or 1000.

The 3 stands for 3 hundreds, or 300.

The 5 stands for 5 tens, or 50.

The 8 stands for 8 ones, or 8.

words   one thousand three hundred fifty-eight

EXERCISES
How many blocks? Give the standard numeral.

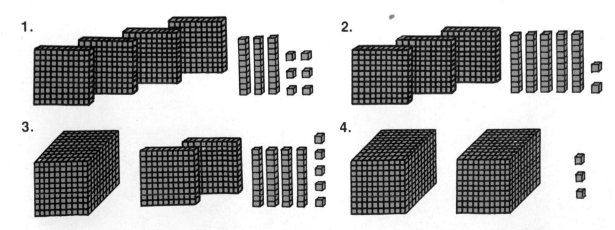

1.

2.

3.

4.

2

What does the red digit stand for?
Give two answers.

5. 8364

3 hundreds
300

6. 3821

7. 7564

8. 5266

9. 4278

10. 9037

11. 7428

12. 3569

13. 4386

14. 5271

Build the standard numeral.

15. 2 in the tens place
8 in the ones place
3 in the thousands place
7 in the hundreds place

16. 5 in the hundreds place
9 in the ones place
0 in the tens place
6 in the thousands place

17. 3 tens
4 thousands
9 hundreds
6 ones

18. 5 hundreds
2 ones
7 thousands
1 ten

Write the standard numeral.

19. four hundred sixty-three

20. nine hundred forty

21. one thousand five hundred

22. three thousand two hundred twelve

23. seven thousand two hundred sixty-one

24. four thousand two hundred ninety

25. eight thousand seventy

26. nine thousand six

We can also write **expanded numerals.**

3475 = 3000 + 400 + 70 + 5

Write as expanded numerals.

27. 586

28. 698

29. 746

30. 839

31. 2816

32. 3574

33. 9281

34. 6453

3

More about thousands

thousands					
Hundreds	Tens	Ones	Hundreds	Tens	Ones
2	8	1	4	3	6

We can use a comma to
separate the thousands.

281,436

- 6 ones, or 6
- 3 tens, or 30
- 4 hundreds, or 400
- 1 thousand, or 1000
- 8 ten thousands, or 80,000
- 2 hundred thousands, or 200,000

Here are two more ways
to write the number.

281 thousand, 436

two hundred eighty-one thousand, four hundred thirty-six

EXERCISES

Which digit is in the   357,168

1. thousands place?

2. ones place?

3. tens place?

4. ten thousands place?

5. hundreds place?

6. hundred thousands place?

4

What does the red digit stand for?
Give two answers.

7. 3**8**2,719

> *8 ten thousands*
> *80,000*

8. **9**1,692

9. 528,3**1**4

10. 2**9**1,754

11. 362,8**4**6

12. 5**5**5,555

13. 44**4**,444

Write the standard numeral.

14. 26 thousand, 219

15. 453 thousand, 506

16. forty-five thousand, two hundred seventy-four

17. two hundred fifty-six thousand, five hundred twenty

18. six hundred thirty thousand, three hundred six

Give the number that is 10,000 less.

19. 38,216

20. 738,172

21. 529,304

22. 521,783

23. 304,216

24. 293,817

Give the number that is 1000 greater.

25. 74,263

26. 382,160

27. 9421

28. 593,741

29. 529,284

30. 199,263

Write each number in expanded form.

42,356 = 40,000 + 2000 + 300 + 50 + 6

31. 38,921

32. 57,496

33. 35,142

34. 238,145

35. 726,574

36. 953,884

Comparing numbers

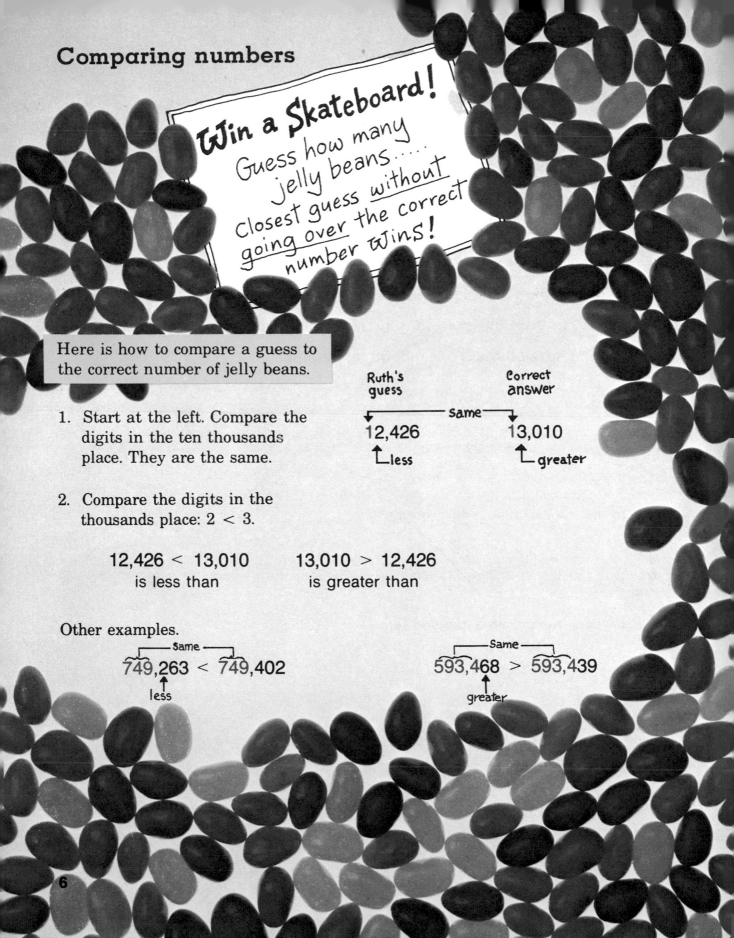

Win a Skateboard!
Guess how many jelly beans.....
Closest guess without going over the correct number wins!

Here is how to compare a guess to the correct number of jelly beans.

1. Start at the left. Compare the digits in the ten thousands place. They are the same.

Ruth's guess — same — Correct answer

12,426 — less   13,010 — greater

2. Compare the digits in the thousands place: 2 < 3.

$$12,426 < 13,010$$
is less than

$$13,010 > 12,426$$
is greater than

Other examples.

— Same —
749,263 < 749,402
less

— Same —
593,468 > 593,439
greater

EXERCISES

Less than (<) or greater than (>)?

1. 532 ◯ 534
2. 682 ◯ 79
3. 742 ◯ 651

4. 6905 ◯ 6991
5. 5934 ◯ 5926
6. 8342 ◯ 8432

7. 783 ◯ 2873
8. 6914 ◯ 6710
9. 3999 ◯ 4000

10. 56,984 ◯ 6884
11. 34,291 ◯ 35,384
12. 72,916 ◯ 75,388

13. 26,593 ◯ 26,504
14. 391,782 ◯ 390,700

15. 458,371 ◯ 453,871
16. 100,000 ◯ 99,999

River	Length in Kilometers
Arkansas	2333
Mississippi	3778
Missouri	3725
Ohio	1578
Red	1855
Rio Grande	3033
Snake	1670

17. Which river is longest?

18. Which river is shortest?

19. Which river is the second longest?

20. How many of the rivers are longer than 2500 kilometers?

21. How many of the rivers are longer than the Rio Grande?

22. How many of the rivers are shorter than 3000 kilometers?

7

The *exact* seating capacity of the Colorado Stadium is

50,126.

This number, **rounded to the nearest thousand**, is

50,000.

Here are more examples.

1. 67,634 rounded to the nearest thousand is 68,000.

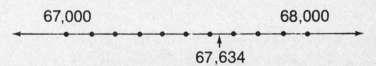

2. 8435 rounded to the nearest hundred is 8400.

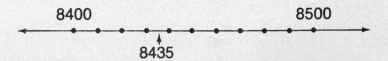

3. 950 is exactly halfway between 900 and 1000. We round up to 1000.

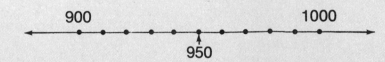

College Football Stadium	Seating Capacity
Auburn	62,291
Colorado	50,126
Georgia Tech	59,245
Louisiana State	67,510
Michigan	101,001
Notre Dame	59,075
Ohio State	81,455
Oregon	41,097
Pennsylvania	60,546
Tulane	80,985

EXERCISES

1. Which stadium has the greatest seating capacity?

2. Which has the least?

3. How many stadiums can hold more than 75,000?

4. Round the seating capacity of each stadium to the nearest thousand.

5. What is the capacity of the Ohio State Stadium, rounded to the nearest ten thousand?

6. What is the capacity of the Michigan Stadium, rounded to the nearest ten thousand?

Round each of these numbers to the nearest hundred.

7. 743   8. 695   9. 850   10. 4763   11. 45

Round each of these numbers to the nearest ten.

12. 52   13. 87   14. 45   15. 9672   16. 803

Millions

A million is 1000 thousands.

On your tenth birthday you have lived about this many seconds.

millions			thousands					
Hundreds	Tens	Ones	Hundreds	Tens	Ones	Hundreds	Tens	Ones
3	1	5	5	3	2	8	0	0

We start at the right and use commas to set off groups of three digits, called periods. The commas separate the thousands and millions.

315,532,800

315 million, 532 thousand, 800

three hundred fifteen million, five hundred thirty-two thousand, eight hundred

EXERCISES
Read aloud.

1. 8,234,512

2. 5,067,825

3. 7,208,310

4. 52,259,186

5. 73,429,381

6. 60,716,429

7. 293,160,824

8. 301,298,634

9. 597,005,320

10. 400,290,067

11. 502,820,006

12. 840,312,968

10

Give the digit that is in the   463,572,100

13. tens place.

14. hundred thousands place.

15. hundreds place.

16. ten millions place.

17. thousands place.

18. ten thousands place.

19. millions place.

20. hundred millions place.

Write the standard numeral.

21. eight million, two hundred forty-five thousand, nine hundred five

22. sixty-two million, seven hundred forty-three thousand, two hundred eighty-four

23. one hundred eighty-one million, five hundred eleven thousand, two hundred

24. six hundred nineteen million, three hundred sixty-two thousand, twenty-five

Use the table below to answer the questions.

25. Which ocean has the greatest area?

26. Which is the third largest?

27. How many bodies of water have an area that is greater than 20,000,000 square kilometers?

28. Which have an average depth greater than 2 kilometers (2000 meters)?

Name	Area (square kilometers)	Average Depth (meters)
Arctic Ocean	14,090,100	1205
Atlantic Ocean	82,400,900	3926
Bering Sea	2,291,900	1547
Caribbean Sea	1,942,500	2647
Gulf of Mexico	1,592,900	1486
Indian Ocean	65,527,000	3963
Mediterranean Sea	2,965,800	1429
Sea of Okhotsk	1,589,700	838
Pacific Ocean	165,760,000	4027
South China Sea	2,319,100	1652

11

Billions

Would you believe...

The United States is less than 7 billion seconds old!

A billion is 1000 million.
A billion is a *very* large number.

billions			millions			thousands					
H	T	O	H	T	O	H	T	O	H	T	O
3	8	2	5	1	6	3	0	5	4	1	7

382,516,305,417

382 billion, 516 million, 305 thousand, 417

Three hundred eighty-two billion, five hundred
sixteen million,
three hundred five thousand, four hundred seventeen

EXERCISES
Read aloud.

1. 6,382,534
2. 29,782,568
3. 583,297,156
4. 9,348,291,765
5. 8,429,635,218
6. 6,382,491,708
7. 25,296,481,107
8. 98,364,273,081
9. 63,829,543,000
10. 237,642,812,438
11. 400,360,298,000
12. 370,400,000,000
13. 863,000,000,000
14. 890,000,000,000
15. 604,003,200,010
16. 502,060,300,020
17. 700,040,000,330
18. 200,002,020,200

12

Tell which digit is in the   538,264,527,019

19. millions place.   20. billions place.

21. thousands place.   22. ten millions place.

23. hundred billions place.   24. hundred thousands place.

25. hundred millions place.   26. ten billions place.

Write the standard numeral.

27. 325 billion, 426 million, 843

28. 247 billion

29. 86 billion, 926 million

30. sixty-seven billion, three hundred million,
    one thousand, seventy-five

31. two hundred billion, five hundred twelve
    million, forty-two thousand, fifty-eight

Round to the nearest million.

32. 8,319,406   33. 34,952,164   34. 258,500,000

Round to the nearest billion.

35. 7,861,752,000   36. 59,261,493,280   37. 356,281,743,500

What is the greatest number that you can build with these digits?

38.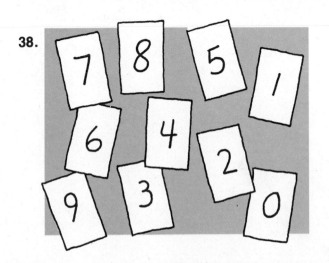

39.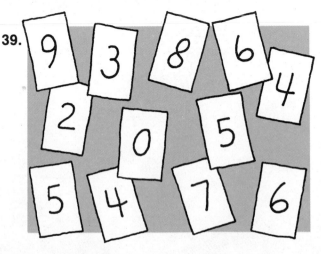

Roman numerals

The Romans of long ago used letters to write numerals.

Here are the symbols they used for the numbers 1 through 10.

1	2	3	4	5	6	7	8	9	10
I	II	III	IV	V	VI	VII	VIII	IX	X

The Romans did not use a place-value system. They wrote the symbols side by side and usually added the values.

III = 3   VII = 7

XV = 15   XVIII = 18

XXV = 25   XXVI = 26

The Romans had a special rule.

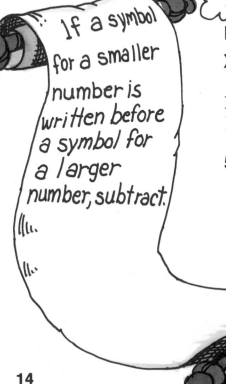

If a symbol for a smaller number is written before a symbol for a larger number, subtract.

IV = 4   IX = 9

XIV = 14   XXIX = 29

Here are some more symbols that were used by the Romans.

50	100	500	1000
L	C	D	M

XL = 40

XC = 90

DCXIV = 614

MCD = 1400

EXERCISES

Write standard numerals.

1. III	2. V	3. VII	4. IX	5. XVI
6. XXXV	7. XXIII	8. XL	9. LX	10. XLV
11. LXVII	12. XC	13. CX	14. CLXV	15. CCL
16. DC	17. CD	18. DCL	19. CDLXXV	20. DCXLI

Write Roman numerals.

21. 9	22. 14	23. 16	24. 45	25. 58
26. 73	27. 91	28. 140	29. 282	30. 356
31. 400	32. 468	33. 527	34. 802	35. 920

Write the dates of these famous inventions in standard numerals.

36. Magnetic Compass

MC

37. Adding Machine

MDCXLII

38. Gasoline Automobile

MDCCCLXXXV

39. Safety Match

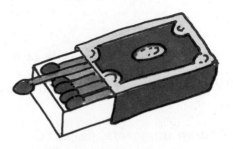

MDCCXLIV

What does the red digit stand for?
Give two answers. [pages 2–5]

1. 853**9**

2. 71,6**4**2

3. 46,9**8**3

4. 2**7**3,416

5. **8**03,251

6. 6**6**9,382

< or >? [pages 6, 7]

7. 382 ⬤ 392

8. 425 ⬤ 415

9. 8964 ⬤ 900

10. 58,132 ⬤ 59,423

11. 7803 ⬤ 7964

12. 637,812 ⬤ 637,714

Round. [pages 8, 9]

13. 3756 to the nearest ten

14. 28,165 to the nearest thousand

15. 494,250 to the nearest hundred thousand

16. 665,000 to the nearest ten thousand

[pages 10, 11]
In 463,198,027, which digit is in the

17. millions place?

18. ten thousands place?

19. thousands place?

20. ten millions place?

21. hundred thousands place?

22. hundred millions place?

Write as standard numerals. [pages 14, 15]

23. XXXIV

24. LXXXVII

25. MDC

26. MCDXCII

Write as Roman numerals. [pages 14, 15]

27. 42

28. 96

29. 354

30. 1776

16

Project

841
814
481
418
184
14

1. Make these digit cards:

   3 4 2 5

2. How many 2-digit numbers can you build with these digits?

   4 2

3. How many 2-digit numbers can you build with these digits?

   5 4 2

4. How many 3-digit numbers can be built with these digits?

   5 4 2

5. How many 4-digit numbers can be built with these digits?

   3 5 2 4

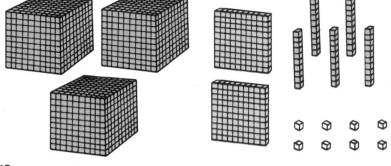

3258

1. The 3 stands for 3 _?_.

2. The 2 stands for 2 _?_.

3. The 5 stands for 5 _?_.

4. The 8 stands for 8 _?_.

5. There are _?_ small blocks.

6. The number of small blocks (in words) is three thousand two hundred _?_.

Round.

7. 3284 to the nearest thousand

8. 3284 to the nearest ten

Less than (<) or greater than (>)?

9. 3258 3285

10. 6001 5968

Millions			Thousands					
Hundreds	Tens	Ones	Hundreds	Tens	Ones	Hundreds	Tens	Ones
7	1	8	3	4	6	2	0	5

Which digit is in the

11. ten thousands place?

12. ten millions place?

13. hundred thousands place?

14. hundred millions place?

More than 5000 years ago, the Egyptians developed a system for writing about numbers.

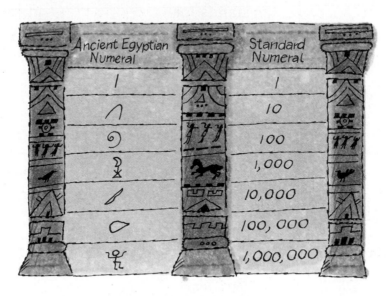

The Egyptians simply combined the symbols and added their values. Since they did not have a place-value system, they could write the symbols in any order.

18 = ⌒ |||| / |||| 123 = ⌒⌒⌒ / ||| 4362 = ...

Write, using Egyptian numerals.

1. 6   2. 34   3. 201   4. 524

5. 1241   6. 24,352   7. 242,100   8. 1,240,000

Give standard numerals.

9.   10.   11.   12.

MAJOR CHECKUP
Standardized Format

Choose the correct letter.

---

1. In 9634 the 9 stands for

    a. 9 tens
    b. 9 thousands
    c. 9 hundreds
    d. none of these

2. In 8216 the 2 stands for

    a. 20
    b. 2000
    c. 200
    d. none of these

3. In 374,927 the digit in the ten thousands place is

    a. 2
    b. 7
    c. 4
    d. none of these

---

4. The number 100,000 greater than 638,125 is

    a. 639,125
    b. 638,225
    c. 637,125
    d. none of these

5. Which number is less than 82,156?

    a. 735,216
    b. 83,000
    c. 82,099
    d. none of these

6. Which number is greatest?

    a. 567,834
    b. 576,834
    c. 574,834
    d. 577,834

---

7. 38,265 rounded to the nearest thousand is

    a. 40,000
    b. 38,000
    c. 39,000
    d. none of these

8. 362,489 rounded to the nearest 100,000 is

    a. 362,000
    b. 400,000
    c. 360,000
    d. none of these

9. 255,000 rounded to the nearest ten thousand is

    a. 260,000
    b. 250,000
    c. 255,000
    d. none of these

---

10. In 38,649,254 the 8 is in the

a. thousands place
b. hundred thousands place
c. millions place
d. none of these

11. The number 10 million greater than 694,831,725 is

    a. 695,831,725
    b. 684,831,725
    c. 704,831,725
    d. none of these

12. The Roman numeral for 46 is

    a. XLVI
    b. LXVI
    c. XLIV
    d. none of these

2
Addition
and
Subtraction

Basic addition facts

When I first learned to add, I had to count to get sums.

$$3 + 5 = 8$$

addends   sum

Now addition is easier. I have memorized the basic facts. These two properties help me to remember the basic facts.

The Order Property
Changing the order of the addends does not change the sum.

$$4 + 3 = 3 + 4$$

The Adding 0 Property
The sum of any number and 0 is that same number.

$$7 + 0 = 7$$

EXERCISES

Give each sum.

1. If $9 + 2 = 11$, then $2 + 9 = \underline{?}$.

2. If $8 + 5 = 13$, then $5 + 8 = \underline{?}$.

3. If $7 + 5 = 12$, then $5 + 7 = \underline{?}$.

4. If $9 + 6 = 15$, then $6 + 9 = \underline{?}$.

5. If $8 + 4 = 12$, then $4 + 8 = \underline{?}$.

6. If $9 + 7 = 16$, then $7 + 9 = \underline{?}$.

7. $5 + 3 = \underline{?}$ and $3 + 5 = \underline{?}$.

8. $7 + 3 = \underline{?}$ and $3 + 7 = \underline{?}$.

9. $6 + 4 = \underline{?}$ and $4 + 6 = \underline{?}$.

10. $6 + 0 = \underline{?}$ **11.** $7 + 0 = \underline{?}$ **12.** $5 + 0 = \underline{?}$ **13.** $0 + 0 = \underline{?}$

14. $9 + 0 = \underline{?}$ **15.** $4 + 0 = \underline{?}$ **16.** $8 + 0 = \underline{?}$ **17.** $27 + 0 = \underline{?}$

Study the shortcut. Then use the shortcut to find each sum.

18. If $5 + 5 = 10$, then $5 + 6 = \underline{?}$.

19. If $6 + 6 = 12$, then $6 + 7 = \underline{?}$.

20. If $9 + 9 = 18$, then $9 + 8 = \underline{?}$.

21. If $7 + 7 = 14$, then $7 + 6 = \underline{?}$.

22. If $8 + 8 = 16$, then $8 + 7 = \underline{?}$.

23. If $8 + 2 = 10$, then $8 + 3 = \underline{?}$.

24. If $8 + 2 = 10$, then $8 + 4 = \underline{?}$.

25. If $8 + 2 = 10$, then $8 + 5 = \underline{?}$.

26. If $7 + 3 = 10$, then $7 + 4 = \underline{?}$.

27. If $7 + 3 = 10$, then $7 + 6 = \underline{?}$.

28. If $5 + 5 = 10$, then $5 + 7 = \underline{?}$.

Find the missing addends.

29. $8 + \underline{?} = 10$ **30.** $8 + \underline{?} = 11$ **31.** $8 + \underline{?} = 12$

32. $7 + \underline{?} = 10$ **33.** $7 + \underline{?} = 12$ **34.** $7 + \underline{?} = 13$

35. $9 + \underline{?} = 10$ **36.** $9 + \underline{?} = 11$ **37.** $9 + \underline{?} = 14$

38. $9 + \underline{?} = 15$ **39.** $9 + \underline{?} = 16$ **40.** $9 + \underline{?} = 17$

Basic addition facts

All the basic addition facts are listed below.
See how quickly you can list the sums.

1. 0 +3	2. 1 +0	3. 2 +5	4. 0 +8	5. 1 +5	6. 2 +8	7. 0 +2	8. 7 +5
9. 2 +1	10. 9 +2	11. 6 +3	12. 1 +7	13. 2 +4	14. 3 +8	15. 5 +8	16. 2 +6
17. 4 +8	18. 5 +4	19. 8 +2	20. 1 +4	21. 0 +0	22. 3 +4	23. 8 +7	24. 3 +7
25. 3 +2	26. 1 +8	27. 1 +6	28. 1 +9	29. 0 +4	30. 8 +6	31. 2 +9	32. 2 +3
33. 5 +7	34. 2 +7	35. 1 +2	36. 8 +4	37. 7 +9	38. 0 +5	39. 4 +5	40. 7 +4
41. 4 +0	42. 4 +3	43. 1 +3	44. 2 +0	45. 7 +8	46. 3 +3	47. 1 +1	48. 6 +2
49. 3 +0	50. 6 +0	51. 5 +3	52. 8 +5	53. 9 +7	54. 4 +7	55. 7 +1	56. 8 +3
57. 3 +6	58. 9 +8	59. 7 +3	60. 4 +9	61. 9 +1	62. 0 +9	63. 3 +9	64. 7 +2
65. 0 +7	66. 4 +6	67. 9 +6	68. 2 +2	69. 9 +0	70. 9 +5	71. 0 +1	72. 7 +7
73. 5 +2	74. 9 +9	75. 4 +2	76. 3 +5	77. 6 +6	78. 6 +7	79. 6 +8	80. 5 +6
81. 0 +6	82. 4 +1	83. 4 +4	84. 3 +1	85. 6 +5	86. 6 +4	87. 7 +0	88. 9 +3
89. 5 +0	90. 8 +0	91. 5 +9	92. 6 +1	93. 8 +8	94. 5 +5	95. 7 +6	96. 5 +1
		97. 6 +9	98. 8 +1	99. 8 +9	100. 9 +4		

Check your answers.

1. 3	**2.** 1	**3.** 7	**4.** 8	**5.** 6	**6.** 10	**7.** 2	**8.** 12
9. 3	**10.** 11	**11.** 9	**12.** 8	**13.** 6	**14.** 11	**15.** 13	**16.** 8
17. 12	**18.** 9	**19.** 10	**20.** 5	**21.** 0	**22.** 7	**23.** 15	**24.** 10
25. 5	**26.** 9	**27.** 7	**28.** 10	**29.** 4	**30.** 14	**31.** 11	**32.** 5
33. 12	**34.** 9	**35.** 3	**36.** 12	**37.** 16	**38.** 5	**39.** 9	**40.** 11
41. 4	**42.** 7	**43.** 4	**44.** 2	**45.** 15	**46.** 6	**47.** 2	**48.** 8
49. 3	**50.** 6	**51.** 8	**52.** 13	**53.** 16	**54.** 11	**55.** 8	**56.** 11
57. 9	**58.** 17	**59.** 10	**60.** 13	**61.** 10	**62.** 9	**63.** 12	**64.** 9
65. 7	**66.** 10	**67.** 15	**68.** 4	**69.** 9	**70.** 14	**71.** 1	**72.** 14
73. 7	**74.** 18	**75.** 6	**76.** 8	**77.** 12	**78.** 13	**79.** 14	**80.** 11
81. 6	**82.** 5	**83.** 8	**84.** 4	**85.** 11	**86.** 10	**87.** 7	**88.** 12
89. 5	**90.** 8	**91.** 14	**92.** 7	**93.** 16	**94.** 10	**95.** 13	**96.** 6
		97. 15	**98.** 9	**99.** 17	**100.** 13		

101. Your score is the number correct. What is your score?

102. Practice the facts that you missed. See if you can get a better (higher) score.

103. See how fast you can give the sums orally. Have a classmate keep a tally of your mistakes.

104. Make a graph as shown here.

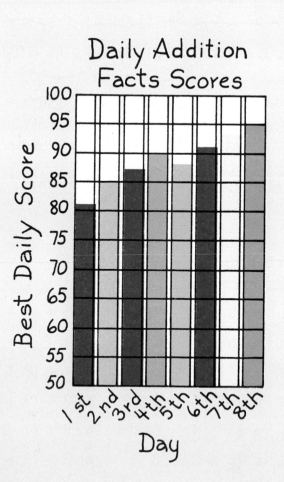

25

More than two addends

The Grouping Property

Changing the grouping of the addends does not change the sum.

$$(3 + 2) + 5 = 3 + (2 + 5)$$

Remember to work inside the grouping symbols first.

Since you can change the order and the grouping of the addends without changing the sum—

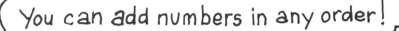

You can **add** numbers in any order!

Add these numbers in different orders.

Did you always get the same sum?

EXERCISES
Give each sum.

1. **a.** (3 + 5) + 4   **b.** 3 + (5 + 4)

2. **a.** (5 + 1) + 6   **b.** 5 + (1 + 6)

3. **a.** (4 + 2) + 6   **b.** 4 + (2 + 6)

4. **a.** (3 + 3) + 5   **b.** 3 + (3 + 5)

5. **a.** (3 + 4) + 5   **b.** 3 + (4 + 5)

6. **a.** (6 + 2) + 3   **b.** 6 + (2 + 3)

Add. Remember that you can add in any order. So, look for a sum of 10.

7. 3
    4
    +7

8. 2
    6
    +8

9. 4
    6
    +5

10. 8
    5
    +5

11. 3
    7
    +7

12. 6
    6
    +4

13. 5
    5
    +4

14. 6
    8
    +4

15. 9
    7
    +1

16. 2
    6
    +8

17. 7
    4
    +6

18. 8
    3
    +7

19. 2
    8
    +7

20. 3
    4
    +7

21. 6
    5
    +4

22. 3
    9
    +1

23. 4
    6
    +3

24. 5
    1
    +9

25. 3
    9
    2
    +1

26. 2
    4
    3
    +8

27. 3
    4
    7
    +2

28. 1
    7
    2
    +8

29. 3
    6
    2
    +7

30. 8
    6
    1
    +2

31. 5
    8
    1
    9
    +5

32. 1
    4
    2
    8
    +6

33. 3
    7
    6
    4
    +4

34. 9
    3
    1
    8
    +2

35. 6
    3
    5
    4
    +7

36. 8
    1
    4
    2
    +7

Give each missing addend.

37. $5 + \underline{3} = 8$

38. $6 + \underline{?} = 10$

39. $4 + \underline{?} = 9$

40. $3 + \underline{?} = 6$

41. $5 + \underline{?} = 5$

42. $7 + \underline{?} = 8$

43. $6 + \underline{?} = 14$

44. $9 + \underline{?} = 15$

45. $8 + \underline{?} = 16$

46. $\underline{?} + 9 = 17$

47. $\underline{?} + 6 = 11$

48. $\underline{?} + 8 = 12$

49. $\underline{?} + 4 = 13$

50. $\underline{?} + 8 = 13$

51. $\underline{?} + 7 = 15$

52. $\underline{?} + 9 = 18$

53. $\underline{?} + 8 = 16$

54. $\underline{?} + 6 = 15$

Adding 2-digit numbers

You can find the total number of blocks by adding
in columns.

Step 1. Add in ones column.

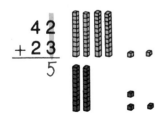

```
  4 2
+ 2 3
    5
```

Step 2. Add in tens column.

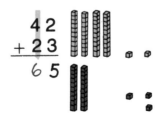

```
  4 2
+ 2 3
  6 5
```

In this example, 10 ones are regrouped for 1 ten.

Step 1. Add ones. **Step 2.** Regroup. **Step 3.** Add tens.

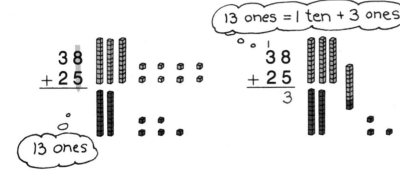

13 ones = 1 ten + 3 ones

```
  3 8          3 8          3 8
+ 2 5        + 2 5        + 2 5
                 3          6 3
```

13 ones

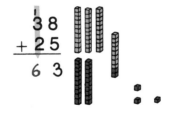

EXERCISES
Add.

1. 24
    +12

2. 43
    +22

3. 40
    +30

4. 50
    +35

5. 53
    +43

6. 30
    +19

7. 32
    +32

8. 54
    +13

9. 25
    +24

10. 51
    +35

11. 41
    +53

12. 44
    +52

13. 42
    +23

14. 23
    +42

15. 31
    +16

16. 52
    +15

17. 26
    +61

18. 45
    +43

| 19. 58 +27 | 20. 39 +25 | 21. 52 +38 | 22. 27 +67 | 23. 39 +38 | 24. 49 +23 |

19. 58
+27

20. 39
+25

21. 52
+38

22. 27
+67

23. 39
+38

24. 49
+23

25. 38
+ 7

26. 56
+38

27. 49
+36

28. 72
+18

29. 35
+55

30. 27
+19

31. 43
+87

32. 58
+46

33. 19
+36

34. 43
+ 8

35. 53
+28

36. 28
+53

37. 56
+48

38. 43
+88

39. 72
+ 9

40. 56
+88

41. 55
+89

42. 75
+49

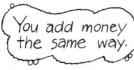

You add money the same way.

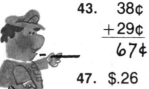

43. 38¢
+29¢
67¢

44. 15¢
+29¢

45. 36¢
+27¢

46. 53¢
+38¢

47. $.26
+ .87
$1.13

48. $.46
+ .29

49. $.36
+ .98

50. $.48
+ .76

Solve.

51.

What is the total price?

52.

What is the total price?

53. Sarah bought two orders of french fries for 47¢ each. How much did she spend?

54. Jon had 92¢. He wanted to buy a 45¢ milk shake and a 49¢ hamburger. Did he have enough money?

Keeping Skills Sharp

Round to the nearest hundred.

1. 168
2. 541
3. 723
4. 1252
5. 1963

Round to the nearest thousand.

6. 3410
7. 2678
8. 5500
9. 78,360
10. 92,500

Adding 3-digit numbers

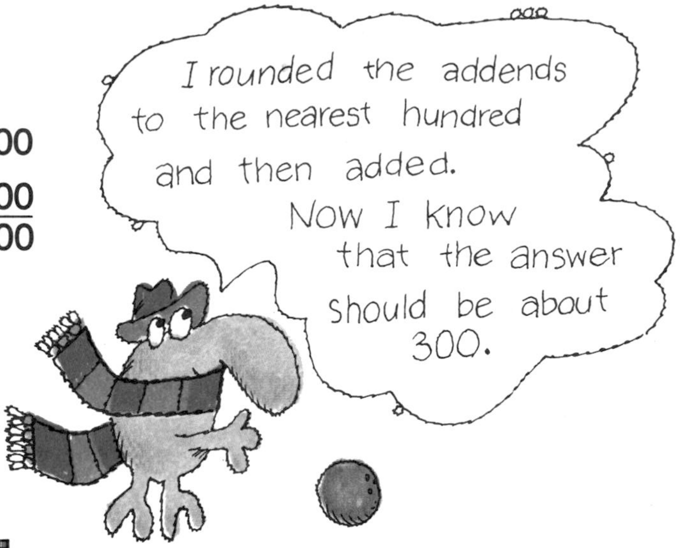

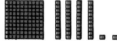

I rounded the addends to the nearest hundred and then added.
Now I know that the answer should be about 300.

EXAMPLE.

142	rounds to	100
+ 163	rounds to	+ 200
		300

Step 1. Add ones.

$$\begin{array}{r} 142 \\ +\,163 \\ \hline 5 \end{array}$$

Step 2. Add tens.

$$\begin{array}{r} 142 \\ +\,163 \\ \hline 5 \end{array}$$

10 tens

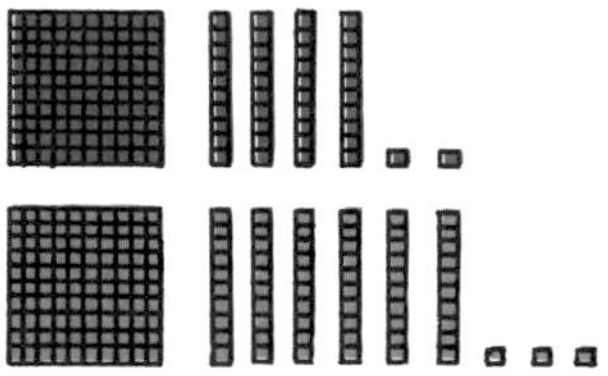

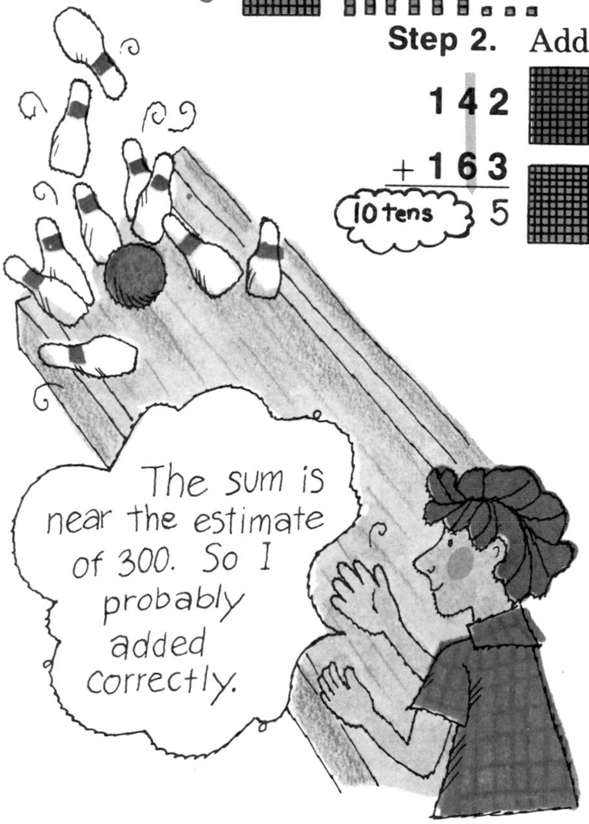

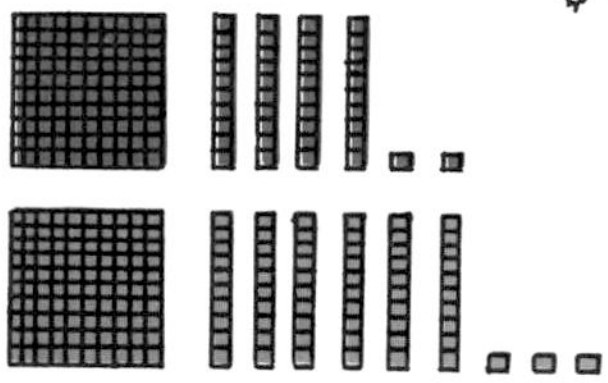

The sum is near the estimate of 300. So I probably added correctly.

Step 3. Regroup.

$$\begin{array}{r} {\scriptstyle 1} \\ 142 \\ +\,163 \\ \hline 05 \end{array}$$

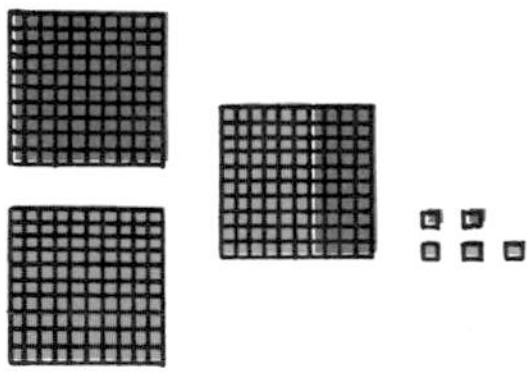

Step 4. Add hundreds.

$$\begin{array}{r} {\scriptstyle 1} \\ 142 \\ +\,163 \\ \hline 305 \end{array}$$

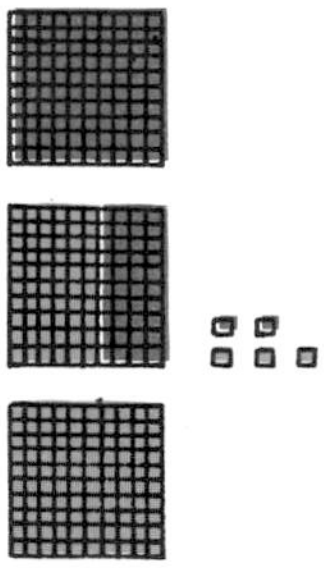

In this example, we regroup twice. First estimate the sum and then study the steps.

Step 1. Add ones and regroup.

$$\begin{array}{r} {\scriptstyle 1} \\ 298 \\ +\,174 \\ \hline 2 \end{array}$$

Step 2. Add tens and regroup.

$$\begin{array}{r} {\scriptstyle 1\,1} \\ 298 \\ +\,174 \\ \hline 72 \end{array}$$

Step 3. Add hundreds.

$$\begin{array}{r} {\scriptstyle 1\,1} \\ 298 \\ +\,174 \\ \hline 472 \end{array}$$

EXERCISES

First estimate the sum. Then add.

1. 242
    +173

2. 439
    +270

3. 272
    + 81

4. 521
    +390

5. 143
    +681

6. 359
    +476

7. 566
    +389

8. 475
    +365

9. 394
    + 78

10. 293
    +529

11. 653
    + 12

12. 553
    +486

13. 443
    +258

14. 345
    +482

15. 521
    +278

16. 976
    +847

17. 627
    +848

18. 902
    +641

19. 578
    +645

20. 438
    +717

21. 845
    +974

22. 478
    +396

23. 846
    +795

24. 296
    +385

25. 574
    + 86

26. $3.58
    +2.74
    $ 6.32

27. $7.56
    +2.43

28. $6.75
    +2.83

29. $8.39
    +3.95

30. $2.95
    +2.95

31. $4.98
    +2.76

32. $7.85
    +5.29

33. $5.29
    + .85

You add money the same way.

BOWLING SCORES

Name	Game 1	Game 2	Game 3
Bill	114	98	117
Joan	125	101	95
Lou	100	106	115
Susan	114	96	118

Solve.

34. What was Bill's total score for his first two games?

35. What was Bill's total for all three games?

36. What was Joan's total score?

37. Who had the greater total, Lou or Susan?

Give the missing digits.

38. 526
    +38▨
    ▨9▨1

39. 4▨6
    +39▨
    823

★40. ▨5▨
    +3▨7
    ▨055

31

Adding larger numbers

You add larger numbers the same way you add smaller numbers.

REMEMBER! When a sum is 10 or greater, regroup!

Step 1. Add ones and regroup.

```
    ¹
  758 4
+ 290 8
      2
```

Step 2. Add tens.

```
    ¹
  75 8 4
+ 29 0 8
     9 2
```

Step 3. Add hundreds and regroup.

```
  ¹
  7 5 84
+ 2 9 08
    4 92
```

Step 4. Add thousands.

```
  ¹
  7 584
+ 2 908
 10,492
```

Other examples.

```
  ¹ ¹ ¹              ¹ ¹ ¹ ¹
  59 678            892 635
+ 24 380          + 142 785
  84,058          1,035,420
```

EXERCISES

Give each sum.

1. 3829 +1746	2. 4973 +9618	3. 5348 + 645	4. 8475 +6397
5. 74235 + 9847	6. 69184 + 5986	7. 35792 +34596	8. 48635 +48635
9. 59483 +72965	10. 71358 +42848	11. 49658 +27498	12. 89653 +17846
13. 593482 + 28567	14. 783619 + 7478	15. 395826 +438599	16. 742856 +174698
17. $354.25 +486.19	18. $736.28 +540.75	19. $483.97 +594.86	20. $562.88 +947.05

Solve.

21.

What is the total price?

22.

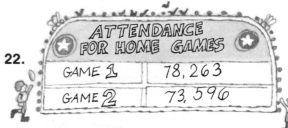

What was the total attendance?

23. The Clark family drove their car 10,483 kilometers one year and 19,768 kilometers the next. How far did they drive during the two years?

24. In 1959, the population of Oakville was 28,746. During the next 20 years the population increased by 19,658. What was the population then?

Add across.
Add down.

25.

228	346	?
491	274	?
?	?	?

26.

395	768	?
419	656	?
?	?	?

27.

519	742	?
385	691	?
?	?	?

Adding 3 or more numbers

Since numbers can be added in any order I look for sums of 10.

Step 1.
Add ones.

```
 58
 26
 34
+45
```
18 +5
23

Step 2.
Regroup.

```
 2
 58
 26
 34
+45
  3
```

Step 3.
Add tens.

```
 2
 58
 26
 34
+45
163
```

Step 1.
Add ones
and regroup.

```
  2
 546
 383
 154
 501
+957
   1
```

Step 2.
Add tens
and regroup.

```
 2 2
 546
 383
 154
 501
+957
  41
```

Step 3.
Add hundreds
and regroup.

```
 2 2
 546
 383
 154
 501
+957
2541
```

EXERCISES
Give each sum.

1.
```
 56
 23
+48
```

2.
```
 29
 74
+63
```

3.
```
 801
 746
+594
```

4.
```
 363
 775
+457
```

5.
```
 955
 145
+628
```

6.
```
 63
 42
 78
+91
```

7.
```
 45
 45
 45
+45
```

8.
```
 258
 346
  91
+759
```

9.
```
 7425
 6813
 4259
+ 647
```

10.
```
 24752
 76874
 80257
+  323
```

11.
```
 51
 38
 29
 74
+51
```

12.
```
 59
 61
 58
 62
+60
```

13.
```
 272
 353
 438
 686
+147
```

14.
```
 3456
 2851
 1234
  659
+ 154
```

15.
```
 76325
 81804
 97235
   936
+ 5563
```

34

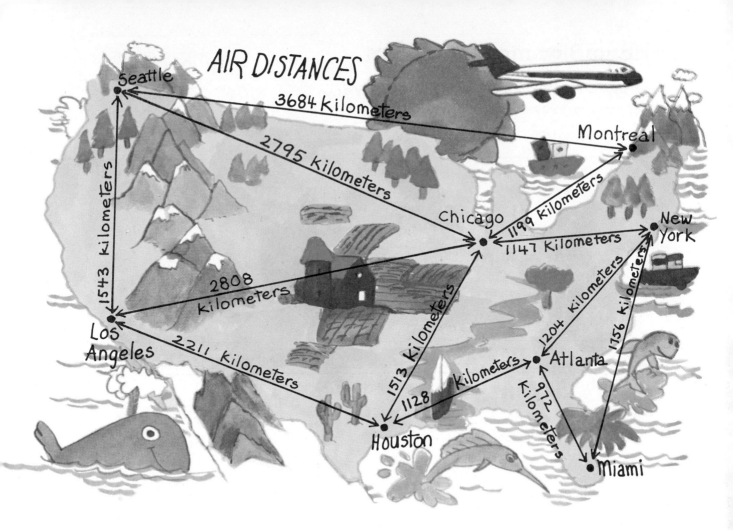

AIR DISTANCES

Seattle — 3684 kilometers — Montreal

2795 kilometers (Seattle to Chicago)

1543 kilometers (Seattle to Los Angeles)

2808 kilometers (Los Angeles to Chicago)

Chicago

1199 Kilometers (Chicago to Montreal)

1147 Kilometers (Chicago to New York)

New York

2211 kilometers (Los Angeles to Houston)

Los Angeles

1513 Kilometers (Chicago to Houston)

1128 Kilometers (Houston to Atlanta)

1204 kilometers (Atlanta to New York)

1756 kilometers (Atlanta to New York)

Atlanta

972 Kilometers (Atlanta to Miami)

Houston

Miami

Solve.

16. How far is it from Montreal to Chicago by air?

17. How many air kilometers is it from New York to Miami?

18. A jet flying from New York to Miami stopped at Atlanta. How far did it fly?

19. How long is the Seattle–Los Angeles–Houston flight?

20. Which is longer, a New York–Atlanta flight or a New York–Chicago flight?

21. How many kilometers is a Montreal–Chicago–Los Angeles flight?

22. How long is a Los Angeles–Houston–Atlanta–New York flight?

23. Find the total distance of a New York–Chicago–Los Angeles–Seattle flight.

Basic subtraction facts

All the basic subtraction facts are listed below.
See how many seconds it takes you to write the differences.

1. 3 −3	2. 1 −0	3. 7 −5	4. 8 −8	5. 6 −5	6. 10 −8	7. 2 −2	8. 12 −5
9. 3 −1	10. 11 −2	11. 9 −3	12. 8 −7	13. 6 −4	14. 11 −8	15. 13 −8	16. 8 −6
17. 12 −8	18. 9 −4	19. 10 −2	20. 5 −4	21. 0 −0	22. 7 −4	23. 15 −7	24. 10 −7
25. 5 −2	26. 9 −8	27. 7 −6	28. 10 −9	29. 4 −4	30. 14 −6	31. 11 −9	32. 5 −3
33. 12 −7	34. 9 −7	35. 3 −2	36. 12 −4	37. 16 −9	38. 5 −5	39. 9 −5	40. 11 −4
41. 4 −0	42. 7 −3	43. 4 −3	44. 2 −0	45. 15 −8	46. 6 −3	47. 2 −1	48. 8 −2
49. 3 −0	50. 6 −0	51. 8 −3	52. 13 −5	53. 16 −7	54. 11 −7	55. 8 −1	56. 11 −3
57. 9 −6	58. 17 −8	59. 10 −3	60. 13 −9	61. 10 −1	62. 9 −9	63. 12 −9	64. 9 −2
65. 7 −0	66. 10 −6	67. 15 −6	68. 4 −2	69. 9 −0	70. 14 −5	71. 1 −0	72. 14 −7
73. 7 −2	74. 18 −9	75. 6 −2	76. 8 −5	77. 12 −6	78. 13 −7	79. 14 −8	80. 11 −6
81. 6 −6	82. 5 −1	83. 8 −4	84. 4 −1	85. 11 −5	86. 10 −4	87. 7 −0	88. 12 −3
89. 5 −0	90. 8 −0	91. 14 −9	92. 7 −1	93. 16 −8	94. 10 −5	95. 13 −6	96. 6 −1
		97. 15 −9	98. 9 −1	99. 17 −9	100. 13 −4		

Remember that subtraction is finding the missing addend. The answer is called the **difference**.

Check your answers.

1. 0	2. 1	3. 2	4. 0	5. 1	6. 2	7. 0	8. 7
9. 2	10. 9	11. 6	12. 1	13. 2	14. 3	15. 5	16. 2
17. 4	18. 5	19. 8	20. 1	21. 0	22. 3	23. 8	24. 3
25. 3	26. 1	27. 1	28. 1	29. 0	30. 8	31. 2	32. 2
33. 5	34. 2	35. 1	36. 8	37. 7	38. 0	39. 4	40. 7
41. 4	42. 4	43. 1	44. 2	45. 7	46. 3	47. 1	48. 6
49. 3	50. 6	51. 5	52. 8	53. 9	54. 4	55. 7	56. 8
57. 3	58. 9	59. 7	60. 4	61. 9	62. 0	63. 3	64. 7
65. 7	66. 4	67. 9	68. 2	69. 9	70. 9	71. 1	72. 7
73. 5	74. 9	75. 4	76. 3	77. 6	78. 6	79. 6	80. 5
81. 0	82. 4	83. 4	84. 3	85. 6	86. 6	87. 7	88. 9
89. 5	90. 8	91. 5	92. 6	93. 8	94. 5	95. 7	96. 5
		97. 6	98. 8	99. 8	100. 9		

101. To find your score, add the number of seconds and the number of mistakes.

102. Practice the facts that you missed. See if you can get a better (lower) score.

103. Work with a classmate. Practice your subtraction facts orally each day. Keep a record of your best daily score.

104. You may wish to graph your score as shown:

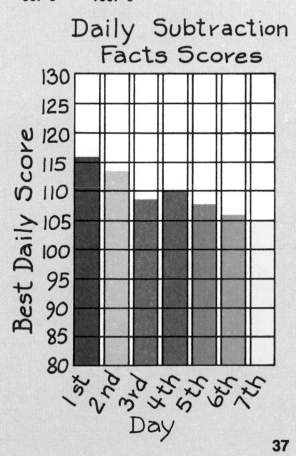

Daily Subtraction Facts Scores

Subtracting 2-digit numbers

You can find the number of blocks
left by subtracting in columns.

Step 1. Subtract in ones column.

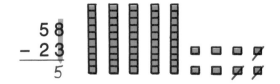

$$\begin{array}{r} 5\,8 \\ -\ 2\,3 \\ \hline 5 \end{array}$$

Step 2. Subtract in tens column.

$$\begin{array}{r} 5\,8 \\ -\ 2\,3 \\ \hline 35 \end{array}$$

Since subtraction is finding a
missing addend, we can check
subtraction by addition.

blocks left	**35**
blocks taken away	**+ 23**
blocks in all	**58**

It checks!

In this example, 1 ten is regrouped
for 10 ones.

Step 1. Not enough ones.

$$\begin{array}{r} 62 \\ -\ 48 \end{array}$$

Step 2. Regroup.

$$\begin{array}{r} {}^{5}\!\!\not{6}{}^{1}2 \\ -\ 48 \end{array}$$

Step 3. Subtract.

$$\begin{array}{r} {}^{5}\!\!\not{6}{}^{1}2 \\ -\ 48 \\ \hline 14 \end{array}$$

check by adding these

EXERCISES

First subtract. Then check by addition.

1. 98 − 58	2. 75 − 53	3. 89 − 26	4. 77 − 36	5. 68 − 42	6. 88 − 35
7. 86 − 35	8. 67 − 40	9. 97 − 27	10. 69 − 28	11. 96 − 35	12. 76 − 42

Give each difference.

13. 52
    − 18

14. 60
    − 22

15. 90
    − 46

16. 73
    − 58

17. 80
    − 39

18. 62
    − 45

19. 92
    − 35

20. 71
    − 58

21. 82
    − 46

22. 53
    − 29

23. 63
    − 48

24. 91
    − 48

25. 72
    − 22

26. 61
    − 56

27. 45
    − 28

28. 81
    − 27

29. 64
    − 9

30. 60
    − 42

31. 93
    − 43

32. 83
    − 7

33. 85
    − 43

34. 94
    − 36

35. 84
    − 35

36. 65
    − 56

37. 52¢
    − 26¢

38. 64¢
    − 29¢

39. 78¢
    − 39¢

40. 58¢
    − 25¢

41. 59¢
    − 38¢

42. 70¢
    − 56¢

43. 82¢
    − 49¢

44. 61¢
    − 27¢

45. 89¢
    − 19¢

Solve.

46.

How much more does the large box cost?

47. Have

Want to Buy

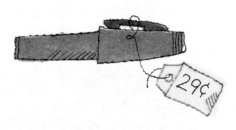

How much money will be left?

48. Greg went on an 80-kilometer bicycle tour. During the first 3 hours he rode 37 kilometers. How many kilometers were left?

49. Sally wants to buy a bicycle that costs $92. She has saved $49. How much more money does she need?

Subtracting 3-digit numbers

EXAMPLE:

$$365 \text{ rounds to } 400$$
$$-182 \text{ rounds to } -200$$
$$200$$

Step 1. Subtract ones.

$$\begin{array}{r} 36\,5 \\ -18\,2 \\ \hline 3 \end{array}$$

Step 2. Regroup.

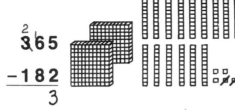

$$\begin{array}{r} \overset{2}{3}65 \\ -182 \\ \hline 3 \end{array}$$

Step 3. Subtract tens.

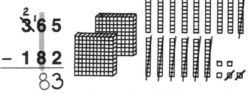

$$\begin{array}{r} \overset{2}{3}\overset{1}{6}5 \\ -182 \\ \hline 83 \end{array}$$

Step 4. Subtract hundreds.

The difference is near my estimate. So, I probably subtracted correctly.

$$\begin{array}{r} \overset{2}{3}\overset{1}{6}5 \\ -182 \\ \hline 183 \end{array}$$

In this example we have to regroup twice before subtracting.

Step 1. Regroup.

$$\begin{array}{r} \overset{3}{4}03 \\ -258 \end{array}$$

Step 2. Regroup.

$$\begin{array}{r} \overset{3}{4}\overset{9}{0}3 \\ -258 \end{array}$$

Step 3. Subtract.

$$\begin{array}{r} \overset{3}{4}\overset{9}{0}3 \\ -258 \\ \hline 145 \end{array}$$

EXERCISES

First estimate the difference.
Then subtract.

1. 537 – 248	**2.** 714 – 80	**3.** 558 – 362	**4.** 693 – 157
5. 946 – 58	**6.** 725 – 258	**7.** 423 – 55	**8.** 628 – 346
9. 532 – 274	**10.** 641 – 185	**11.** 946 – 275	**12.** 835 – 59
13. 624 – 495	**14.** 753 – 299	**15.** 542 – 76	**16.** 502 – 348
17. 701 – 256	**18.** 603 – 48	**19.** 504 – 175	**20.** 800 – 496
21. $5.48 – 2.56	**22.** $6.25 – 3.58	**23.** $5.05 – .68	**24.** $3.56 – 2.99

Solve.

25.

Elm City   149 km
Springfield 227 km

How far from Elm City to Springfield?

26. Have   Buy

$3.25

How much change?

1. 38
  24
+15

2. 821
  465
+378

3. 4625
  718
+2469

4. 36
  78
  95
+43

5. 159
  146
  380
+ 56

6. 3521
  78
  365
+4175

7. 3904
  1283
  572
+ 659

Subtracting larger numbers

Sometimes you will need to regroup before you subtract.

You use the same method to subtract larger numbers that you use to subtract smaller numbers.

Step 1. Regroup and subtract ones.

```
   5
  83̸6̸4
- 251 9
      5
```

Step 2. Subtract tens.

```
    5
  83̸6̸'4
- 25 1 9
     45
```

Step 3. Regroup and subtract hundreds.

```
  7  5
  8̸3̸6̸4
- 2 5 1 9
    845
```

Step 4. Subtract thousands.

```
  7  5
  8̸'3̸6̸4̸
- 2 519
   5845
```

Other examples.

```
  2 9  7
  3̸0̸2̸8̸4
- 1 5 8 1 7
   14,467
```

```
  7 13 11 10
  8̸4̸2̸1̸6̸7
- 3 5 4 5 9 1
    487,576
```

EXERCISES

Give each difference.

1. 7659
   − 2384
	2. 8134
	   − 529
		3. 6052
		   − 1080
			4. 3904
			   − 2465

5. 3829
   − 1469
	6. 5302
	   − 1469
		7. 8204
		   − 3691
			8. 7002
			   − 816

9. 42148
   − 8029
	10. 71253
	   − 14065
		11. 61974
		   − 3895
			12. 82345
			   − 17586

13. 823517
   − 219486
	14. 593475
	   − 16829
		15. 436219
		   − 85774
			16. 369003
			   − 151274

Solve.

City	Population		
	1850	1900	1950
New York	696,115	3,437,202	7,891,957
Chicago	29,963	1,698,575	3,620,962
Los Angeles	1,610	102,479	1,970,358
Philadelphia	121,376	1,293,697	2,071,605

17. What was the population of New York City in 1950?

18. What was the total population of the four cities in 1900?

19. In 1850, how many more people lived in New York City than in Chicago?

20. In 1900, how many more people lived in Philadelphia than in Los Angeles?

21. How much did the population of Los Angeles increase from 1900 to 1950?

22. What was the population of Chicago in 1900, rounded to the nearest thousand?

Complete.

23.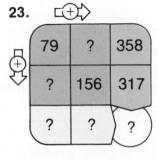

24.

25.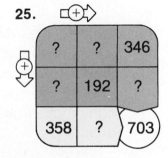

43

Addition and subtraction

$(1603 - 452) + 897 = 2048$

Remember to work inside the grouping symbols first.

EXERCISES
Compute.

1. $(58 + 39) + 26$
2. $58 + (39 + 26)$
3. $(79 + 82) - 56$
4. $79 + (82 - 56)$
5. $(95 - 23) + 47$
6. $95 - (23 + 47)$
7. $(90 - 56) - 28$
8. $90 - (56 - 28)$
9. $(420 + 118) + 276$
10. $420 + (118 + 276)$
11. $(349 + 526) - 235$
12. $349 + (526 - 235)$
13. $(802 - 278) + 149$
14. $802 - (278 + 149)$
15. $(712 - 321) - 257$
16. $712 - (321 - 257)$

Solve.

17.

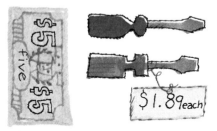

How much money will be left?

18.

How much more money is needed?

19. A fifth-grade class had to sell 275 tickets to the school carnival. They sold 97 tickets the first week and 116 the second week. How many more tickets did they have to sell?

20. A youth club was given 400 trees to plant along a nature trail. They planted 142 one weekend and 178 the next. How many did they have left to plant?

44

I came within 13 of the target number, 500

$$(374 + 852) - 739 \rightarrow 500$$

```
  1
  374          500
 +852         -487
 1226           13
 -739
  487
```

How close did these players come to the target number?

1. Beth
   $$(753 + 258) - 495 \rightarrow 500$$

2. Alan
   $$(826 + 435) - 527 \rightarrow 500$$

3. Juan
   $$(366 + 402) - 265 \rightarrow 500$$

4. Dave
   $$(829 + 648) - 897 \rightarrow 500$$

Play the game.

1. Make a digit card for each of the digits 0 through 9.

2. Choose a leader.

3. Draw a table like this:
   $$(\square\square\square + \square\square\square) - \square\square\square \rightarrow 500.$$

4. Without looking, the leader picks a card. Each player writes the digit in any square of the table.

5. The card is put back and step 4 is repeated until all squares have been filled in.

6. The player who gets closest to the target number, 500, wins the game.

45

Problem solving

In this lesson you will be given some two-step problems. Often such problems can be solved in more than one way. Compare Jane's way with Bill's way.

Jane's Way

1. Read the problem and find the question.

   John had $20. He rented skis for $5.75 and bought a lift ticket for $11.80. How much money did he have left?

2. What are the facts?

   had $20
   spent $5.75
   spent $11.80

3. Decide what to do.

   First add to find the money spent. Then subtract to find the money left.

4. Answer the question.

   $5.75
   + 11.80
   $17.55 amount spent

   $20.00
   − 17.55
   $ 2.45 amount left

5. Estimate! Does your answer seem right?

   Spent $6 + $12 = $18
   Have left $20 − $18 = $2

   The answer seems right.

Bill's Way

1. Read the problem and find the question.

   John had $20. He rented skis for $5.75 and bought a lift ticket for $11.80. How much money did he have left?

2. What are the facts?

   had $20
   spent $5.75
   spent $11.80

3. Decide what to do.

   First subtract to find how much is left after renting the skis. Then subtract to find how much is left after buying the lift ticket.

4. Answer the question.

   $20.00
   − 5.75
   $14.25 left after renting skis
   − 11.80
   $ 2.45 left after buying ticket

5. Estimate! Does your answer seem right?

   $20 − $6 = $14
   $14 − $12 = $2

   The answer seems right.

46

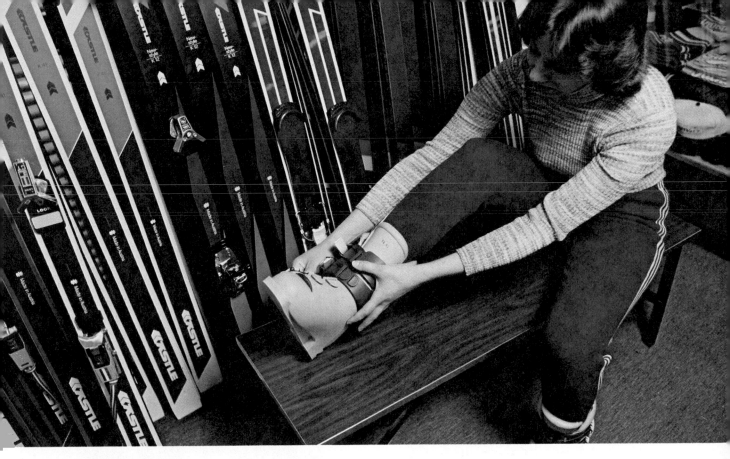

EXERCISES
Try to use the steps to solve these problems.

1. Miss Cooper wanted to buy new skis that cost $149 and new ski boots that cost $119. She had only $229. How much more money did she need?

2. Charles went on a 1000-kilometer bicycle trip. He rode 110 kilometers the first day and 95 kilometers the second. How many kilometers did he have left to ride?

3. Chris bought a baseball that cost $3.79 plus $.19 sales tax. How much change did he get from a $10 bill?

4. Jack bowled three games. His scores were 112, 129, and 145. What was his total score for the three games?

5. Jill bought three tennis balls for $2.79 and a sweat band for $.90. How much change did she get from a $5 bill?

6. Carl wants to buy a bike that costs $189. He can earn $35 a week. How many weeks will he have to work to buy the bike?

Problem solving

1. How many kilometers is it from Ada to Harper?

2. How long is the bike route?

3. The first rest stop for the bikers was at Sidney. How many more kilometers did they have to ride?

4. The second rest stop was 25 kilometers from Sidney. How far from Harper was the second rest stop? How far from Oakville?

BIKE ROUTE

DISTANCES IN KILOMETERS

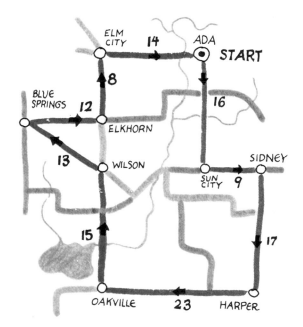

5. The bikers ate lunch at Wilson. How far had they traveled? How far did they have to go?

6. Sarah ordered a super cheeseburger for $1.25 and a milk shake for $.69. What was the total price?

7. Bill had $3. He ordered two hot dogs for $.85 each and a grape drink for $.45. How much money did he have left?

8. A bicycle shop in Ada awarded Karen a $20 gift certificate for first place in the safety contest. She bought 2 tires for $5.29 each and a bike pack for $9.56. How much money did she have left?

CHAPTER CHECKUP

Add. [pages 22–34]

| 1. | 58
 +21 | 2. | 69
 +18 | 3. | 78
 +35 | 4. | 593
 +298 |

5. 658
   +597

6. 3824
   +1536

7. 85674
   + 2981

8. 483673
   +297575

9. 28
   37
   +23

10. 596
    784
    +356

11. 2814
    326
    7821
    + 599

12. 537
    261
    83
    145
    + 21

Subtract. [pages 36–45]

13. 98
    − 46

14. 82
    − 36

15. 473
    − 47

16. 603
    − 459

17. 800
    − 258

18. 4314
    − 1682

19. 54175
    − 17986

20. 836052
    − 38791

Solve. [pages 46–49]

21.

What is the total cost?

22.

·CITY·	·POPULATION·
Sutton	34,251
Palmer	43,020

How many more people live in Palmer?

23. Sandy had 219 football cards. She found 142 more in her attic and bought 57 more at a garage sale. How many did she have then?

24. David had 206 baseball cards. He bought 67 more and then gave 95 cards to his little brother. How many baseball cards did he have left?

Project

1. While playing on the school grounds, pick up any pieces of litter that you see.

2. Make a litter graph like the one shown.

3. After a week or two, make a graph showing how many pieces of litter were picked up each day by your whole class.

4. List some things that the graph shows.

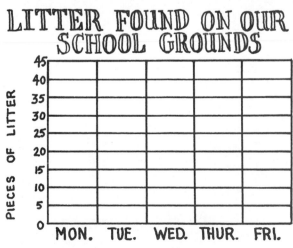

LITTER FOUND ON OUR SCHOOL GROUNDS

PIECES OF LITTER

45
40
35
30
25
20
15
10
5
0

MON. TUE. WED. THUR. FRI.

CHAPTER REVIEW

Add.
Regroup once.

$$\begin{array}{r} \overset{1}{7}461 \\ +1294 \\ \hline 8755 \end{array}$$

1. 542	2. 823	3. 3765
+63	+58	+2712

Regroup more than once.

$$\begin{array}{r} \overset{1}{2}\overset{1}{8}\overset{1}{3}7\overset{1}{1}4 \\ + 59648 \\ \hline 343{,}362 \end{array}$$

4. 8432	5. 76345	6. 370956
+2591	+4738	+839614

Add more than two numbers.

$$\begin{array}{r} \overset{1}{8}\overset{2}{4}\overset{2}{6}5 \\ 374 \\ 158 \\ + 9535 \\ \hline 18{,}532 \end{array}$$

7. 35	8. 263	9. 3521
26	75	759
38	184	2163
+15	+942	+ 97

Subtract.
Regroup once.

$$\begin{array}{r} \overset{4}{\cancel{5}}\overset{1}{2}86 \\ -1943 \\ \hline 3343 \end{array}$$

10. 596	11. 742	12. 826
– 48	– 117	– 353

Regroup more than once.

$$\begin{array}{r} \overset{2}{\cancel{3}}\overset{9}{\cancel{0}}\overset{4}{\cancel{5}}4 \\ -1387 \\ \hline 1667 \end{array}$$

13. 361	14. 9835	15. 6308
– 194	– 2379	– 149

16. 36482	17. 530491	18. 730046
–19536	–206838	–415348

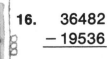

CHAPTER CHALLENGE

Complete each number pattern.

1. 2, 4, 8, 16, <u>?</u>
2. 14, 12, 10, 8, <u>?</u>
3. 1, 2, 1, 3, 1, <u>?</u>
4. 41, 38, 35, 32, 29, <u>?</u>
5. 1, 3, 6, <u>?</u>, 15
6. 29, 25, 22, <u>?</u>, 19
7. 5, 25, 6, 24, 7, 23, 8, <u>?</u>
8. 64, 32, <u>?</u>, 8, 4
9. 15, 17, 16, <u>?</u>, 17, 19, 18
10. 40, 33, 26, 19, <u>?</u>
11. 5, 4, 10, 9, 15, <u>?</u>, 20, 19
12. <u>?</u>, 35, 46, 57, 68
13. 28, 20, 14, 10, <u>?</u>
14. 23, 28, 25, <u>?</u>, 27, 32
15. 9, 10, 18, 19, 27, <u>?</u>, 36, 37
16. <u>?</u>, 6, 5, 9, 8, 12, 11, 15

Copy this square and fill in your answers. If the sum of your answers along each row, column, and diagonal is the same, your answers are correct!

1.	2.	3.	4.
5.	6.	7.	8.
9.	10.	11.	12.
13.	14.	15.	16.

a b c d   a b c d   a b c d   a b c d   a b c d
14   34   14   4   30
a b c d   c d   a b c d
15   31
a b c   Standardized Format   a b c   a b c d

MAJOR CHECKUP
Standardized Format

Choose the correct letter.

1. In 5834, the 8 stands for	**2.** In 267,810, the digit in the ten thousands place is	**3.** The standard numeral for four hundred thousand forty-four is
a. 80 **b.** 8000 **c.** 800 **d.** none of these	**a.** 6 **b.** 7 **c.** 8 **d.** none of these	**a.** 444,000 **b.** 400,044 **c.** 400,440 **d.** none of these
4. Which number is 10,000 greater than 348,961?	**5.** Which number is greatest?	**6.** 547,376 rounded to the nearest thousand is
a. 448,961 **b.** 349,961 **c.** 338,961 **d.** none of these	**a.** 416,382 **b.** 418,015 **c.** 389,996 **d.** 58,361	**a.** 547,000 **b.** 548,000 **c.** 547,400 **d.** none of these
7. 650,000 rounded to the nearest hundred thousand is	**8.** In 356,749,182 the digit in the millions place is	**9.** Add. 47839 +32816
a. 600,000 **b.** 700,000 **c.** 650,000 **d.** none of these	**a.** 6 **b.** 3 **c.** 7 **d.** none of these	**a.** 79,645 **b.** 79,655 **c.** 80,645 **d.** none of these
10. Add. 382 167 593 +142	**11.** Subtract. 59281 −36948	**12.** Subtract. 650378 −149739
a. 1284 **b.** 1274 **c.** 1084 **d.** none of these	**a.** 23,747 **b.** 23,333 **c.** 22,333 **d.** none of these	**a.** 519,441 **b.** 500,639 **c.** 501,639 **d.** none of these

3
Multiplication

The basic multiplication facts

When I first learned to multiply, I had to count to find products.

$2 \times 4 = 8$
factors   product

These properties make it easier to remember the facts.

The Order Property
Changing the order of the factors does not change the product.

$3 \times 2 = 2 \times 3$

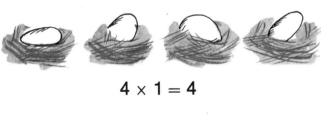

The Multiplying by 1 Property
The product of any number and 1 is that same number.

$4 \times 1 = 4$

The Multiplying by 0 Property
The product of any number and 0 is 0.

$3 \times 0 = 0$

The Grouping Property
Changing the grouping of the factors does not change the product.

$(2 \times 3) \times 4 = 2 \times (3 \times 4)$

EXERCISES

Give each product.

1. If 4 × 2 = 8, then 2 × 4 = _?_.

2. If 5 × 4 = 20, then 4 × 5 = _?_.

3. If 3 × 7 = 21, then 7 × 3 = _?_.

4. If 7 × 6 = 42, then 6 × 7 = _?_.

5. If 8 × 7 = 56, then 7 × 8 = _?_.

6. If 9 × 8 = 72, then 8 × 9 = _?_.

7. If 7 × 9 = _?_, then 9 × 7 = _?_.

8. If 6 × 8 = _?_, then 8 × 6 = _?_.

9. 6 × 1 = _?_   10. 9 × 0 = _?_   11. 1 × 8 = _?_   12. 0 × 7 = _?_

13. 5 × 0 = _?_   14. 1 × 9 = _?_   15. 0 × 0 = _?_   16. 1 × 1 = _?_

Study the shortcut, then use the shortcut to find each product.

Sometimes I forget a fact. I can use another fact to help me figure out the answer.

$7 \times 6 = \blacksquare$ °° 6 less

$8 \times 6 = 48$

$9 \times 6 = \blacksquare$ °° 6 greater

17. If 7 × 7 = 49, then 8 × 7 = _?_.

18. If 8 × 4 = 32, then 9 × 4 = _?_.

19. If 6 × 5 = 30, then 5 × 5 = _?_.

20. If 6 × 9 = 54, then 7 × 9 = _?_.

21. If 8 × 8 = 64, then 9 × 8 = _?_.

22. If 7 × 9 = 63, then 6 × 9 = _?_.

Practicing the basic multiplication facts

All the basic multiplication facts are listed below. See how quickly you can list the products.

WHAT'S YOUR SCORE?

1. 9 ×2	2. 2 ×1	3. 7 ×5	4. 0 ×2	5. 2 ×8	6. 1 ×5	7. 0 ×8	8. 2 ×5
9. 1 ×0	10. 0 ×3	11. 1 ×4	12. 8 ×2	13. 5 ×4	14. 4 ×8	15. 0 ×0	16. 0 ×1
17. 3 ×8	18. 7 ×7	19. 5 ×9	20. 8 ×5	21. 5 ×0	22. 6 ×1	23. 2 ×0	24. 9 ×8
25. 0 ×6	26. 9 ×3	27. 1 ×3	28. 9 ×1	29. 2 ×9	30. 6 ×4	31. 4 ×6	32. 8 ×4
33. 8 ×0	34. 2 ×6	35. 4 ×7	36. 3 ×4	37. 5 ×8	38. 9 ×5	39. 7 ×9	40. 7 ×0
41. 8 ×8	42. 8 ×6	43. 3 ×6	44. 9 ×0	45. 1 ×6	46. 4 ×1	47. 2 ×2	48. 0 ×9
49. 3 ×3	50. 5 ×3	51. 2 ×3	52. 5 ×2	53. 9 ×7	54. 2 ×4	55. 1 ×1	56. 8 ×7
57. 1 ×9	58. 6 ×3	59. 8 ×3	60. 4 ×9	61. 0 ×7	62. 1 ×8	63. 3 ×9	64. 4 ×0
65. 9 ×6	66. 1 ×2	67. 5 ×5	68. 7 ×8	69. 2 ×7	70. 6 ×0	71. 3 ×1	72. 9 ×9
73. 1 ×7	74. 4 ×4	75. 3 ×7	76. 7 ×1	77. 5 ×6	78. 4 ×5	79. 7 ×6	80. 6 ×7
81. 7 ×2	82. 3 ×2	83. 4 ×2	84. 6 ×2	85. 0 ×4	86. 3 ×5	87. 5 ×1	88. 6 ×9
89. 6 ×6	90. 8 ×1	91. 6 ×5	92. 0 ×5	93. 4 ×3	94. 5 ×7	95. 6 ×8	96. 8 ×9
		97. 7 ×4	98. 7 ×3	99. 3 ×0	100. 9 ×4		

58

Check your answers.

1. 18	**2.** 2	**3.** 35	**4.** 0	**5.** 16	**6.** 5	**7.** 0	**8.** 10
9. 0	**10.** 0	**11.** 4	**12.** 16	**13.** 20	**14.** 32	**15.** 0	**16.** 0
17. 24	**18.** 49	**19.** 45	**20.** 40	**21.** 0	**22.** 6	**23.** 0	**24.** 72
25. 0	**26.** 27	**27.** 3	**28.** 9	**29.** 18	**30.** 24	**31.** 24	**32.** 32
33. 0	**34.** 12	**35.** 28	**36.** 12	**37.** 40	**38.** 45	**39.** 63	**40.** 0
41. 64	**42.** 48	**43.** 18	**44.** 0	**45.** 6	**46.** 4	**47.** 4	**48.** 0
49. 9	**50.** 15	**51.** 6	**52.** 10	**53.** 63	**54.** 8	**55.** 1	**56.** 56
57. 9	**58.** 18	**59.** 24	**60.** 36	**61.** 0	**62.** 8	**63.** 27	**64.** 0
65. 54	**66.** 2	**67.** 25	**68.** 56	**69.** 14	**70.** 0	**71.** 3	**72.** 81
73. 7	**74.** 16	**75.** 21	**76.** 7	**77.** 30	**78.** 20	**79.** 42	**80.** 42
81. 14	**82.** 6	**83.** 8	**84.** 12	**85.** 0	**86.** 15	**87.** 5	**88.** 54
89. 36	**90.** 8	**91.** 30	**92.** 0	**93.** 12	**94.** 35	**95.** 48	**96.** 72

97. 28 **98.** 21 **99.** 0 **100.** 36

101. Practice the facts that you missed.

102. Work with a classmate. See how quickly you can give the products orally. Have your partner keep a tally of your mistakes.

103. To find your score, add the number of seconds and the number of mistakes. Try for a better (lower) score.

104. Practice your facts for the next several days and keep a line graph of your scores as shown:

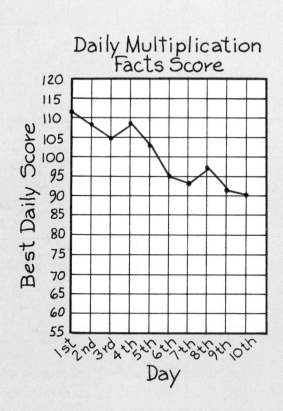

Daily Multiplication Facts Score

59

Multiples and common multiples

0, 4, 8, 12, 16, and 20 are **multiples** of 4. What are the next two multiples of 4? 10 is not a multiple of 4, because no whole number times 4 is 10.

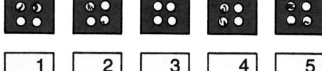
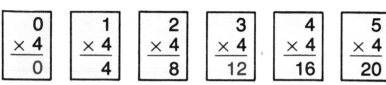

0	1	2	3	4	5
× 4	× 4	× 4	× 4	× 4	× 4
0	4	8	12	16	20

Here are the first few multiples of 6.

0	1	2	3	4	5
× 6	× 6	× 6	× 6	× 6	× 6
0	6	12	18	24	30

0 and 12 are multiples of both 4 and 6. They are called **common multiples.** What is the next common multiple of 4 and 6? The smallest common multiple, other than 0, is called the **least common multiple.** 12 is the least common multiple of 4 and 6.

EXERCISES

1. **a.** Give the first 12 multiples of 4.
   b. Give the first 12 multiples of 5.
   c. What are the first 3 common multiples of 4 and 5?
   d. What is the least common multiple of 4 and 5?

2. **a.** Give the first 10 multiples of 9.
   b. Give the first 10 multiples of 6.
   c. What are the first 3 common multiples of 9 and 6?
   d. What is the least common multiple of 9 and 6?

Give the least common multiple of the two numbers.

3. 2, 4   4. 3, 4   5. 2, 9   6. 4, 5

7. 4, 6   8. 10, 6   9. 5, 3   10. 9, 3

11. 5, 6   12. 3, 12   13. 4, 10   14. 7, 8

Multiples of 2 are called **even numbers.** Whole numbers that are not multiples of 2 are called odd numbers.

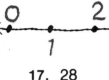
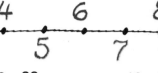

Even or odd?

15. 10   16. 17   17. 28   18. 23   19. 39

20. If you add two even numbers, the sum is ?.

21. The sum of two odd numbers is ?.

22. The difference of two even numbers is ?.

23. The product of two odd numbers is ?.

24. If you multiply two even numbers the product is ?.

The ones digit has been painted over.
Tell what the number could be.

25.
26.
27.
28.

Multiplying a 2-digit number

There are 2 sets of blocks with 34 blocks in each set. To find the total number of blocks, multiply.

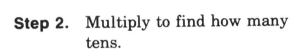

Step 1. Multiply to find how many ones.

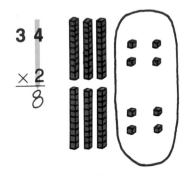

Step 2. Multiply to find how many tens.

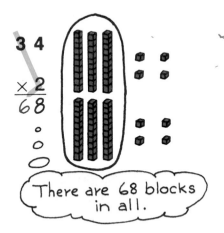

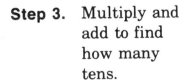

There are 68 blocks in all.

In this example 10 ones are regrouped for 1 ten.

Step 1. Multiply to find how many ones.

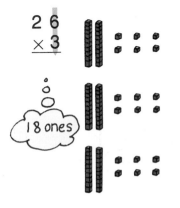

18 ones

Step 2. Regroup.

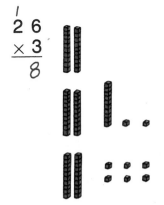

Step 3. Multiply and add to find how many tens.

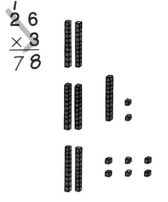

EXERCISES
Multiply.

1. 23
   ×3

2. 22
   ×4

3. 10
   ×5

4. 21
   ×4

5. 32
   ×3

6. 10
   ×6

7. 20
   ×4

8. 32
   ×3

9. 12
   ×4

10. 23
    ×2

11. 10
    ×5

12. 11
    ×6

13. 26
    ×3

14. 35
    ×2

15. 45
    ×2

16. 28
    ×3

17. 16
    ×4

18. 18
    ×5

19. 68
    ×2

20. 46
    ×5

21. 38
    ×6

22. 49
    ×4

23. 76
    ×8

24. 53
    ×9

25. 74
    ×7

26. 58
    ×4

27. 66
    ×9

28. 93
    ×6

29. 87
    ×8

30. 75
    ×5

31. 53
    ×5

32. 74
    ×8

33. 85
    ×9

34. 67
    ×5

35. 39
    ×7

36. 58
    ×6

37. $.28
    ×2

38. $.38
    ×6

39. $.41
    ×7

40. $.68
    ×9

41. $.57
    ×3

42. $.85
    ×6

43. $.92
    ×8

44. $.49
    ×5

45. $.79
    ×8

46. $.57
    ×9

47. 8 minutes
    How many
    seconds?

48. 7 hours
    How many
    minutes?

49. 6 days
    How many
    hours?

Multiplying a 3-digit number

EXAMPLE.   264   rounds to   300

       × 3   × 3
                                  ———
                                   900

My estimate is 900. Will the product be less than or greater than my estimate?

Step 1.   Multiply to find how many ones.

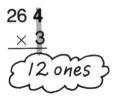

26**4**
× **3**
———
12 ones

Step 2.   Regroup.

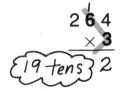

12 ones = 1 ten + 2 ones

  ¹ ∘ ∘
264
× 3
———
    2

Step 3.   Multiply and add to find how many tens.

2⁶4
× **3**
———
19 tens 2

Step 4.   Regroup.

19 tens = 1 hundred + 9 tens

 ∘∘∘∘
 ¹ ¹
264
× 3
———
 92

Step 5.   Multiply and add to find how many hundreds.

/ /
2⁶4
× 3
———
792

Is the product reasonable?

EXERCISES

First estimate the product.
Then multiply.

1. 124
   ×3

2. 238
   ×4

3. 316
   ×3

4. 278
   ×2

5. 156
   ×4

6. 387
   ×5

7. 425
   ×6

8. 800
   ×8

9. 742
   ×5

10. 502
    ×9

11. 726
    ×4

12. 656
    ×3

13. 529
    ×5

14. 599
    ×7

15. 680
    ×6

16. 538
    ×5

17. 742
    ×8

18. 613
    ×7

19. 467
    ×9

20. 962
    ×5

21. $2.58
    ×7

22. $4.93
    ×3

23. $9.02
    ×4

24. $7.83
    ×6

25. $6.75
    ×8

Solve.

26.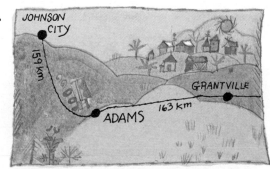

    Each week, a truck driver drives 5 round trips from Johnson City to Grantville. How far is that?

27. There are 144 screws in 1 box. How many screws are in 6 boxes?

28. A certain kind of bus seats 46 people. How many people will 9 such buses seat?

29. Each member of a youth club wants to collect 375 kilograms of paper. There are 8 members. How much should they collect in all?

Find the missing digits.

30. 8
    ×4
    3140

31. 94
    ×
    4164

★ 32.
    ×8
    2864

65

Multiplying larger numbers

You multiply a larger number the same way you multiply a smaller number.

Step 1. Multiply and regroup.

$$\begin{array}{r} \overset{3}{9}36\;4 \\ \times\;8 \\ \hline 2 \end{array}$$

Step 2. Multiply, add, and regroup.

$$\begin{array}{r} 9\overset{5}{3}\;\overset{3}{6}\;4 \\ \times\;8 \\ \hline 1\;2 \end{array}$$

Step 3. Multiply, add, and regroup.

$$\begin{array}{r} \overset{2}{9}\;\overset{5}{3}\;\overset{3}{6}4 \\ \times\;8 \\ \hline 9\;1\;2 \end{array}$$

Step 4. Multiply and add.

$$\begin{array}{r} \overset{2}{9}\;\overset{5}{3}64 \\ \times\;8 \\ \hline 74{,}912 \end{array}$$

Other examples.

$$\begin{array}{r} \overset{4412}{37824} \\ \times\;6 \\ \hline 226{,}944 \end{array} \qquad \begin{array}{r} \overset{21132}{753296} \\ \times\;4 \\ \hline 3{,}013{,}184 \end{array}$$

EXERCISES

Multiply.

1. 3274
   ×5

2. 9106
   ×4

3. 3582
   ×6

4. 7136
   ×3

5. 52816
   ×4

6. 39428
   ×2

7. 74385
   ×3

8. 60342
   ×5

9. 216342
   ×3

10. 516394
    ×8

11. 491763
    ×6

12. 378219
    ×5

13. 258 × 6

14. 423 × 9

15. 8 × 7421

16. 3506 × 7

17. 5106 × 5

18. 4 × 39174

Solve.

19. How many pictures can you take with 6 rolls of this film?

20. What is the total price of 4 rolls of film?

Use your product (Exercise 21) to give these products. Do not multiply.

Multiply.

21. 12345679
    ×9

22. 12345679
    ×18

23. 12345679
    ×27

Multiplying by 10 and 100

There are 10 bottle caps in each stack. To find the total number of bottle caps, you can multiply.

$$\begin{array}{r} 10 \\ \times\,7 \\ \hline 70 \end{array} \qquad \begin{array}{r} 7 \\ \times\,10 \\ \hline 70 \end{array}$$

Study these products.

$$\begin{array}{r} 9 \\ \times\,10 \\ \hline 90 \end{array} \quad \begin{array}{r} 25 \\ \times\,10 \\ \hline 250 \end{array} \quad \begin{array}{r} 84 \\ \times\,10 \\ \hline 840 \end{array} \quad \begin{array}{r} 186 \\ \times\,10 \\ \hline 1860 \end{array} \quad \begin{array}{r} 925 \\ \times\,10 \\ \hline 9250 \end{array} \quad \begin{array}{r} 2436 \\ \times\,10 \\ \hline 24,360 \end{array}$$

What is an easy way to multiply a number by 10?

There are 100 bottle caps in each pile.

$$\begin{array}{r} 100 \\ \times\,3 \\ \hline 300 \end{array} \qquad \begin{array}{r} 3 \\ \times\,100 \\ \hline 300 \end{array}$$

Study these products.

$$\begin{array}{r} 6 \\ \times\,100 \\ \hline 600 \end{array} \quad \begin{array}{r} 12 \\ \times\,100 \\ \hline 1200 \end{array} \quad \begin{array}{r} 152 \\ \times\,100 \\ \hline 15,200 \end{array} \quad \begin{array}{r} 283 \\ \times\,100 \\ \hline 28,300 \end{array} \quad \begin{array}{r} 3426 \\ \times\,100 \\ \hline 342,600 \end{array}$$

What is an easy way to multiply a number by 100?

EXERCISES

Multiply.

1. 16 ×10	**2.** 19 ×10	**3.** 25 ×10	**4.** 37 ×10	**5.** 68 ×10
6. 125 ×10	**7.** 150 ×10	**8.** 246 ×10	**9.** 373 ×10	**10.** 658 ×10
11. 5214 ×10	**12.** 3782 ×10	**13.** 5963 ×10	**14.** 4000 ×10	**15.** 7800 ×10
16. 18 ×100	**17.** 35 ×100	**18.** 64 ×100	**19.** 80 ×100	**20.** 92 ×100
21. 130 ×100	**22.** 152 ×100	**23.** 268 ×100	**24.** 642 ×100	**25.** 867 ×100
26. 3214 ×100	**27.** 2178 ×100	**28.** 4320 ×100	**29.** 5000 ×100	**30.** 3871 ×100

Complete.

31.

Dimes	7	13	25	140	165	348
Cents	?	?	?	?	?	?

32.

Meters	24	68	142	236	458	698
Centimeters	?	?	?	?	?	?

Remember:
1 meter = 100 centimeters

Solve.

33. There were 15 players on a Little League team. Each player sold 10 tickets. How many tickets did the team sell?

34. To raise money, 825 students at Lowry Elementary School each ran 100 meters in a school relay. How many meters was the relay?

35. Guess the product of these ten numbers.

1 2 3 4 5 6 7 8 9 10

36. Find the product. How close was your guess?

Multiplying by multiples of 10 and 100

Notice that there are 24 stamps on each sheet, 3 sheets in each stack, and 10 stacks.

Here is how to find the total number of stamps.

24	stamps on each sheet
×3	sheets in each stack
72	stamps in each stack
×10	stacks
720	stamps

$$\begin{array}{r} 24 \\ \times 30 \\ \hline 720 \end{array}$$

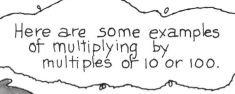

A shortcut is to write the 0 in the product first and then multiply by 3.

Here are some examples of multiplying by multiples of 10 or 100.

$$\begin{array}{r} 154 \\ \times 80 \\ \hline 12,320 \end{array} \qquad \begin{array}{r} 256 \\ \times 200 \\ \hline 57,200 \end{array} \qquad \begin{array}{r} 593 \\ \times 400 \\ \hline 237,200 \end{array} \qquad \begin{array}{r} 742 \\ \times 600 \\ \hline 445,200 \end{array}$$

EXERCISES
Multiply.

1.   24
   ×20
	2. 42
	   ×50
		3. 63
		   ×70
			4. 82
			   ×40
				5. 56
				   ×60

6. 125
   ×50
	7. 156
	   ×30
		8. 240
		   ×70
			9. 356
			   ×80
				10. 456
				   ×60

11. 571
   ×50
	12. 602
	   ×60
		13. 800
		   ×90
			14. 456
			   ×70
				15. 783
				   ×80

16. 295
  ×200
	17. 746
	  ×400
		18. 519
		  ×300
			19. 920
			  ×600
				20. 693
				  ×500

21. 527
  ×800
	22. 640
	  ×700
		23. 806
		  ×600
			24. 758
			  ×900
				25. 846
				  ×500

Solve.

26.

How many cookies in 30 boxes?

27.

How many sheets of paper in 200 packages?

28. A truck farmer planted 260 tomato plants in each of 60 rows. How many tomato plants did he plant?

29. To build a section of fence for her dog, Miss Bailey needs 512 nails. She plans to build 20 sections. How many nails does she need?

Multiply across.
Multiply down.

30.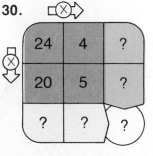

24	4	?
20	5	?
?	?	?

31.

52	6	?
8	5	?
?	?	?

32.

68	5	?
20	4	?
?	?	?

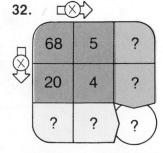

Multiplying by a 2-digit number

Twenty-one cases of soup have been delivered to the supermarket. How many cans of soup is that?

There are 24 cans in each case. We can find the total number of cans by using the **distributive property:**

$$24 \times 21 = (24 \times 20) + (24 \times 1)$$

Step 1. Multiply by 1.

$$
\begin{array}{r}
24 \\
\times\ 21 \\
\hline
24
\end{array}
$$
24 *cans in 1 case*

Step 2. Multiply by 20.

$$
\begin{array}{r}
24 \\
\times\ 21 \\
\hline
24 \\
480
\end{array}
$$
480 *cans in 20 cases*

Step 3. Add.

$$
\begin{array}{r}
24 \\
\times\ 21 \\
\hline
24 \\
480 \\
\hline
504
\end{array}
$$
504 *cans in all 21 cases*

Another example.

$$
\begin{array}{r}
\overset{32}{\overset{53}{574}} \\
\times\ 58 \\
\hline
4592 \\
28700 \\
\hline
33{,}292
\end{array}
$$

EXERCISES

Give each product.

1. 53 ×24	2. 37 ×25	3. 73 ×32	4. 95 ×43	5. 60 ×38
6. 49 ×49	7. 83 ×45	8. 54 ×53	9. 78 ×64	10. 95 ×58
11. 96 ×25	12. 57 ×36	13. 74 ×62	14. 62 ×40	15. 81 ×74
16. 158 ×31	17. 296 ×45	18. 342 ×62	19. 506 ×51	20. 821 ×78
21. $1.42 ×46	22. $6.95 ×70	23. $9.24 ×43	24. $5.38 ×97	25. $8.26 ×64

Solve.

26.

How many apples in 24 boxes?

27.

How much will 18 tickets cost?

28. Bill can read 23 pages in an hour. How many pages can he read in 12 hours?

29. While on a 4-day car trip, Miss Johnson averaged 61 kilometers an hour. How far did she drive if she drove 8 hours each day?

Who am I?

30. I am 68 greater than the product of 42 and 16.

31. I am 54 less than the product of 232 and 34.

32. I am the product of 89 multiplied by the sum of 25 and 37.

73

Multiplying by a 3-digit number

The example below shows how to multiply by a
3-digit number.

EXAMPLE.
$$\begin{array}{r} 364 \\ \times\ 123 \end{array}$$

$$\begin{array}{r} 400 \\ \times 100 \\ \hline 40,000 \end{array}$$

Step 1.	**Step 2.**	**Step 3.**	**Step 4.**
Multiply by 3.	Multiply by 20.	Multiply by 100.	Add.

Step 1. Multiply by 3.

$$\begin{array}{r} 364 \\ \times\ 123 \\ \hline 1092 \end{array}$$

Step 2. Multiply by 20.

$$\begin{array}{r} 364 \\ \times\ 123 \\ \hline 1092 \\ 7280 \end{array}$$

Step 3. Multiply by 100.

$$\begin{array}{r} 364 \\ \times\ 123 \\ \hline 1092 \\ 7280 \\ 36400 \end{array}$$

Step 4. Add.

$$\begin{array}{r} 364 \\ \times\ 123 \\ \hline 1092 \\ 7280 \\ 36400 \\ \hline 44,772 \end{array}$$

EXERCISES

First estimate the product.
Then multiply.

1. 52
   ×38 $\begin{Bmatrix} 50 \\ ×40 \end{Bmatrix}$

2. 61
   ×52

3. 78
   ×39

4. 85
   ×64

5. 298
   ×42

6. 321
   ×39

7. 468
   ×126

8. 705
   ×283

9. 883
   ×327

Multiply.

10. 374
    ×152

11. 495
    ×344

12. 784
    ×285

13. 714
    ×329

14. 866
    ×304

15. 589
    ×206

★16. 7419
     ×340

★17. 3659
     ×428

★18. 8953
     ×765

Solve.

19. At a sports arena there are 168 rows of seats with 92 seats in each row. How many seats are in the arena?

20. Ms. Allison works 7 hours a day, 5 days a week. How many hours does she work in 48 weeks?

1. 93
   − 21

2. 78
   − 40

3. 58
   − 39

4. 80
   − 43

5. 453
   − 271

6. 526
   − 152

7. 642
   − 395

8. 834
   − 456

9. 903
   − 275

10. 600
    − 458

11. 2319
    − 528

12. 5678
    − 1759

13. 32005
    − 6384

14. 91063
    − 30847

15. 827609
    − 59318

16. 508394
    − 186503

Practice

Give each product.

1. 372
   × 26

2. 406
   × 37

3. 293
   × 83

4. 756
   × 48

5. 872
   × 70

6. 935
   × 45

7. 225
   × 88

8. 248
   × 25

9. 394
   × 27

10. 630
    × 19

11. 803
    × 59

12. 159
    × 73

13. 562
    × 143

14. 781
    × 222

15. 457
    × 300

16. 283
    × 500

17. 743
    × 302

18. 643
    × 507

19. 231
    × 421

20. 775
    × 806

21. 504
    × 276

22. 703
    × 543

23. 805
    × 607

24. 906
    × 505

25. 619
    × 342

26. 879
    × 131

27. 608
    × 773

28. 159
    × 638

29. 580
    × 179

30. 176
    × 389

31. 460
    × 527

32. 908
    × 709

33. 638
    × 419

34. 456
    × 911

35. 920
    × 105

Remember that these steps can help you solve problems.

1. Read the problem and find the question.

2. What are the facts?

3. Decide what to do.

4. Answer the question.

5. Estimate! Does your answer seem right?

36. In a 500-kilometer stock car race all 17 starters were able to finish. How many kilometers were driven in all?

37. In a theater there are 25 rows with 32 seats in each row and 25 rows with 36 seats in each row. How many seats are there in all?

38. There are 12 classes in the Marshall School. Each class has 34 students. If 37 students are absent, how many students are present?

39. A library ordered 24 books that cost $9.95 each and 16 records that cost $4.98 each. What was the total amount of the order?

40. Captain Rogers flies an airliner between Seattle, Washington and Atlanta, Georgia, a distance of 3512 kilometers. In 8 round trips, how far would he fly?

41. Mrs. Steiner drives a school bus. Her route is 45 kilometers long. One year she drove the route twice a day for 180 days. How far did she drive?

PROBLEM SOLVING

Make up a problem to fit.

NUMBER NEWS

$(6 \times 25) + 8 = 158$

Problem solving

1. One year Bob McAdoo scored 934 field goals. Each field goal is worth 2 points. How many points did McAdoo score on field goals that year?

2. One year Rick Barry scored 1011 field goals and 753 free throws. Each field goal is worth 2 points and each free throw is worth 1 point. How many points did he score?

3. One year Jerry West scored a total of 2309 points. He scored 831 field goals. How many free throws did he make?

4. a. In 1962 Wilt Chamberlain averaged about 50 points a game. At that rate, how many points did he score in 20 games?
   b. If Chamberlain played in 80 games in 1962, what was his total for the year?

5. a. In 1965, Chamberlain averaged about 35 points a game. How many points did he score in 50 games?
   b. If he played in 73 games in 1965, what was his point total for the year?

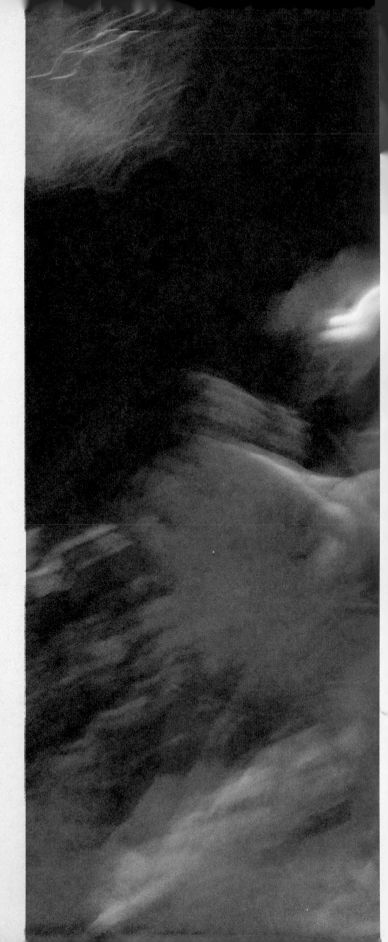

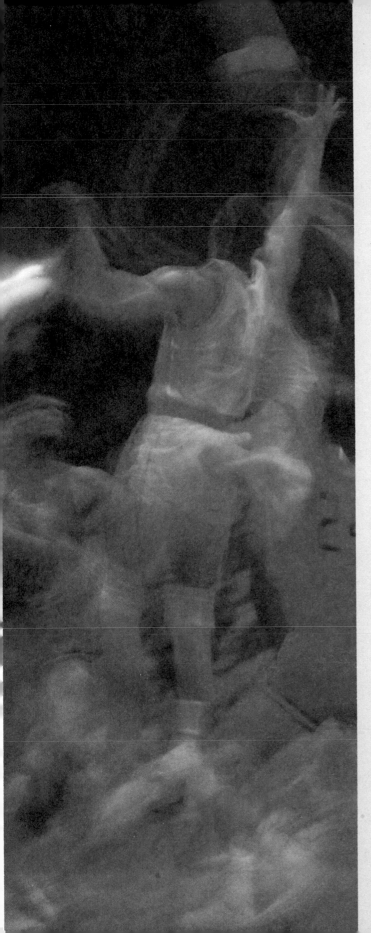

6. Our basketball stadium has 3 sections, A, B, and C. Section A has 3842 seats, and section B has 468 more seats than section A. If there are 13,284 seats in all, how many seats are in section C?

7. a. In one basketball stadium a section contains 32 rows with 26 seats in each row. How many seats are in the section?
   b. How many seats are there in 18 such sections?

8. If tickets for a game cost $3.50, how much would 10 tickets cost? 24 tickets?

9. Season tickets for 41 home games cost $130. Single tickets sell for $3.50 each. How much cheaper are season tickets?

10. a. One program seller sold 748 programs. If they cost $.75 each, how much did she take in?
    b. If the programs cost her $.40 each, what was her profit? (Profit is the difference between the cost to the seller and the selling price.)

CHAPTER CHECKUP

Give the least common multiple. [pages 60, 61]

1. 4, 6   2. 3, 7   3. 6, 8   4. 9, 6   5. 8, 4

Find each product. [pages 62–75]

6. 42
   ×2

7. 28
   ×4

8. 279
   ×6

9. 1496
   ×7

10. 84252
    ×8

11. 342
    ×10

12. 3482
    ×100

13. 3938
    ×60

14. 253
    ×52

15. 792
    ×68

16. 384
    ×200

17. 391
    ×125

Solve. [pages 77–79]

18.

How many paper clips
in 9 boxes?

19.

How many tacks in 36 boxes?

20. Ms. Davis owns a school supply
    store. She has 78 boxes of ball
    point pens with 120 pens in each
    box. How many pens does she
    have?

21. Ms. Davis has 124 boxes of
    pencils with 144 pencils in each
    box. How many pencils does she
    have?

Project

1. What was the date of your birth?

2. How many years old are you?

3. How many days old are you?

4. Determine about how many hours you have lived.

5. About how many minutes have you lived?

6. About how many seconds have you lived?

Remember—

60 seconds = 1 minute
60 minutes = 1 hour
24 hours = 1 day
365 days = 1 year
366 days = 1 leap year

CHAPTER REVIEW

Multiply.

1. $\overset{1}{3}6$
    $\times 3$
    $\overline{108}$

2. 254
    $\times 9$

3. 1326
    $\times 7$

4. 42
    $\times 10$
    $\overline{420}$

5. 256
    $\times 10$

6. 384
    $\times 100$

7. $\overset{1}{8}3$
    $\times 60$
    $\overline{4980}$

8. 78
    $\times 40$

9. 453
    $\times 200$

10. $\overset{1}{8}5$
    $\times 23$
    $\overline{255}$ ◦◦ (3 × 85)
    1700 ◦◦ (20 × 85)
    $\overline{1955}$

11. 79
    $\times 46$

12. 58
    $\times 85$

13. $\overset{1}{5}23$
    $\times 146$
    $\overline{3138}$ ◦ (6 × 523)
    20920 ◦◦ (40 × 523)
    52300 ◦◦ (100 × 523)
    $\overline{76,358}$

14. 642
    $\times 234$

15. 859
    $\times 357$

CHAPTER CHALLENGE

Find this sum.

$1 + 2 + 3 + 4 + 5 + 6 = \underline{\ ?\ }$

Now find the same sum by multiplying.

ATTENTION
SHORTCUT
AHEAD

SHORTCUT

The sum of each pair is 7. There are 3 pairs.

Use the multiplication shortcut to find these sums.

1. $1 + 2 + 3 + 4 = \underline{\ ?\ }$

2. $1 + 2 + 3 + 4 + 5 + 6 + 7 + 8 = \underline{\ ?\ }$

3. $1 + 2 + 3 + \ \ + 8 + 9 + 10 = \underline{\ ?\ }$

4. $1 + 2 + \ \ + 15 + 16 = \underline{\ ?\ }$

5. $2 + 4 + \ \ + 18 + 20 = \underline{\ ?\ }$

★6. $1 + 2 + 3 + \ \ + 97 + 98 + 99 = \underline{\ ?\ }$

a b c d   a b c d   a b c d   a b c d   a b c d   a b c d
14   34   14   4   30
a b c d   a b c d   a b c d
15   31
a b c

MAJOR CHECKUP
Standardized Format

Choose the correct letter.

1. The expanded numeral for 578 is
   a. five hundred seventy-eight
   b. $500 + 70 + 8$
   c.

Hundreds	Tens	Ones
5	7	8

   d. none of these

2. In 94,167, the digit in the ten thousands place is
   a. 1
   b. 9
   c. 4
   d. none of these

3. In 563,740, the 5 stands for
   a. 5 ten thousands
   b. 5000
   c. 500
   d. none of these

4. 743,500 rounded to the nearest thousand is
   a. 743,500
   b. 743,000
   c. 744,000
   d. none of these

5. In 438,715,602, the 3 stands for
   a. 3 ten thousands
   b. 3 million
   c. 3 ten millions
   d. none of these

6. Add.
   35281
   +7896
   a. 32,077
   b. 42,177
   c. 33,177
   d. none of these

7. Add.
   521
   78
   256
   +642
   a. 1497
   b. 1487
   c. 1397
   d. none of these

8. Subtract.
   705
   − 156
   a. 651
   b. 559
   c. 549
   d. none of these

9. Subtract.
   753214
   − 85392
   a. 732,182
   b. 667,822
   c. 668,822
   d. none of these

10. The least common multiple of 8 and 6 is
    a. 2
    b. 48
    c. 24
    d. none of these

11. Multiply.
    3821
    ×7
    a. 26,747
    b. 26,757
    c. 21,647
    d. none of these

12. Multiply.
    164
    ×258
    a. 33,312
    b. 42,312
    c. 42,302
    d. none of these

4
Division

The basic division facts

You don't have to learn any new facts, because division is just finding a missing factor. If you remember the multiplication facts, you know the division facts.

If you remember: $6 \times 4 = 24$

then you know: $24 \div 6 = 4$

and

$24 \div 4 = 6$

divisor   quotient

To solve a division problem, think about a multiplication fact.

$9 \times \underline{?} = 72$

$72 \div 9 = \underline{?}$

Here is another way to write a division problem.

divisor ⟶ $9\overline{)36}$ 4 ⟵ quotient

$36 \div 9 = 4$

In some division problems there is a remainder.

$$9\overline{)38} \quad 4\ R2$$
$$\underline{-36}$$
$$2$$

86

EXERCISES

Give each missing factor.

1. $6 \times \underline{?} = 30$

2. $3 \times \underline{?} = 27$

3. $4 \times \underline{?} = 24$

4. $8 \times \underline{?} = 56$

5. $4 \times \underline{?} = 32$

6. $7 \times \underline{?} = 63$

7. $6 \times \underline{?} = 36$

8. $5 \times \underline{?} = 40$

9. $6 \times \underline{?} = 42$

10. $8 \times \underline{?} = 72$

11. $6 \times \underline{?} = 48$

12. $9 \times \underline{?} = 81$

Give each quotient.

$6 \times 7 = 42$

13. $42 \div 6 = \underline{?}$

$8 \times 6 = 48$

14. $48 \div 8 = \underline{?}$

$4 \times 9 = 36$

15. $36 \div 4 = \underline{?}$

$5 \times ? = 45$

16. $45 \div 5 = \underline{?}$

$9 \times ? = 54$

17. $54 \div 9 = \underline{?}$

$9 \times ? = 63$

18. $63 \div 9 = \underline{?}$

19. $45 \div 9 = \underline{?}$

20. $63 \div 7 = \underline{?}$

21. $72 \div 8 = \underline{?}$

22. $64 \div 8 = \underline{?}$

23. $81 \div 9 = \underline{?}$

24. $49 \div 7 = \underline{?}$

25. $4 \overline{)24}$

26. $3 \overline{)27}$

27. $7 \overline{)49}$

28. $2 \overline{)18}$

29. $5 \overline{)40}$

30. $4 \overline{)32}$

31. $8 \overline{)32}$

32. $7 \overline{)21}$

33. $8 \overline{)24}$

34. $9 \overline{)27}$

35. $6 \overline{)48}$

36. $9 \overline{)63}$

37. $8 \overline{)72}$

38. $5 \overline{)35}$

39. $6 \overline{)42}$

Give each quotient and remainder.

40. $4 \overline{)17}$

41. $3 \overline{)16}$

42. $3 \overline{)17}$

43. $5 \overline{)24}$

44. $6 \overline{)23}$

45. $8 \overline{)53}$

46. $9 \overline{)48}$

47. $7 \overline{)51}$

48. $6 \overline{)50}$

49. $8 \overline{)43}$

50. $7 \overline{)41}$

51. $8 \overline{)62}$

52. $9 \overline{)71}$

53. $9 \overline{)65}$

54. $9 \overline{)75}$

55. $8 \overline{)46}$

56. $4 \overline{)33}$

57. $5 \overline{)39}$

58. $4 \overline{)29}$

59. $6 \overline{)38}$

Basic division facts

All the basic division facts are listed below.
See how many seconds it takes you to write the quotients.

1. 4$\overline{)4}$ 2. 9$\overline{)0}$ 3. 2$\overline{)4}$ 4. 7$\overline{)49}$ 5. 2$\overline{)2}$

6. 7$\overline{)21}$ 7. 1$\overline{)8}$ 8. 9$\overline{)18}$ 9. 5$\overline{)5}$ 10. 6$\overline{)6}$

11. 1$\overline{)7}$ 12. 8$\overline{)16}$ 13. 5$\overline{)20}$ 14. 3$\overline{)24}$ 15. 3$\overline{)15}$

16. 7$\overline{)0}$ 17. 9$\overline{)9}$ 18. 7$\overline{)56}$ 19. 8$\overline{)40}$ 20. 7$\overline{)42}$

21. 4$\overline{)0}$ 22. 6$\overline{)12}$ 23. 1$\overline{)6}$ 24. 6$\overline{)48}$ 25. 3$\overline{)3}$

26. 5$\overline{)35}$ 27. 4$\overline{)36}$ 28. 9$\overline{)27}$ 29. 3$\overline{)12}$ 30. 2$\overline{)6}$

31. 3$\overline{)0}$ 32. 4$\overline{)24}$ 33. 1$\overline{)0}$ 34. 6$\overline{)36}$ 35. 4$\overline{)8}$

36. 8$\overline{)24}$ 37. 1$\overline{)9}$ 38. 1$\overline{)3}$ 39. 7$\overline{)35}$ 40. 4$\overline{)16}$

41. 6$\overline{)18}$ 42. 7$\overline{)7}$ 43. 5$\overline{)30}$ 44. 2$\overline{)0}$ 45. 5$\overline{)10}$

46. 8$\overline{)8}$ 47. 9$\overline{)36}$ 48. 4$\overline{)32}$ 49. 1$\overline{)1}$ 50. 5$\overline{)15}$

51. 3$\overline{)18}$ 52. 8$\overline{)72}$ 53. 7$\overline{)63}$ 54. 9$\overline{)45}$ 55. 9$\overline{)63}$

56. 5$\overline{)45}$ 57. 2$\overline{)8}$ 58. 8$\overline{)32}$ 59. 4$\overline{)12}$ 60. 9$\overline{)81}$

61. 2$\overline{)12}$ 62. 8$\overline{)64}$ 63. 6$\overline{)24}$ 64. 8$\overline{)0}$ 65. 1$\overline{)2}$

66. 3$\overline{)6}$ 67. 6$\overline{)42}$ 68. 3$\overline{)27}$ 69. 6$\overline{)54}$ 70. 7$\overline{)14}$

71. 2$\overline{)18}$ 72. 5$\overline{)0}$ 73. 8$\overline{)48}$ 74. 2$\overline{)14}$ 75. 5$\overline{)25}$

76. 7$\overline{)28}$ 77. 5$\overline{)40}$ 78. 2$\overline{)10}$ 79. 4$\overline{)28}$ 80. 1$\overline{)4}$

81. 9$\overline{)72}$ 82. 9$\overline{)54}$ 83. 3$\overline{)9}$ 84. 4$\overline{)20}$ 85. 6$\overline{)0}$

86. 1$\overline{)5}$ 87. 8$\overline{)56}$ 88. 2$\overline{)16}$ 89. 3$\overline{)21}$ 90. 6$\overline{)30}$

Check your answers.

1. 1	**2.** 0	**3.** 2	**4.** 7	**5.** 1
6. 3	**7.** 8	**8.** 2	**9.** 1	**10.** 1
11. 7	**12.** 2	**13.** 4	**14.** 8	**15.** 5
16. 0	**17.** 1	**18.** 8	**19.** 5	**20.** 6
21. 0	**22.** 2	**23.** 6	**24.** 8	**25.** 1
26. 7	**27.** 9	**28.** 3	**29.** 4	**30.** 3
31. 0	**32.** 6	**33.** 0	**34.** 6	**35.** 2
36. 3	**37.** 9	**38.** 3	**39.** 5	**40.** 4
41. 3	**42.** 1	**43.** 6	**44.** 0	**45.** 2
46. 1	**47.** 4	**48.** 8	**49.** 1	**50.** 3
51. 6	**52.** 9	**53.** 9	**54.** 5	**55.** 7
56. 9	**57.** 4	**58.** 4	**59.** 3	**60.** 9
61. 6	**62.** 8	**63.** 4	**64.** 0	**65.** 2
66. 2	**67.** 7	**68.** 9	**69.** 9	**70.** 2
71. 9	**72.** 0	**73.** 6	**74.** 7	**75.** 5
76. 4	**77.** 8	**78.** 5	**79.** 7	**80.** 4
81. 8	**82.** 6	**83.** 3	**84.** 5	**85.** 0
86. 5	**87.** 7	**88.** 8	**89.** 7	**90.** 5

91. To find your score, multiply the number of mistakes by 2 and add that number to the number of seconds.

92. Practice the facts that you missed. Try for a better (lower) score.

93. Work with a classmate. Give the facts orally. Keep a record of your best daily score.

94. If you wish, make a graph of your scores as shown:

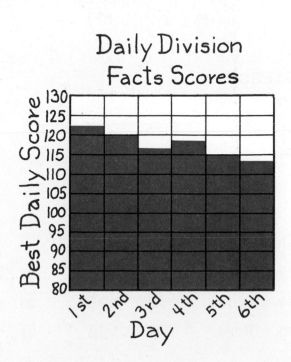

89

Factors and common factors

Since $4 \times 3 = 12$, 4 and 3 are **factors**, or **divisors**, of 12.

$$\begin{array}{r} 4 \\ \times\ 3 \\ \hline 12 \end{array}$$

$$\begin{array}{r} 6 \\ \times\ 2 \\ \hline 12 \end{array}$$

$$\begin{array}{r} 12 \\ \times\ 1 \\ \hline 12 \end{array}$$

Factors of 12: 1, 2, 3, 4, 6, 12

Is 10 a factor of 12? Why or why not?

1, 2, 3, and 6 are factors of both 18 and 24. They are called **common factors**, or **common divisors**, of 18 and 24. The **greatest common factor**, or **greatest common divisor**, of 18 and 24 is 6.

EXERCISES

List all factors.

1. 3	2. 8	3. 9	4. 12	5. 17	6. 16
7. 18	8. 21	9. 20	10. 24	11. 23	12. 25
13. 26	14. 27	15. 28	16. 30	17. 32	18. 36

List all common factors.

19. 8, 12	20. 6, 8	21. 7, 10	22. 8, 24	23. 15, 25
24. 10, 12	25. 16, 18	26. 9, 12	27. 15, 18	28. 10, 20
29. 16, 24	30. 12, 16	31. 18, 24	32. 24, 36	33. 12, 18

True or false?

34. 1 is a divisor of every number.

35. 1 is a common divisor of any two numbers.

36. 2 is a divisor of every even number.

37. 3 is a divisor of every odd number.

38. Every number has at least two divisors.

Give the greatest common factor.

39. 9, 12   40. 10, 35   41. 8, 12   42. 9, 24   43. 14, 35

44. 18, 36   45. 16, 20   46. 16, 48   47. 18, 45   48. 18, 42

49. Complete: $\underline{?} \times 0 = 7$

50. Complete: $\underline{?} \times 0 = 0$

51. Complete: $6 \div 0 = \underline{?}$ $\underline{?} \times 0 = 6$

52. Complete: $0 \div 0 = \underline{?}$ $\underline{?} \times 0 = 0$

Exercises 49–52 show why
WE DON'T DIVIDE BY 0.

91

Problem solving

These steps can help you solve problems.

1. Read the problem and find the question.
2. What are the facts?
3. Decide what to do.
4. Answer the question.
5. Estimate! Does your answer seem right?

In this lesson you will be asked to think about just
the first three steps. Here are some examples.

48 apples
Divided equally into 6 boxes
How many in each box?
Divide.

48 apples in each box
6 boxes
How many apples?
Multiply.

48 apples, divided equally
6 in a box
How many boxes?
Divide.

Two-step Problem

48 apples in each box
6 boxes
12 extra apples
How many apples?
First multiply.
Then add.

EXERCISES

The numbers have been covered.
Add, subtract, multiply, or divide?
Decide what to do.

1. ■ trees
   ■ in each row
   How many rows?

2. ■ trees in one row
   ■ more trees put into the row
   How many trees?

3. ■ apples
   ■ are thrown away
   How many are left?

4. ■ apples in each basket
   ■ baskets
   How many apples in all?

5. ■ apples in one box
   ■ apples in another
   How many fewer apples in the second box?

6. ■ apples
   ■ boxes with the same number in each box
   How many apples in each box?

7. ■ apples fill a bag
   ■ apples in the bag
   How many more apples are needed?

Here are some two-step problems.
Decide what to do. *Hint:* There may be more than one answer.

8. Had $■
   Bought ■ red apples
   Bought ■ yellow apples
   How much money was left?

9. Had ■ boxes
   ■ apples in each box
   Sold ■ apples
   How many apples were left?

10. ■ red apples
    ■ yellow apples
    ■ apples in a box
    How many boxes?

11. Had ■ boxes of apples
    Picked ■ more boxes
    ■ apples in each box
    How many apples?

12. Had $■
    Picked ■ boxes of apples
    Was paid $■ per box
    How much money then?

13. ■ apples
    Put ■ apples in each box
    Was paid $■ per box
    What was the total pay?

Dividing a 2-digit number

Study the examples to see how to divide a 2-digit number by a 1-digit number.

EXAMPLE 1. We can find the quotient by dividing up the blocks.

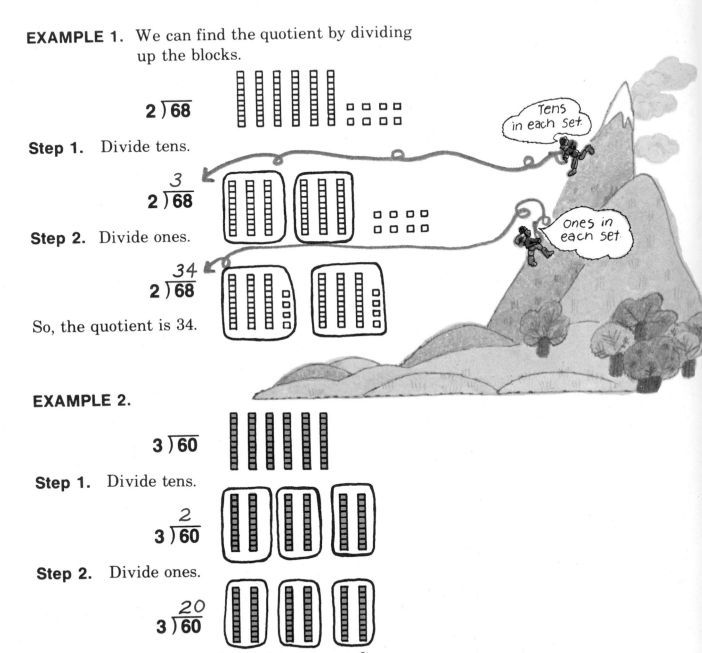

$2\overline{)68}$

Step 1. Divide tens.

$2\overline{)68}$ with 3 above

Tens in each set

Step 2. Divide ones.

$2\overline{)68}$ with 34 above

ones in each set

So, the quotient is 34.

EXAMPLE 2.

$3\overline{)60}$

Step 1. Divide tens.

$3\overline{)60}$ with 2 above

Step 2. Divide ones.

$3\overline{)60}$ with 20 above

The 0 in the quotient tells us that we put 0 ones in each of the 3 sets. What would happen if we didn't write the 0 in the quotient?

EXERCISES

Divide.

1. $2\overline{)68}$
2. $3\overline{)36}$
3. $4\overline{)40}$
4. $4\overline{)44}$
5. $3\overline{)39}$

6. $2\overline{)64}$
7. $4\overline{)88}$
8. $2\overline{)86}$
9. $4\overline{)80}$
10. $3\overline{)33}$

11. $2\overline{)42}$
12. $2\overline{)84}$
13. $4\overline{)84}$
14. $2\overline{)44}$
15. $2\overline{)62}$

16. $4\overline{)48}$
17. $3\overline{)30}$
18. $3\overline{)99}$
19. $2\overline{)88}$
20. $2\overline{)80}$

21. $2\overline{)46¢}$
22. $3\overline{)66¢}$
23. $6\overline{)66¢}$
24. $3\overline{)63¢}$
25. $5\overline{)55¢}$

Solve.

26. Stella made some sandwiches for a hiking trip. She used 48 slices of bread. How many sandwiches did she make?

27. A club sandwich requires 3 slices of bread. If Stanley has 60 slices of bread, how many club sandwiches can he make?

28. Jerry baked 96 cookies. He wants to put the same number of cookies in each of 3 bags. How many should he put in each bag?

29. Jan collected 66 bottles. She wants to put them in cartons of 6. How many cartons does she need?

Division with regrouping

In some division problems you need to regroup.
Study the examples.

EXAMPLE.

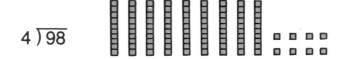

4) 98

Step 1. Divide tens. Put 2 tens in each of
the 4 sets. That leaves 1 ten.

Used 8 tens. There is 1 ten remaining

$$\begin{array}{r} 2 \\ 4\overline{)98} \\ -8 \\ \hline 1 \end{array}$$

Step 2. Regroup 1 ten for 10 ones.

$$\begin{array}{r} 2 \\ 4\overline{)98} \\ -8 \\ \hline 18 \end{array}$$

Write the 8 here and think of this as 18 ones.

Step 3. Divide ones. Put 4 ones in each of
the four sets.

2 ones left

$$\begin{array}{r} 24 \\ 4\overline{)98} \\ -8 \\ \hline 18 \\ -16 \\ \hline 2 \end{array}$$

96

EXERCISES
Divide.

1. 4$\overline{)88}$ 2. 3$\overline{)57}$ 3. 2$\overline{)75}$ 4. 7$\overline{)98}$ 5. 7$\overline{)86}$

6. 3$\overline{)42}$ 7. 6$\overline{)88}$ 8. 3$\overline{)85}$ 9. 6$\overline{)78}$ 10. 4$\overline{)80}$

11. 2$\overline{)52}$ 12. 5$\overline{)80}$ 13. 7$\overline{)84}$ 14. 8$\overline{)96}$ 15. 5$\overline{)90}$

16. 3$\overline{)87}$ 17. 3$\overline{)54}$ 18. 6$\overline{)96}$ 19. 7$\overline{)91}$ 20. 5$\overline{)65}$

21. 2$\overline{)64}$ 22. 5$\overline{)78}$ 23. 5$\overline{)60}$ 24. 6$\overline{)90}$ 25. 2$\overline{)96}$

26. 3$\overline{)45¢}$ 27. 5$\overline{)95¢}$ 28. 3$\overline{)48¢}$ 29. 4$\overline{)76¢}$ 30. 6$\overline{)72¢}$

Solve.

31. 24 tomato plants in a box
8 boxes
How many plants?

32. 84 pepper plants
7 in each row
How many rows?

33. 96 watermelon seeds
6 planted in each hill
How many hills?

34. 18 potato plants in each row
9 rows
How many plants?

Who am I?

35. If you divide me by 4, you get 19.

36. If you multiply me by 3, you get 72.

Dividing greater numbers

You can divide larger numbers in the same way
you divide 2-digit numbers.

EXAMPLE 1. 3) 442

Step 1. Divide hundreds. Subtract.

```
      1
 3 ) 442
    - 3
      1
```

Step 2. Regroup.

```
      1
 3 ) 442
    - 3
      14
```

Step 3. Divide tens. Subtract.

```
      14
 3 ) 442
    - 3
      14
    - 12
       2
```

Step 4. Regroup.

```
      14
 3 ) 442
    - 3
      14
    - 12
      22
```

Step 5. Divide ones. Subtract.

```
      147 R1
 3 ) 442
    - 3
      14
    - 12
      22
    - 21
       1
```

EXAMPLE 2. 5) 3512

Step 1. Not enough thousands.

```
 5 ) 3512
```

Step 2. Regroup and divide
hundreds. Subtract.

```
      7
 5 ) 3512
    - 35
```

Step 3. Not enough tens.

```
      70
 5 ) 3512
    - 35
       1
```

Step 4. Regroup and divide ones.
Subtract.

```
      702 R2
 5 ) 3512
    - 35
       12
     - 10
        2
```

EXERCISES
Divide.

1. 3)521 2. 6)719 3. 7)926 4. 3)742 5. 2)725

6. 5)653 7. 3)842 8. 4)664 9. 3)500 10. 8)976

11. 6)$8.34 12. 4)$6.44 13. 4)$8.32 14. 8)$9.04 15. 4)$8.28

16. 4)152 17. 6)321 18. 8)415 19. 5)329 20. 8)726

21. 7)526 22. 9)456 23. 6)394 24. 9)498 25. 7)645

26. 5)4173 27. 6)3818 28. 4)3042 29. 4)2815 30. 4)2882

31. 7)1675 32. 2)3416 33. 9)9314 34. 6)5151 35. 6)5436

Sometimes, people forget to write 0s
in quotients.

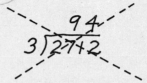

If you estimate first you may not make that
mistake. Here's a way to estimate a quotient.

EXAMPLE 1.
Step 1. Find the first digit of the
quotient.

$$\frac{9}{3)2712}$$

Step 2. Write 0s in *all* remaining
places.

$$\frac{900}{3)2712} \leftarrow estimate$$

EXAMPLE 2.
Step 1. Find the first digit.

$$\frac{6}{4)257}$$

Step 2. Write 0s.

$$\frac{60}{4)257} \leftarrow estimate$$

Estimate. Then find each quotient.

36. 5)512 37. 4)831 38. 6)362 39. 2)157 40. 3)919

41. 6)7153 42. 2)9674 43. 5)3517 44. 8)2403 45. 6)5418

Finding an average

The table below shows the students who entered the rope-jumping contest.

NAME	Jumps Without a Miss		
	First Try	Second Try	Third Try
Ann	45	28	23
Bill	37	36	29
David	18	42	39
Mickey	29	53	26
Ruth	36	37	59
Terry	51	26	40

Ann had a total of 96 jumps. If you divide this total by 3, you get the **average** number of jumps she made on each try.

$$
\begin{array}{r}
45 \\
28 \\
+23 \\
\hline
96
\end{array}
$$

Ann's average $\rightarrow$ 32

3)96

EXERCISES

1. What was Bill's average?

2. What was Ruth's average?

3. Find the average number of jumps for the first try.

4. Find the average number of jumps for the second try.

5. Who had the higher average, David or Terry? How much higher?

6. Who had the highest average? the lowest average?

7. What was Carol's average long jump?

8. Who had the greater average, Al or Paige?

9. Find the average length of the jumps on the first try.

10. How does the first-jump average compare with the last-jump average?

NAME	Standing Long Jump in Centimeters				
	1st Try	2nd Try	3rd Try	4th Try	5th Try
Al	132	136	127	130	125
Carol	138	135	138	132	122
Dennis	121	118	129	128	124
Mimi	130	126	120	125	134
Jill	116	118	125	123	123
Paige	133	136	132	128	131
Ralph	126	132	119	120	123

The bar graph shows the number of baskets made in the free-throw contest.

11. What was the average number of baskets?

12. Did anyone make the average score? Who scored above the average? Who scored below?

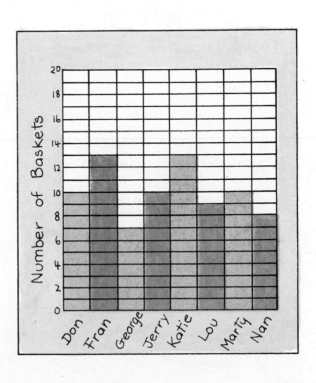

Dividing by a 2-digit number

We divide by a 2-digit number the same way that we divide by a 1-digit number. Here are the multiplication facts for 24. Let's use them to do a division problem.

Step 1.   Not enough hundreds.

$$24\overline{)786}$$

Step 2.   Think 78 tens.
Divide and subtract.

$$
\begin{array}{r}
3 \\
24\overline{)78\,6} \\
-72 \\
\hline
6
\end{array}
$$

This is the fact we need.

Step 3.   Regroup, divide, and subtract.
Think 66 ones.

$$
\begin{array}{r}
32\ R18 \\
24\overline{)786} \\
-72 \\
\hline
66 \\
-48 \\
\hline
18
\end{array}
$$

Use the given multiplication facts to help you with the division problems.

| 27
× 0
0 | 27
× 1
27 | 27
× 2
54 | 27
× 3
81 | 27
× 4
108 | 27
× 5
135 | 27
× 6
162 | 27
× 7
189 | 27
× 8
216 | 27
× 9
243 |

1. 27)864   2. 27)962   3. 27)298   4. 27)513   5. 27)729

6. 27)803   7. 27)958   8. 27)742   9. 27)690   10. 27)899

| 19
× 0
0 | 19
× 1
19 | 19
× 2
38 | 19
× 3
57 | 19
× 4
76 |

11. 19)258   12. 19)374   13. 19)526

| 19
× 5
95 | 19
× 6
114 | 19
× 7
133 | 19
× 8
152 | 19
× 9
171 |

14. 19)675   15. 19)400   16. 19)793

17. 19)877   18. 19)370   19. 19)964

To estimate quotients, find the first digit:

$$\frac{5}{57)\overline{31562}}$$

write 0s in the remaining places.

$$\frac{500}{57)\overline{31562}} \leftarrow \text{estimate}$$

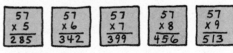

| 57
× 0
0 | 57
× 1
57 | 57
× 2
114 | 57
× 3
171 | 57
× 4
228 |

| 57
× 5
285 | 57
× 6
342 | 57
× 7
399 | 57
× 8
456 | 57
× 9
513 |

Estimate each quotient. Then divide.

20. 57)3675   21. 57)1077   22. 57)16772

23. 57)39564   24. 57)84165   25. 57)564

26. 57)63141   27. 57)459   28. 57)48348

More about dividing by a 2-digit number

In the last lesson you were given all the multiplication facts. In this lesson you will have to work out your own multiplication facts as you divide. The examples show how to use rounding to decide which multiplication facts are needed.

EXAMPLE 1.   32) 870

Step 1. Round the divisor to the nearest 10. Think about dividing by 30.

30

32) 870

Step 2. Think about the multiplication facts for 30.

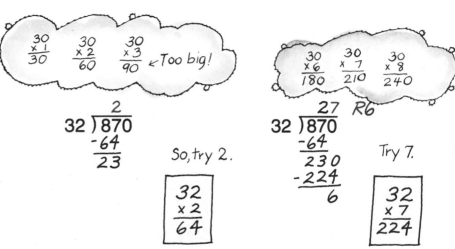

$$\begin{array}{c} 30 \\ \times\ 1 \\ \hline 30 \end{array} \quad \begin{array}{c} 30 \\ \times\ 2 \\ \hline 60 \end{array} \quad \begin{array}{c} 30 \\ \times\ 3 \\ \hline 90 \end{array} \leftarrow \text{Too big!}$$

```
        2
32 ) 870
    -64
     23
```

So, try 2.

```
 32
× 2
 64
```

Step 3. Think about the multiplication facts for 30.

$$\begin{array}{c} 30 \\ \times\ 6 \\ \hline 180 \end{array} \quad \begin{array}{c} 30 \\ \times\ 7 \\ \hline 210 \end{array} \quad \begin{array}{c} 30 \\ \times\ 8 \\ \hline 240 \end{array}$$

```
       27  R6
32 ) 870
    -64
     230
    -224
       6
```

Try 7.

```
 32
× 7
224
```

EXAMPLE 2.   36) 754

Step 1. 40

$$\begin{array}{c} 40 \\ \times\ 1 \\ \hline 40 \end{array} \quad \begin{array}{c} 40 \\ \times\ 2 \\ \hline 80 \end{array} \leftarrow \text{Too big!}$$

Try 1.

```
        1
36 ) 754
    -36
     39
```

Since this remainder is greater than 36, we need to use 2.

Step 2.

```
        2
36 ) 754
    -72
      3
```

```
 36
× 2
 72
```

Step 3.

```
       20  R34
36 ) 754
    -72
     34
    - 0
     34
```

104

EXERCISES

To what number would you round the divisor?

1. $23\overline{)783}$ 2. $49\overline{)956}$ 3. $71\overline{)803}$ 4. $36\overline{)916}$ 5. $54\overline{)642}$

Tell which multiplication fact you would work out first.

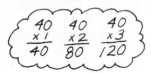

$$\begin{array}{ccc} 40 & 40 & 40 \\ \times 1 & \times 2 & \times 3 \\ \hline 40 & 80 & 120 \end{array}$$

6. $42\overline{)926}$

$$\begin{array}{ccc} 20 & 20 & 20 \\ \times 2 & \times 3 & \times 4 \\ \hline 40 & 60 & 80 \end{array}$$

7. $19\overline{)683}$

$$\begin{array}{ccc} 30 & 30 & 30 \\ \times 1 & \times 2 & \times 3 \\ \hline 30 & 60 & 90 \end{array}$$

8. $33\overline{)697}$

Divide.

9. $18\overline{)927}$ 10. $40\overline{)900}$ 11. $61\overline{)765}$ 12. $16\overline{)699}$ 13. $34\overline{)742}$

14. $33\overline{)683}$ 15. $23\overline{)374}$ 16. $43\overline{)894}$ 17. $47\overline{)963}$ 18. $42\overline{)826}$

19. $27\overline{)958}$ 20. $22\overline{)695}$ 21. $31\overline{)9012}$ 22. $58\overline{)8376}$ 23. $24\overline{)7658}$

24. $43\overline{)8935}$ 25. $36\overline{)4916}$ 26. $50\overline{)7800}$ 27. $57\overline{)65912}$ 28. $38\overline{)97434}$

Solve.

29.

a. How many rolls of film would you have to buy to take 110 pictures?

b. What would be the total price?

30.

a. How many boxes of screws would you have to buy to get 600 screws?

b. What would be the total price?

Keeping Skills Sharp

1. $\begin{array}{r} 39 \\ 74 \\ +81 \\ \hline \end{array}$ 2. $\begin{array}{r} 253 \\ 79 \\ +179 \\ \hline \end{array}$ 3. $\begin{array}{r} 688 \\ 599 \\ +73 \\ \hline \end{array}$ 4. $\begin{array}{r} 652 \\ 891 \\ +375 \\ \hline \end{array}$ 5. $\begin{array}{r} 3916 \\ 803 \\ +2174 \\ \hline \end{array}$ 6. $\begin{array}{r} 5378 \\ 929 \\ +1625 \\ \hline \end{array}$

Division practice

EXAMPLE. $72 \overline{)59863}$

Step 1.

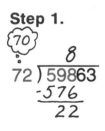

```
        8
72 )59863
   -576
     22
```

I just think about dividing 7 into 59.

$72 \overline{)59863}$ with 8

Step 2.

```
       83
72 )59863
   -576
     226
    -216
      10
```

I just think about dividing 7 into 22.

```
       83
72 )59863
   -576
     226
```

Step 3.

```
      831 R31
72 )59863
   -576
     226
    -216
     103
    - 72
      31
```

I just think about dividing 7 into 10.

```
       831
72 )59863
   -576
     226
    -216
     103
```

We can check a division problem by multiplying the quotient by the divisor and then adding the remainder.

```
    831
   ×72
   1662
  58170
  59,832
```

```
  59832
  + 31 ← remainder
  59,863  It checks!
```

106

EXERCISES

Divide.

1. 8)9367

2. 5)8291

3. 7)6403

4. 9)2853

5. 4)28345

6. 3)70652

7. 8)916304

8. 6)523068

9. 25)2834

10. 32)7136

11. 64)9284

12. 42)9035

13. 37)38216

14. 59)74555

15. 48)92307

16. 27)56283

Round each answer to the nearest cent.

EXAMPLE.

```
         $ 24.46
32 ) $782.98
      -64
      ───
      142
     -128
     ────
      149
     -128
     ────
      218
     -192
     ────
       26.₀₀°
```

17. 5)$94.28

18. 8)$37.43

19. 7)$666.35

20. 9)$597.80

21. 15)$946.74

22. 25)$859.73

23. 47)$496.78

24. 39)$654.32

The remainder is more than half the divisor, so the quotient to the nearest cent is $24.47.

Solve. Give answers to the nearest cent.

25. One dozen doughnuts cost $1.85. What is the price of one doughnut?

26. The 27 students in Bill's class gave $8.70 to the United Fund. How much was the average gift?

Find the missing digits.

27.
```
        6■7 R3
    6 ) 3■2■
      - 36
      ────
        22
      - 18
      ────
        45
      - ■■
      ────
        ■
```

28.
```
         6■■ R■
    14 ) 91■5
       - ■■
       ────
         ■7
       - 70
       ────
         75
       - 70
       ────
         ■
```

★29.
```
          199■ R12
    ■■ ) ■■9■6
       - 38
       ────
         37■
       - ■■■
       ─────
         373
       - 342
       ─────
         ■■■
       - 304
       ─────
         ■■
```

Addition, subtraction, multiplication, and division

Remember to work inside the grouping symbols first.

$(3905 - 193) \div 64 = 58$

$$\begin{array}{r} 3905 \\ -193 \\ \hline 3712 \end{array}$$

$$\begin{array}{r} 58 \\ 64\overline{)3712} \\ 320 \\ \hline 512 \\ 512 \\ \hline 0 \end{array}$$

EXERCISES

Complete.

1. $(258 + 367) - 367 = \underline{?}$

2. $(582 + 453) - 453 = \underline{?}$

3. $(942 + 365) + 218 = \underline{?}$

4. $942 + (365 + 218) = \underline{?}$

5. $(782 - 526) - 142 = \underline{?}$

6. $782 - (256 - 142) = \underline{?}$

7. $(512 \div 16) \div 4 = \underline{?}$

8. $512 \div (16 \div 4) = \underline{?}$

9. $(256 \times 25) \div 25 = \underline{?}$

10. $(874 \times 39) \div 39 = \underline{?}$

11. $(4144 \div 74) + 125 = \underline{?}$

12. $238 \times (1932 \div 28) = \underline{?}$

13. $(1024 - 512) \div 32 = \underline{?}$

14. $1024 - (512 \div 32) = \underline{?}$

15. $(238 \times 5) + 17 = \underline{?}$

16. $238 \times (5 + 17) = \underline{?}$

Solve.

17.
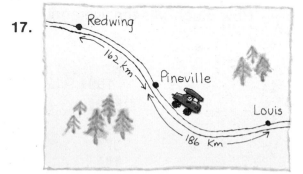

If you average 58 kilometers per hour, how long will it take you to drive from Redwing to Louis?

18. An apple grower ordered 1200 trees. If 42 trees are planted in each row, how many rows can be planted? How many trees will be left over?

19. A farmer wants to build a fence that is 1026 meters long. If the posts are 3 meters apart, How many will be needed? (Careful! The answer is not 342.)

Tell which division has the greater remainder.

1. $47\overline{)9135}$ $14\overline{)5793}$

2. $60\overline{)1397}$ $19\overline{)6307}$

3. $48\overline{)5271}$ $47\overline{)2815}$

4. $36\overline{)2750}$ $72\overline{)5306}$

Play the game.

1. Make a card for each of the digits.

2. Choose a leader.

3. Each player draws a table.

   $\boxed{}\overline{)\boxed{}}$

4. As the leader picks the cards, each player writes the digit in his or her table.

5. Repeat step 4 until your table is filled in.

6. The player who has the greatest remainder wins!

109

Problem solving

1. Bought a rake for $7.75 and a spade for $13.49. What was the total cost?

2. Spent $16.45 for seeds. Gave the clerk a $20 bill. How much change?

3. Set out 8 dozen tomato plants. How many plants?

4. Planted 48 onions in each of 12 rows. How many onions?

5. Had 115 watermelon seeds. Planted 5 in each hill. How many hills?

6. Bought 132 pepper plants. Planted 8 in each row. How many rows? How many were left over?

7. Hired a friend for $2.35 an hour. He worked 15 hours. How much did he earn?

8. A pump pumped 645 liters of water per minute for 2 hours. How much water did it pump?

Use the table below to compute each total price.

9.

CLARK'S MARKET

	PRICE
2 lb spinach	
4 lb potatoes	

10.

CLARK'S MARKET

	PRICE
2 lb beans	
5 peppers	

11.

CLARK'S MARKET

	PRICE
2 lb onions	
3 lb peas	
1 cucumber	

12.

CLARK'S MARKET

	PRICE
2 lb beans	
2 lb cabbage	
12 lb potatoes	
6 peppers	

CLARK'S FRESH VEGETABLES

BEANS	69¢ lb
SPINACH	79¢ lb
CABBAGE	23¢ lb
CUCUMBERS	17¢ each
PEAS	57¢ lb
POTATOES	25¢ lb
ONIONS	48¢ lb
PEPPERS	29¢ each

CHAPTER CHECKUP

Give the greatest common factor (divisor). [pages 90–91]

1. 6, 9
2. 8, 12
3. 12, 18
4. 15, 21
5. 16, 24

Divide. [pages 94–99, 102–104]

6. 3⟌96
7. 2⟌84
8. 3⟌54
9. 5⟌75
10. 6⟌84

11. 8⟌93
12. 4⟌78
13. 5⟌653
14. 9⟌695
15. 7⟌853

16. 42⟌966
17. 35⟌980
18. 53⟌1961
19. 81⟌6000
20. 68⟌6835

Solve. [pages 92–93, 100–101, 110–111]

21. a. What is the average test score?
    b. How many scored above the average? below the average?

22. 322 days
    How many weeks?

23. 672 hours
    How many days?

24. The Appalachian Trail stretches from Mt. Katahdin in Maine to Springer Mountain in Georgia. It is 3210 kilometers long. If you hiked 55 kilometers a day, how long would it take you to hike the trail?

Project

1. **a.** Find out how many minutes each of your classmates watched television yesterday. Compute the class average.

   b. How does your time compare to the class average?

   c. How many classmates watched television less than the average time? more than the average time?

2. **a.** Determine the average after-school playtime of your classmates.

   b. Graph your findings on a graph like this:

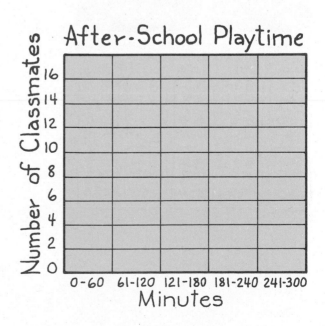

After-School Playtime

Number of Classmates

16
14
12
10
8
6
4
2
0

0-60   61-120   121-180   181-240   241-300

Minutes

CHAPTER REVIEW

Divide.

1. $\begin{array}{r} 24 \\ 2\overline{)48} \end{array}$

2. $3\overline{)93}$

3. $4\overline{)80}$

4. $\begin{array}{r} 13 \\ 6\overline{)78} \\ \underline{-6} \\ 18 \\ \underline{-18} \\ 0 \end{array}$

5. $5\overline{)95}$

6. $7\overline{)91}$

7. $\begin{array}{r} 19\ R2 \\ 3\overline{)59} \\ \underline{-3} \\ 29 \\ \underline{-27} \\ 2 \end{array}$

8. $6\overline{)83}$

9. $8\overline{)99}$

10. $\begin{array}{r} 75\ R1 \\ 7\overline{)526} \\ \underline{-49} \\ 36 \\ \underline{-35} \\ 1 \end{array}$

11. $8\overline{)756}$

12. $9\overline{)700}$

$\begin{array}{r}32\\ \times 0\\ \hline 0\end{array}$	$\begin{array}{r}32\\ \times 1\\ \hline 32\end{array}$	$\begin{array}{r}32\\ \times 2\\ \hline 64\end{array}$	$\begin{array}{r}32\\ \times 3\\ \hline 96\end{array}$	$\begin{array}{r}32\\ \times 4\\ \hline 128\end{array}$
$\begin{array}{r}32\\ \times 5\\ \hline 160\end{array}$	$\begin{array}{r}32\\ \times 6\\ \hline 192\end{array}$	$\begin{array}{r}32\\ \times 7\\ \hline 224\end{array}$	$\begin{array}{r}32\\ \times 8\\ \hline 256\end{array}$	$\begin{array}{r}32\\ \times 9\\ \hline 288\end{array}$

13. $\begin{array}{r} 24\ R17 \\ 32\overline{)785} \\ \underline{-64} \\ 145 \\ \underline{-128} \\ 17 \end{array}$

14. $32\overline{)982}$

15. $32\overline{)896}$

16. $\begin{array}{r} 70\ R54 \\ 56\overline{)3974} \\ \underline{-392} \\ 54 \\ \underline{-0} \\ 54 \end{array}$

17. $61\overline{)8306}$

18. $78\overline{)9973}$

1. Copy and complete this dot graph.

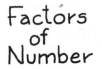

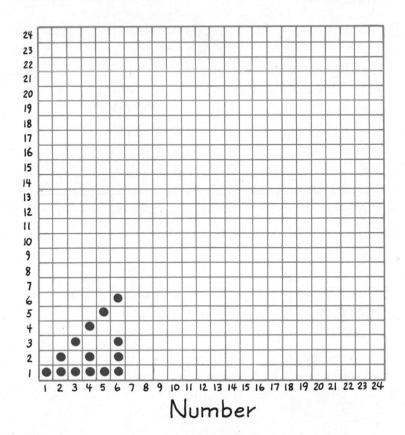

Use your completed graph to answer the following questions.

2. How many factors does 12 have? does 18 have?

3. Which number has the most factors?

4. Which numbers have exactly 3 factors?

5. A **prime number** has exactly two factors. Which numbers on your graph are prime numbers?

6. How can you use your graph to find the common factors of 12 and 18? the greatest common factor of 12 and 18?

Choose the correct letter.

1. In 748,192, the digit in the hundred thousands place is

    a. 8
    b. 4
    c. 7
    d. none of these

2. 295,634 rounded to the nearest thousand is

    a. 200,000
    b. 296,000
    c. 290,000
    d. none of these

3. 450,000 rounded to the nearest thousand is

    a. 500,000
    b. 450,000
    c. 400,000
    d. none of these

4. Which number is the least?

    a. 5,963,849
    b. 5,874,026
    c. 43,281,752
    d. 49,714,260

5. In 738,964,021, the 8 stands for

    a. 80 million
    b. 8 thousand
    c. 800 thousand
    d. none of these

6. Add.
    4639
    +2817

    a. 6446
    b. 6456
    c. 7456
    d. none of these

7. Add.
    7813
    942
    1604
    + 97

    a. 10,456
    b. 10,446
    c. 8346
    d. none of these

8. Subtract.
    7421
    − 3859

    a. 4438
    b. 4672
    c. 3672
    d. none of these

9. Subtract.
    8203
    − 856

    a. 7357
    b. 7347
    c. 8653
    d. none of these

10. Which number is a common multiple of 6 and 9?

    a. 3
    b. 15
    c. 36
    d. none of these

11. Multiply.
    613
    ×8

    a. 4884
    b. 4804
    c. 4904
    d. none of these

12. Multiply.
    7296
    ×75

    a. 88,552
    b. 529,370
    c. 547,200
    d. none of these

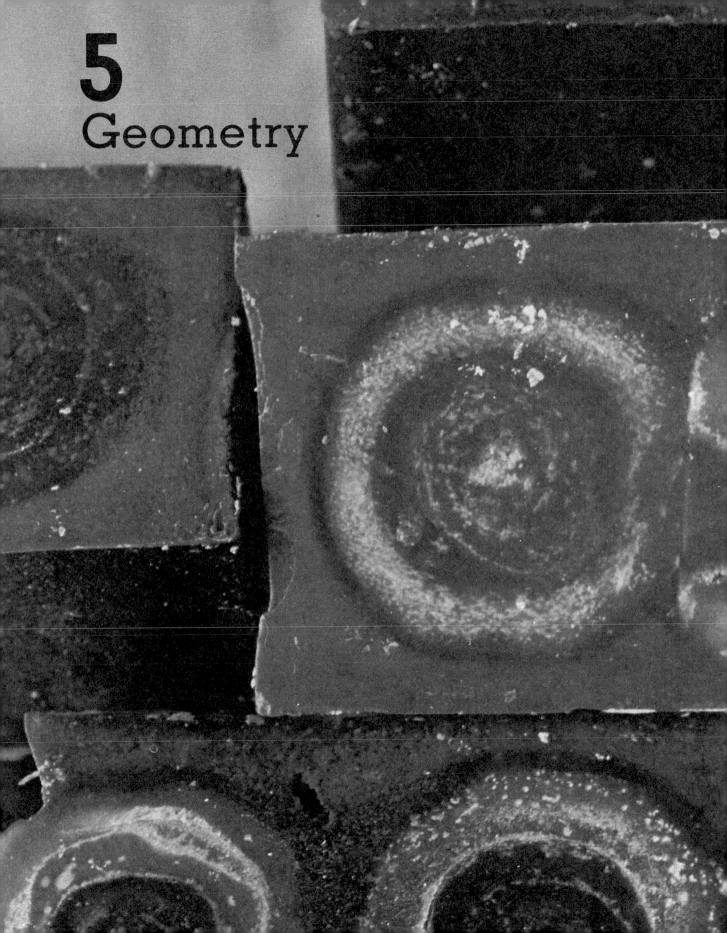

5
Geometry

1.   a. square

    b. triangle

    c. segment

2.   d. line

    e. circle

3.   f. ray

    g. point

    h. rectangle

4.

5.

6.

7.

8.

Points and segments

Sylvester the Space Spider can travel any place in space. He marks his path with a thin spider web. Sometimes he takes the shortest path between two points, a **segment**.

A segment is named by its **endpoints**. Here are two ways to name the segment:

$\overline{MN}$ (segment *MN*) $\overline{NM}$ (segment *MN*)

One day Sylvester was caught speeding. He had to spend the next week in a flat surface, a **plane**. He could go as far as he wanted in that plane, but he could not leave the plane. Here are some plane figures that Sylvester made:

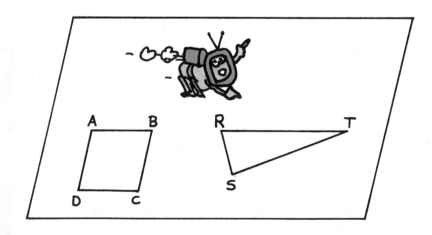

[Remember that the corner points are called **vertices** (plural of **vertex**), and the segments are called **sides**.]

EXERCISES

Which figures are plane figures? (*Hint:* Could Sylvester make the figure by staying on a flat surface?)

1.

sphere

2.

cylinder

3.

cone

4.

triangle

5.

rectangular solid

6.

rectangle

7.

cube

8.

segment

9.

square

10. Give the endpoints of the segment.

11. Give two ways to name the segment.

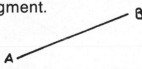

12. List the vertices of the plane figure.

13. How many sides does it have? List the sides.

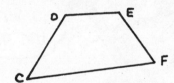

14. Complete this table.

Name	Figure	Number of vertices	Number of sides
triangle			
square			
pentagon			
hexagon			

119

Rays, angles, and lines

Hester, another spider, wanted to spend her whole life traveling. She started at point *A*, went straight through *B*, and then continued along the straight path. Her path is a **ray**. It has an endpoint and goes on and on in one direction.

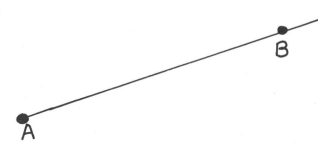

This is ray *AB*.

We write $\overrightarrow{AB}$.

Notice that we write the endpoint first.

$\overrightarrow{MX}$ and $\overrightarrow{MY}$ together form a **line**. Notice that a line has no endpoints. It goes on and on in two directions.

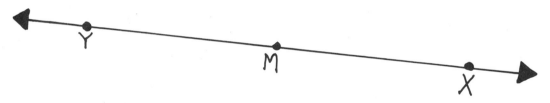

We name a line by using any two points of the line. Here are some names for the line above:

$\overleftrightarrow{XY}$ (line *XY*) $\overleftrightarrow{YX}$ $\overleftrightarrow{XM}$

$\overrightarrow{SR}$ and $\overrightarrow{ST}$ together form an **angle.** Point *S* is the endpoint of both rays. It is called the **vertex** of the angle. The two rays are the **sides** of the angle. Here are three ways of naming the angle:

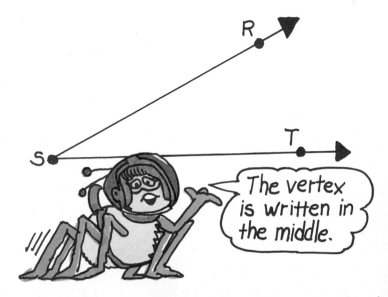

The vertex is written in the middle.

∠*S* (angle *S*)   ∠*RST*   ∠*TSR*

120

EXERCISES

True or false?

1. A segment has two endpoints.
2. A line has two endpoints.
3. A ray has one endpoint.
4. E is the vertex of $\angle DEF$.
5. $\overrightarrow{FE}$ is a side of $\angle DEF$.
6. $\angle DEF$ can be called $\angle E$.
7. $\overleftrightarrow{ED}$ is a side of the angle.

Use three letters to name each angle.

8.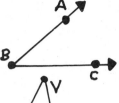

9.

10.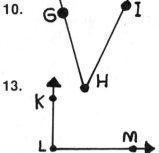

11.

12.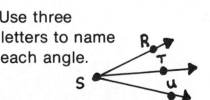

13.

14. a. Use three letters to name each angle.

    b. Why can't you use "$\angle S$" to name one of the angles?

15. Angle R is called an angle of the triangle. Name the other angles of the triangle.

Keeping Skills Sharp

1. 56 ×8	2. 72 ×5	3. 193 ×7	4. 1523 ×4	5. 2580 ×6	6. 83 ×15
7. 74 ×26	8. 54 ×91	9. 158 ×32	10. 195 ×146	11. 783 ×250	12. 709 ×623

Measuring angles

The **degree** is a unit used for measuring angles.

Read "1°" as "one degree."

The measure of ∠ABC is 25°.

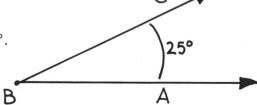

A **protractor** is used to measure angles.

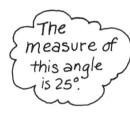

The measure of this angle is 25°.

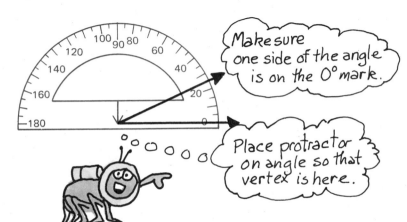

Make sure one side of the angle is on the 0° mark.

Place protractor on angle so that vertex is here.

EXERCISES

Give the measure of each angle.

1.
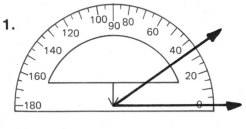

2.
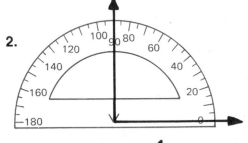

3.
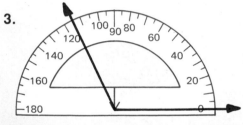

4.
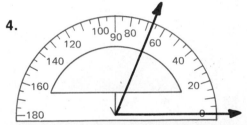

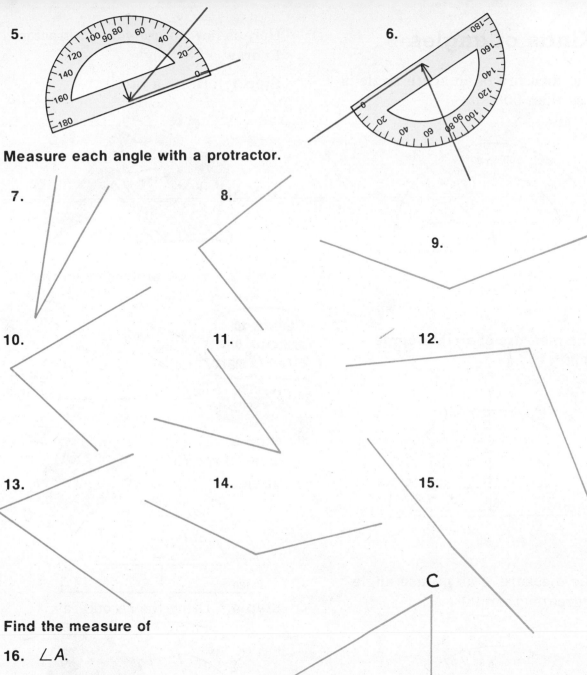

5.

6.

Measure each angle with a protractor.

7.

8.

9.

10.

11.

12.

13.

14.

15.

Find the measure of

16. ∠A.

17. ∠B.

18. ∠C.

19. Add the measures of ∠A, ∠B, and ∠C.

20. Draw a triangle of your own. Determine the sum of the angles. Did you get the same sum as you did in Exercise 19?

Kinds of angles

The measure of an **acute angle** is less than 90°.

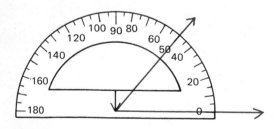

The measure of a **right angle** is 90°.

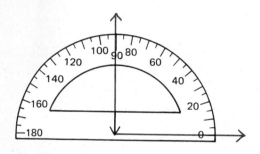

The measure of an **obtuse angle** is greater than 90°.

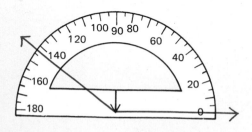

Here is how to use your protractor to draw a 75° angle.

Step 1.   Draw a ray.

Step 2.   Place protractor on ray as shown.

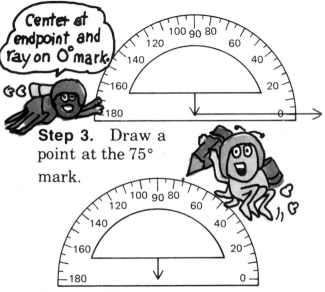

Step 3.   Draw a point at the 75° mark.

Step 4.   Draw the second ray.

EXERCISES

Tell whether the angle is acute, right, or obtuse.

1.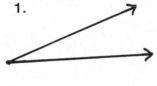

2.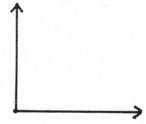

3.

4.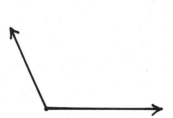

5.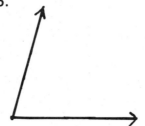

6.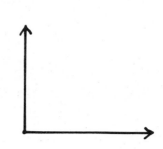

7. ∠BAD   8. ∠BAC

9. ∠CAD   10. ∠CAE

11. ∠BAE   12. ∠CAF

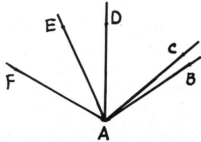

Draw angles having these measures.

13. 35°   14. 115°   15. 90°

16. 38°   17. 152°

True or false? (If you need to, make a sketch.)

18. A square has 4 right angles.

19. All rectangles have 4 right angles.

20. No triangle has 3 acute angles.

21. Some triangles have 1 obtuse angle.

22. No triangle has 2 obtuse angles.

125

Parallel and perpendicular lines

Sometimes Esther and Sylvester fly straight paths in formation. Their paths look like this:

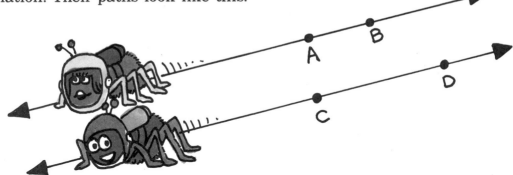

The two lines are called **parallel lines.** They are in the same plane, they never meet, and they are always the same distance apart. $\overleftrightarrow{AB}$ is parallel to $\overleftrightarrow{CD}$.

We also say that two segments are parallel if they are parts of two parallel lines.

$\overline{MN}$ is parallel to $\overline{ST}$.

Two lines that intersect to form right angles are called **perpendicular** lines.

$\overleftrightarrow{XY}$ is perpendicular to $\overleftrightarrow{TU}$.

Two segments are perpendicular if they belong to perpendicular lines.

$\overline{XY}$ is perpendicular to $\overline{TU}$.

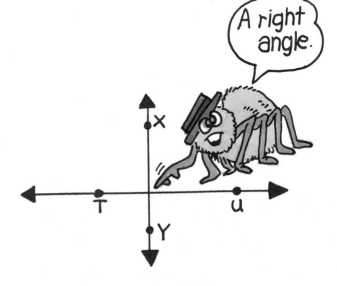

A right angle.

126

EXERCISES

The blue lines shown in each exercise were torn from a large piece of paper. Do you think that the lines are parallel, perpendicular, or neither?

1.

2.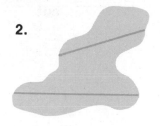

3.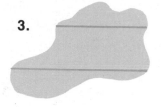

Tell which segments are parallel and which are perpendicular.

4.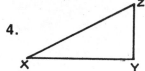

5.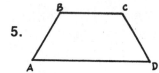

6.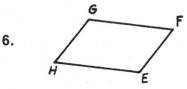

7.

8.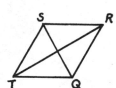

9.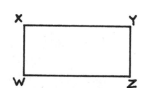

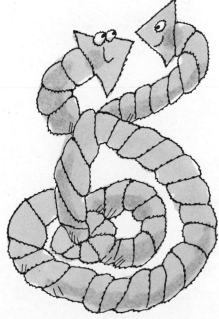

Draw a figure to go with each sentence.

10. $\overleftrightarrow{AB}$ is perpendicular to $\overleftrightarrow{CD}$.

11. $\overleftrightarrow{RS}$ is parallel to $\overleftrightarrow{XY}$.

12. $\overleftrightarrow{TU}$ intersects $\overleftrightarrow{WX}$ at point P.

13. $\overleftrightarrow{EF}$ is perpendicular to $\overleftrightarrow{EG}$.

14. $\overleftrightarrow{AB}$ is parallel to $\overleftrightarrow{CD}$, $\overleftrightarrow{RS}$ is perpendicular to $\overleftrightarrow{AB}$, $\overleftrightarrow{RS}$ intersects $\overleftrightarrow{AB}$ at point M, and $\overleftrightarrow{CD}$ intersects $\overleftrightarrow{RS}$ at point P.

Circles

When Sylvester was just a little spider and couldn't fly, his mother sometimes put him in the yard to play. To be sure that he didn't run out into the street, she used a thin spider web to tie him to a stake. Sylvester would run around and around and around.

His path was a **circle**. The stake was the **center** of the circle.

$\overline{CD}$ is a **radius** of this circle.

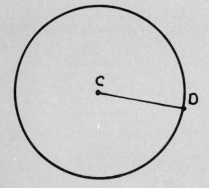

C is the center and D is on the circle.

$\overline{RS}$ is a **diameter** of this circle.

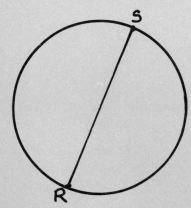

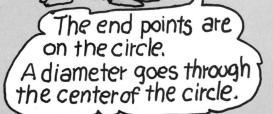

The end points are on the circle.
A diameter goes through the center of the circle.

EXERCISES
Name the red part.

1.
2.
3.
4.

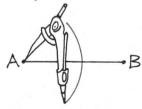

Get a centimeter ruler and a compass.
Draw a circle with a radius of:

5. 2 cm   6. 3 cm   7. 4 cm

Draw a circle with a diameter of:

8. 2 cm   9. 4 cm   10. 6 cm

The word *bisect* means to cut into halves.
These steps show how to bisect a segment.

Step 1. 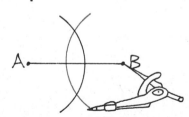   **Step 2.**   **Step 3.**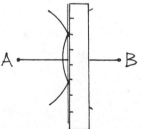

11. Draw a segment and bisect it.

Here is how to bisect an angle.

Step 1.    **Step 2.** 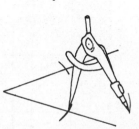   **Step 3.**    **Step 4.**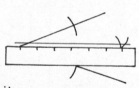

12. Draw an angle and bisect it.

129

Congruent figures

Figures that are the same size and
shape are **congruent** figures. Are
these two figures congruent?

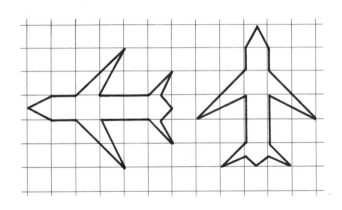

EXERCISES
Match congruent figures.

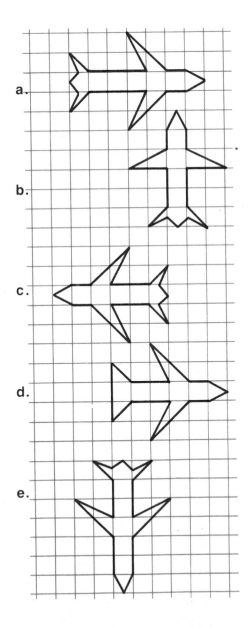

1.

2.

3.

4.

5.

a.

b.

c.

d.

e.

Esther had three rubber stamps. She used them to make the red figures shown below. Tell whether the blue figures could have been made with the same stamps.

(*Hint:* Try making tracings.)

6.

7.

8.

9.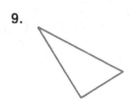

10.

11.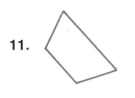

12.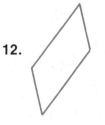

13.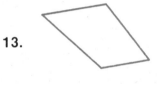

14.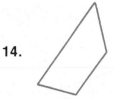

15.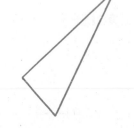

Keeping Skills Sharp

1. $9\overline{)468}$ 2. $7\overline{)658}$ 3. $8\overline{)536}$ 4. $5\overline{)7385}$ 5. $3\overline{)1596}$

6. $14\overline{)784}$ 7. $26\overline{)621}$ 8. $37\overline{)1702}$ 9. $52\overline{)1976}$ 10. $81\overline{)5265}$

11. $27\overline{)596}$ 12. $48\overline{)889}$ 13. $63\overline{)1596}$ 14. $95\overline{)3784}$ 15. $74\overline{)6289}$

131

More about congruent figures

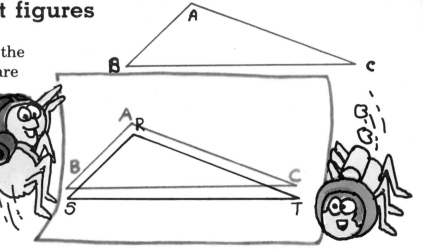

A tracing of the red triangle fits the black triangle. So, the triangles are congruent.

The parts that fit are called **corresponding parts**.

Corresponding angles

$\angle A \longleftrightarrow \angle R$ Read as "$\angle A$ corresponds to $\angle R$."

$\angle B \longleftrightarrow \angle S$

$\angle C \longleftrightarrow \angle T$

Corresponding sides

$\overline{AB} \longleftrightarrow \overline{RS}$

$\overline{BC} \longleftrightarrow \overline{ST}$

$\overline{CA} \longleftrightarrow \overline{TR}$

Notice that if two figures are congruent, then their corresponding parts are congruent. What angle is congruent to $\angle B$? What side is congruent to $\overline{CA}$?

EXERCISES

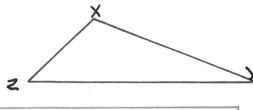

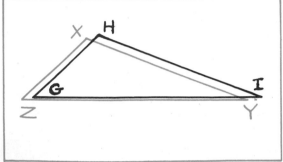

Complete.

Corresponding angles

1. $\angle X \longleftrightarrow$?
2. $\angle Y \longleftrightarrow$?
3. $\angle Z \longleftrightarrow$?

Corresponding sides

4. $\overline{XY} \longleftrightarrow$?
5. $\overline{YZ} \longleftrightarrow$?
6. $\overline{ZX} \longleftrightarrow$?

132

**The two triangles are congruent.
Complete the corresponding parts that fit.**

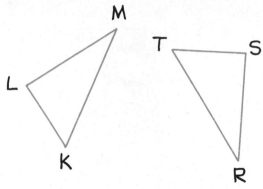

7. $\angle K \longleftrightarrow$?

8. $\angle M \longleftrightarrow$?

9. $\angle L \longleftrightarrow$?

10. $\overline{KL} \longleftrightarrow$?

11. $\overline{LM} \longleftrightarrow$?

12. $\overline{MK} \longleftrightarrow$?

**The two triangles are congruent.
Complete.**

13. $\angle A$ is congruent to ?.

14. $\overline{FE}$ is congruent to ?.

15. $\angle E$ is congruent to ?.

16. $\overline{AB}$ is congruent to ?.

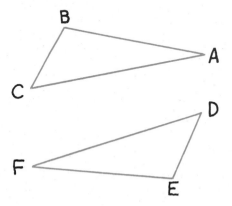

**Part of each triangle has been covered.
Study the facts. Then decide whether the
triangles are congruent.**

17.

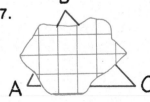

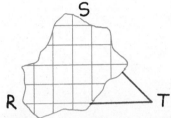

$\overline{AB}$ is congruent to $\overline{RS}$.

$\overline{BC}$ is congruent to $\overline{ST}$.

$\overline{CA}$ is congruent to $\overline{TR}$.

18.

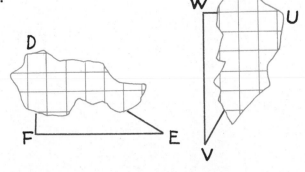

$\angle F$ is congruent to $\angle W$.

$\overline{FE}$ is congruent to $\overline{WV}$.

$\angle E$ is congruent to $\angle V$.

Line of symmetry

Sylvester and Esther cut out a triangle and then folded it along the dotted line.

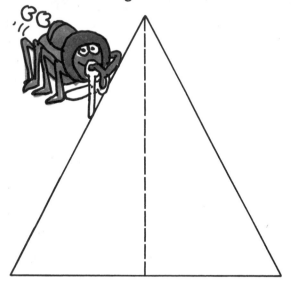 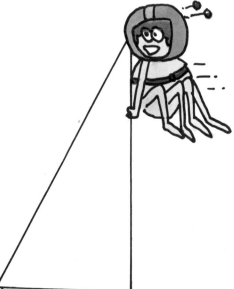

The two parts fit together. This means that the dotted line is a **line of symmetry** of the triangle.

EXERCISES

Is the red line a line of symmetry?

1.
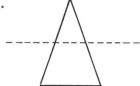

2.
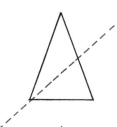

3.

4.
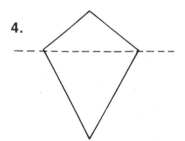

5.
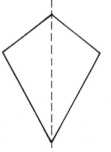

6.
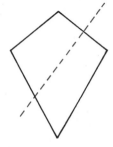

134

How many lines of symmetry? If you need to, trace each figure and draw all lines of symmetry.

7.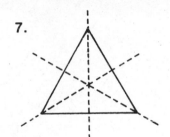

8.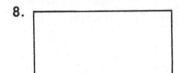

9.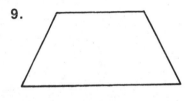

10.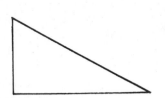

11.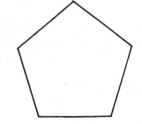

12.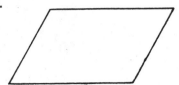

13.

14.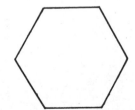

15.

16. Which printed capital letters have a horizontal line of symmetry?

17. Which have a vertical line of symmetry?

18. Which have both a vertical and a horizontal line of symmetry?

19. Can you find *words* that have a line of symmetry?

135

Triangles and quadrilaterals

In this lesson you will study some triangles and quadrilaterals (4-sided figures). You don't have to learn all the names now.

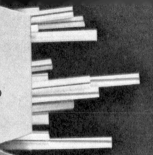

QUADRILATERALS

SQUARE

RECTANGLE

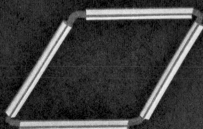

RHOMBUS

PARALLELOGRAM

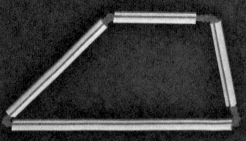

TRAPEZOID

QUADRILATERAL

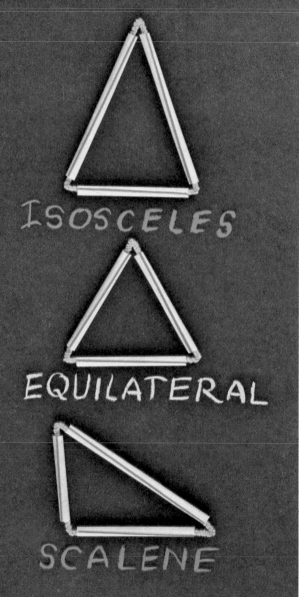

TRIANGLES

ISOSCELES

EQUILATERAL

SCALENE

EXERCISES

Which triangle has

1. no two sides congruent?

2. all three sides congruent?

3. exactly two sides congruent?

4. all three angles congruent?

5. exactly two congruent angles?

6. no lines of symmetry?

7. exactly one line of symmetry?

8. exactly three lines of symmetry?

Study the clues. Then name the quadrilateral.

9. 4 sides are congruent
   4 angles are not congruent

10. 4 congruent sides
    4 congruent angles

11. 2 pairs of congruent sides
    4 congruent angles

12. 1 pair of parallel sides

★13. How many of the quadrilaterals shown on page 136 have lines of symmetry? *Warning:* The answer is **not** 4.

★14. Can you draw a quadrilateral that has just one line of symmetry?

137

Locating points on a grid

A **number pair** is used to locate a point on a grid.

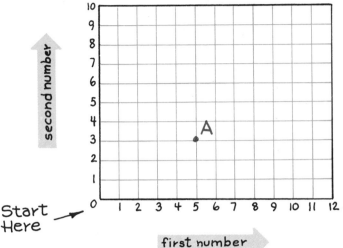

To locate point A we start at 0 and count 5 units to the right. Then we count 3 units up.

To give the location of point A, we use the number pair (5, 3). The first number tells us the number of units to the right and the second number tells us the number of units up.

EXERCISES

Give the number pair for each point.

1. A   2. E   3. F
4. G   5. B   6. I
7. D   8. H   9. C

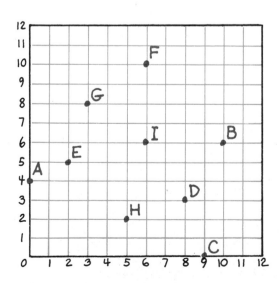

Make a grid like the one shown. Put these points on your grid.

10. A(6, 1)   11. B(7, 1)
12. C(1, 7)   13. D(2, 10)
14. E(5, 11)   15. F(7, 8)
16. G(9, 13)   17. H(10, 14)
18. I(12, 13) 19. J(11, 12)
20. K(12, 11) 21. L(11, 10)
22. M(12, 7)   23. N(9, 2)
24. O(10, 1)

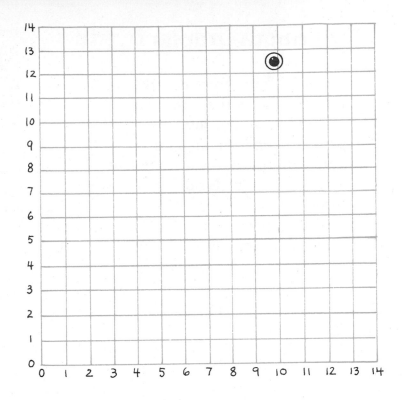

25. On your graph draw these segments.

$\overline{AB}$ $\overline{BC}$ $\overline{CD}$ $\overline{DE}$ $\overline{EF}$

$\overline{FG}$ $\overline{GH}$ $\overline{HI}$ $\overline{IJ}$ $\overline{JK}$

$\overline{KL}$ $\overline{LM}$ $\overline{MN}$ $\overline{NO}$

26. Graph the number pairs.

Rule
Add 3
(0, 3)
(1, 4)
(2, 5)
(3, 6)
(4, 7)
(5, 8)
(6, 9)

27. Graph some number pairs for
Rule
Subtract 1

More about graphs

How well a plant grows depends on such conditions as the type of soil, the amount of water, the temperature, and the amount of sunlight. Plant scientists study how well plants grow under different conditions.

A fifth-grade class planted a corn seed in a large clay pot. They kept the plant in the sunlight and watered it every 3 days. They kept this record of how the corn plant grew.

OUR CORN PLANT

Age in weeks	Height in centimeters
(2	2)
(3	4)
(4	7)
(5	10)
(6	13)
(7	15)
(8	17)

1. Copy and complete the line graph of how the first corn plant grew.

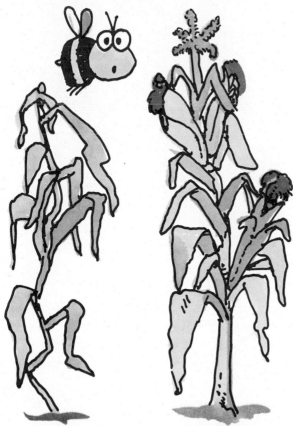

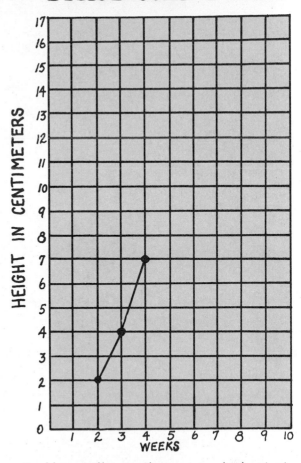

FIRST CORN PLANT

This graph shows the growth of a second corn plant that was given less water.

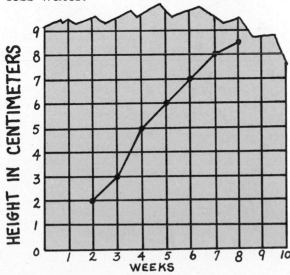

2. How tall was the second plant at 3 weeks?

3. At what week was the second plant 7 cm tall?

4. How much did the plant grow between the third and fourth weeks?

5. What was the difference in height between the two plants at the end of the fifth week?

6. You may wish to work with some classmates and do some plant research of your own. Keep a graph of your results.

141

CHAPTER CHECKUP

True or false?

1. A segment has two endpoints.

2. A ray has two endpoints.

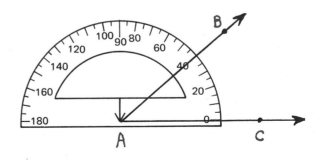

3. We can write ∠ABC to name the angle pictured.

4. The measure of ∠A is 40°.

5. The measure of a right angle is 90°.

6. Two lines in a plane that do not cross are called *perpendicular lines*.

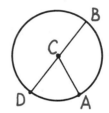

7. Point C is on the circle.

8. $\overline{BD}$ is a diameter of the circle.

9. ∠A and ∠D are corresponding parts.

CONGRUENT TRIANGLES

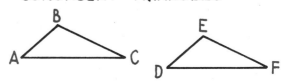

10. ∠C is congruent to ∠F.

11. A rectangle has two lines of symmetry.

12. Some triangles have 3 lines of symmetry.

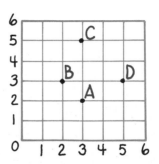

13. Give the number pair for point A.

14. What letter is at (3, 5)?

Project

The art shown above was done by connecting points on the sides of angles. You can make your own segment art by following these steps.

1. Draw an angle.

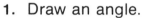

2. Use a ruler and mark off equally spaced dots as shown. Mark off the same number of dots on each side of the angle.

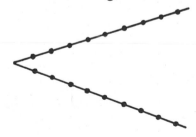

3. Use a sharp pencil and straightedge to connect the dots in the order shown.

4. Design and draw your own segment art. You may wish to work with more than one angle.

143

CHAPTER REVIEW

Match.

1. point   **2.** segment   **3.** ray   **4.** angle   **5.** line

a.    **b.** 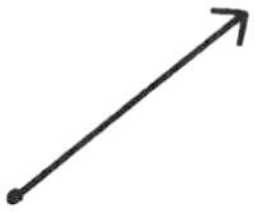   **c.** •   **d.**    **e.**

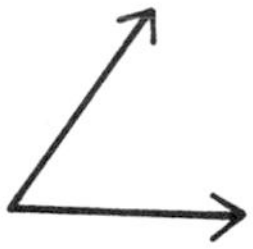

Complete.

6. In ∠S, point S is called the _?_.

7. The angle can be named in any of these three ways: ∠S, ∠RST, or _?_.

8. The measure of ∠RST is _?_°.

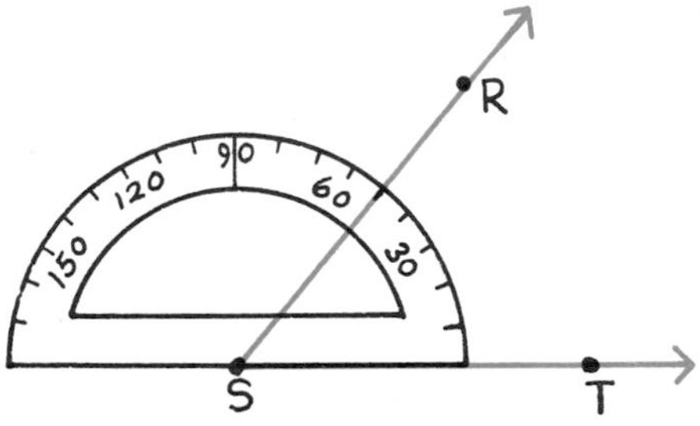

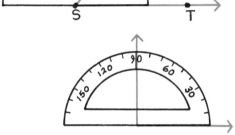

9. A right angle measures _?_.

10. Two lines that intersect to form right angles are called _____?_____ lines.
parallel/ perpendicular

11. Point _?_ is the center of the circle.

12. $\overline{CD}$ is a radius and $\overline{AB}$ is a _?_.

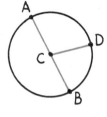

13. The congruent triangles are A and _?_

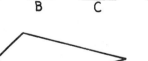

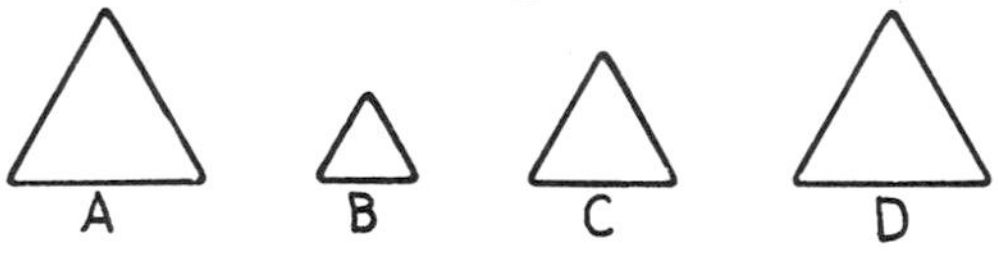

14. This quadrilateral (a 4-sided figure) has _?_ line(s) of symmetry.

15. The number pair for point A is _?_.

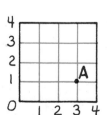

CHAPTER CHALLENGE

The red segments are called diagonals of the figure.

Complete the following table.

	Picture	Number of sides	Number of diagonals
1.			
2.			
3.			
4.			
5.			

6. Study the numbers in your diagonals column. Do you see a pattern? *Hint:* What is the difference of the first and second numbers? The second and third? The third and fourth?

7. How many diagonals do you think an 8-sided figure has? Check your answer with a drawing.

8. How many diagonals does a 9-sided figure have?

Form

a b c d   a b c d   a b c d   a b c d   a b c d   a b c d

14   34   14   4   30

a b c d   c d   a b c d

15   31

a b c   a b c   a b c   a b c d

MAJOR CHECKUP
Standardized Format

Choose the correct letter.

1. In 26,948, the 6 stands for

  a. 6 hundreds
  b. 6 ten thousands
  c. 6 thousands
  d. none of these

2. 578,500 rounded to the nearest thousand is

  a. 579,000
  b. 578,000
  c. 580,000
  d. none of these

3. Which number is greatest?

  a. 63,829,174
  b. 64,279,356
  c. 63,841,200
  d. 9,778,215

4. Add.
   297
  4283
   197
 + 65

  a. 4832
  b. 4522
  c. 4732
  d. none of these

5. Subtract.
  4902
 − 578

  a. 4476
  b. 4434
  c. 4324
  d. none of these

6. Which number is the least common multiple of 6 and 8?

  a. 14
  b. 48
  c. 24
  d. none of these

7. Multiply.
  5308
   ×7

  a. 35,106
  b. 35,156
  c. 37,106
  d. none of these

8. Multiply.
  328
 ×59

  a. 19,352
  b. 18,352
  c. 4592
  d. none of these

9. Divide.
  3)744

  a. 211
  b. 248
  c. 244
  d. none of these

10. What is the remainder?
  3)7537

  a. 1
  b. 9
  c. 3
  d. 7536

11. What is the average price?

  a. 80¢
  b. 75¢
  c. 85¢
  d. none of these

12. Divide.
  58)7946

  a. 138
  b. 127
  c. 137
  d. none of these

6

Fractions–
Addition
and
Subtraction

Using fractions

What fraction is colored?

1.

2.

3.

4.

5.

6.

7.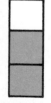

8.

9.

10.

3 green balls

5 balls in all

numerator → $\dfrac{3}{5}$ of the balls are green
denominator →

Read as "three-fifths."
The numerator and denominator of
a fraction are sometimes called the
terms of the fraction.

EXERCISES

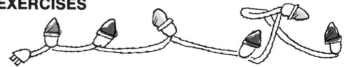

What fraction of the bulbs are

1. blue?
2. yellow?
3. red?
4. not yellow?

Give the fraction.

5.

   a. red pencils
   b. blue pencils

6.

   a. empty bottles
   b. full bottles

7. What fraction of the figures are

   a. red?

   b. blue?

   c. yellow?

   d. squares?

   e. large circles?

   f . not triangles?

Give the fraction.

8.

   _?_ of a cup

9.

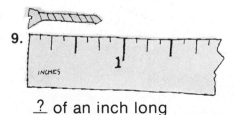

   _?_ of an inch long

10.

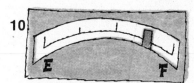

   _?_ of a tank of gasoline

11.

   _?_ of a pound

What fraction of the students in your class

12. are boys?

13. are girls?

14. wear glasses?

15. do not wear glasses?

16. have first names beginning with the letter D?

17. have last names beginning with a vowel?

Ratios

There are 5 puppies in all. The **ratio** of brown puppies to spotted puppies is 3 to 2. Here are some ways that you can write the ratio of brown puppies to spotted puppies:

3 to 2 $\qquad$ $\frac{3}{2}$

Read each ratio as "3 to 2." What is the ratio of spotted to brown puppies?

EXERCISES

Give the ratio.

1. green pencils to yellow pencils

2. yellow pencils to green pencils

3. small drinks to large drinks

4. large drinks to small drinks

5. red buttons to blue buttons

6. blue buttons to red buttons

Give each ratio for your class.

7. girls to boys

8. boys to girls

9. last names beginning with vowels to last names beginning with consonants

10. students wearing glasses to students not wearing glasses

11. students not wearing blue jeans to students wearing blue jeans

12. students who walk to school to students who ride to school

Think about mixing these 3 cans of paint together. The ratio of yellow to red in the mixture would be $\frac{1}{2}$.

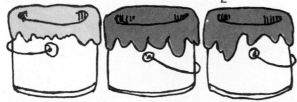

Complete this table of ratios to get the same mixture.

	13.	14.	15.	16.
Liters of yellow	1	2	3	4	5	6
Liters of red	2	4				

17. The ratio of girls to boys in a certain class is 3 to 2. Are there more girls or boys in the class?

18. The ratio of red marbles to blue marbles is $\frac{1}{3}$. There are 24 marbles in all. How many red marbles and how many blue marbles are there?

Probability

Two students put some red, yellow, and blue marbles in the bag. One student mixed up the marbles and the other, without looking in the bag, took out a marble and recorded its color. The marble was replaced in the bag and the experiment repeated. Here is the record they kept of their experiment.

EXPERIMENT: Picking a marble from a bag.			
Possible Outcomes	🔴	🔵	🟡
Tally of Outcomes	ⅢⅢ III	IIII	ⅢⅢ ⅢⅢ II
Fraction of all outcomes	8/24	4/24	12/24

1. What were the possible outcomes of the experiment?

2. How many times was a yellow marble picked?

3. How many times was a blue marble picked?

4. What fraction of the outcomes were red marbles?

5. If you had to guess, would you guess that there were more blue marbles in the bag, or more yellow marbles?

10. Toss a penny 40 times and complete this record of your experiment.

Possible Outcomes	Heads	Tails
Tally of outcomes		
Fraction of all outcomes		

Andrew tossed a paper cup and recorded the outcomes on a bar graph.

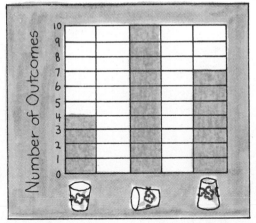

EXPERIMENT: Tossing a Thumbtack

Possible Outcomes		
Tally of Outcomes	TH TH TH III	TH II
Fraction of all Outcomes.	?	?

6. How many outcomes?

7. How many times did the thumbtack land "point down"? "point up"?

8. What fraction of the outcomes were "point up"?

9. If you were to toss the thumbtack once, how do you think that it would land?

11. How many possible outcomes?

12. How many times did he toss the cup?

13. What fraction of the outcomes were "right side up"?

14. If you were to toss the cup one time, how do you think it would land?

Equivalent fractions

When you multiply both terms of a fraction by the same number, you get an equivalent fraction.

 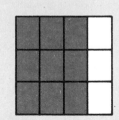 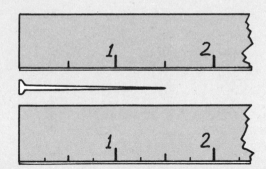

Multiply both terms by 3. $\dfrac{3}{4} \overset{\times 3}{\underset{\times 3}{=}} \dfrac{9}{12}$

Multiply both terms by 2. $\dfrac{3}{2} \overset{\times 2}{\underset{\times 2}{=}} \dfrac{6}{4}$

EXERCISES
Complete.

1.

$\dfrac{1}{2} = ?$

2.

$\dfrac{1}{3} = ?$

3.

$\dfrac{1}{4} = ?$

4.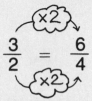

$\dfrac{1}{2} = ?$

5.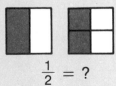

$\dfrac{2}{3} = ?$

6.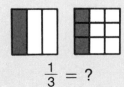

$\dfrac{3}{4} = ?$

7.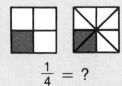

$\dfrac{3}{8} = ?$

8.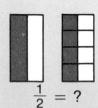

$\dfrac{2}{3} = ?$

9.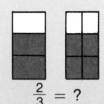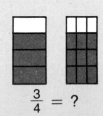

$\dfrac{3}{4} = ?$

Complete.

10. 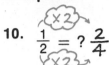 $\frac{1}{2} = ?\ \frac{2}{4}$

11. $\frac{1}{4} = ?$ (×3, ×3)

12. $\frac{1}{8} = ?$ (×4, ×4)

13. $\frac{0}{4} = ?$ (×2, ×2)

14. $\frac{2}{3} = ?$ (×4, ×4)

15. $\frac{1}{3} = ?$ (×2, ×2)

16. $\frac{5}{3} = ?$ (×4, ×4)

17. $\frac{7}{8} = ?$ (×2, ×2)

18. $\frac{3}{2} = ?$ (×3, ×3)

19. $\frac{2}{5} = ?$ (×4, ×4)

20. $\frac{3}{4} = ?$ (×2, ×2)

21. $\frac{4}{5} = ?$ (×3, ×3)

22. $\frac{3}{5} = ?$ (×4, ×4)

23. $\frac{1}{1} = ?$ (×6, ×6)

24. $\frac{5}{8} = ?$ (×3, ×3)

25. $\frac{4}{3} = ?$ (×2, ×2)

Look for a pattern.
Give the next three equivalent fractions.

26. $\frac{1}{2}, \frac{2}{4}, \frac{3}{6}, \underline{?}, \underline{?}, \underline{?}$

27. $\frac{1}{3}, \frac{2}{6}, \frac{3}{9}, \underline{?}, \underline{?}, \underline{?}$

28. $\frac{1}{4}, \frac{2}{8}, \frac{3}{12}, \underline{?}, \underline{?}, \underline{?}$

29. $\frac{2}{3}, \frac{4}{6}, \underline{?}, \underline{?}, \underline{?}$

30. $\frac{3}{4}, \underline{?}, \underline{?}, \underline{?}$

31. $\frac{3}{2}, \underline{?}, \underline{?}, \underline{?}$

32. $\frac{4}{3}, \underline{?}, \underline{?}, \underline{?}$

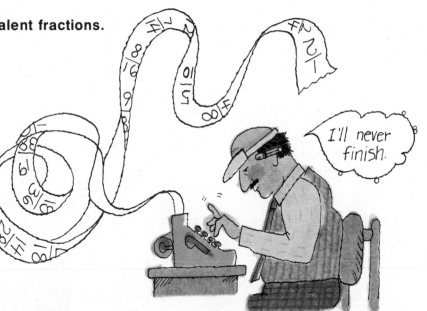

I'll never finish.

Solve.

33.

BUTTER

What fraction of the butter has been used? Give two fractions.

34.

What fraction of the eggs have been used? Give two fractions.

Reducing fractions to lower terms

You can get an equivalent fraction by dividing both terms of a fraction by the same number.

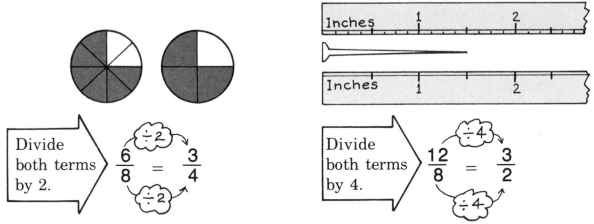

When we divide both terms of a fraction by a whole number greater than 1, we get an equivalent fraction with smaller terms. This is called **reducing** the terms of a fraction, or simply **reducing a fraction** to lower terms.

A fraction that cannot be reduced to lower terms is in **lowest terms.**

EXERCISES
Complete.

1.
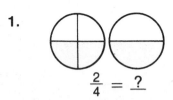

$$\frac{2}{4} = \frac{?}{\_}$$

2.
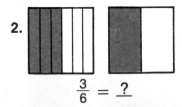

$$\frac{3}{6} = \frac{?}{\_}$$

3.
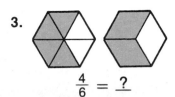

$$\frac{4}{6} = \frac{?}{\_}$$

4.
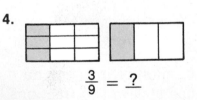

$$\frac{3}{9} = \frac{?}{\_}$$

5.
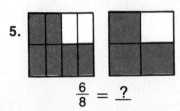

$$\frac{6}{8} = \frac{?}{\_}$$

6.
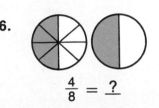

$$\frac{4}{8} = \frac{?}{\_}$$

Complete.

7. 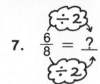 $\frac{6}{8} = \frac{?}{?}$ (÷2 / ÷2)

8. $\frac{4}{8} = \frac{?}{?}$ (÷4 / ÷4)

9. $\frac{6}{9} = \frac{?}{?}$ (÷3 / ÷3)

10. $\frac{6}{2} = \frac{?}{?}$ (÷2 / ÷2)

11. $\frac{9}{6} = \frac{?}{?}$ (÷3 / ÷3)

12. $\frac{12}{8} = \frac{?}{?}$ (÷4 / ÷4)

13. $\frac{12}{16} = \frac{?}{?}$ (÷4 / ÷4)

14. $\frac{10}{15} = \frac{?}{?}$ (÷5 / ÷5)

15. $\frac{8}{16} = \frac{?}{?}$ (÷8 / ÷8)

16. $\frac{12}{4} = \frac{?}{?}$ (÷4 / ÷4)

17. $\frac{24}{16} = \frac{?}{?}$ (÷8 / ÷8)

18. $\frac{18}{24} = \frac{?}{?}$ (÷6 / ÷6)

Reduce to lowest terms.

19. $\frac{3}{6}$
20. $\frac{2}{6}$
21. $\frac{4}{8}$
22. $\frac{4}{12}$
23. $\frac{5}{10}$
24. $\frac{6}{8}$

25. $\frac{3}{12}$
26. $\frac{4}{6}$
27. $\frac{6}{9}$
28. $\frac{6}{3}$
29. $\frac{12}{16}$
30. $\frac{3}{9}$

31. $\frac{12}{15}$
32. $\frac{9}{6}$
33. $\frac{12}{18}$
34. $\frac{16}{12}$
35. $\frac{18}{12}$
36. $\frac{20}{16}$

Who am I?

37. I am equivalent to $\frac{18}{24}$. I am in lowest terms.

38. I am equivalent to $\frac{2}{3}$. My numerator is 6.

39. I am equivalent to $\frac{3}{4}$. My denominator is 12.

More about reducing fractions

Dividing both terms of a fraction by their greatest common factor reduces the fraction to lowest terms.

$\dfrac{6}{8} = \dfrac{3}{4}$

The greatest common factor is 2.

Here is a shortcut that you can sometimes use.

$\dfrac{\overset{3}{\cancel{6}}}{\underset{4}{\cancel{8}}}$

One way to decide whether two fractions are equivalent is to reduce both to lowest terms.

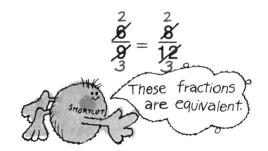

$\dfrac{\overset{2}{\cancel{6}}}{\underset{3}{\cancel{9}}} = \dfrac{\overset{2}{\cancel{8}}}{\underset{3}{\cancel{12}}}$

These fractions are equivalent.

To write a fraction with a denominator of 1 in lowest terms, write it as a whole number.

EXAMPLE. $\dfrac{\overset{4}{\cancel{8}}}{\underset{1}{\cancel{2}}} = 4$

EXERCISES
Reduce to lowest terms.

1. $\dfrac{5}{10}$ 2. $\dfrac{6}{8}$ 3. $\dfrac{8}{12}$ 4. $\dfrac{9}{3}$ 5. $\dfrac{4}{6}$ 6. $\dfrac{15}{10}$

7. $\dfrac{3}{9}$ 8. $\dfrac{15}{18}$ 9. $\dfrac{16}{12}$ 10. $\dfrac{8}{24}$ 11. $\dfrac{0}{6}$ 12. $\dfrac{24}{6}$

13. $\dfrac{10}{2}$ 14. $\dfrac{4}{16}$ 15. $\dfrac{10}{20}$ 16. $\dfrac{10}{15}$ 17. $\dfrac{12}{3}$ 18. $\dfrac{12}{8}$

Are the two fractions equivalent? *Hint:* **Reduce both to lowest terms.**

19. $\dfrac{3}{12}, \dfrac{4}{16}$ 20. $\dfrac{6}{12}, \dfrac{7}{14}$ 21. $\dfrac{10}{12}, \dfrac{8}{10}$ 22. $\dfrac{5}{15}, \dfrac{6}{18}$

158

CONSTRUCTION BLUEPRINT

$\frac{1}{3}$

Use the digits to build as many fractions as you can that are equivalent to the "red" fraction.

1. $\frac{1}{2}$ [4] [6] [1] [2]   Answer: $\frac{1}{2}$, $\frac{2}{4}$, $\frac{6}{12}$ 2. $\frac{3}{4}$ [9] [2] [1] [0]

3. $\frac{6}{9}$ [3] [6] [2] [4]   4. $\frac{6}{8}$ [3] [2] [4] [2]   5. $\frac{9}{6}$ [3] [9] [4] [2]

Play the game.

1. Make a set of digit cards.

2. Choose a game leader and divide the class into two teams, Team A and Team B.

3. The leader writes a fraction on the chalkboard.

4. The leader shows Team A four digits. Team A gets one point for each equivalent fraction that they can build with the digits.

5. The leader replaces the cards and step 4 is repeated with Team B.

6. Next the leader writes a different fraction on the chalkboard and it is Team A's turn.

7. When both teams have had ten turns, the team with more points wins!

Comparing fractions

Two fractions that have the same denominator are easy to compare. Both of these fractions have 5 as denominator. We call 5 their **common denominator**.

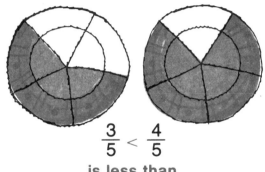

$$\frac{3}{5} < \frac{4}{5}$$

is less than

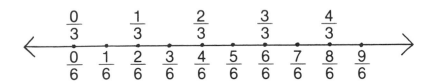

$$\frac{4}{3} > \frac{5}{6}$$

is greater than

To compare two fractions with different denominators, think about equivalent fractions with a common denominator.

$$\frac{2}{3} < \frac{3}{4}$$

EXERCISES

< or >?

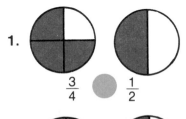

1.
$$\frac{3}{4} \bigcirc \frac{1}{2}$$

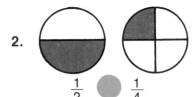

2.
$$\frac{1}{2} \bigcirc \frac{1}{4}$$

3.
$$\frac{1}{3} \bigcirc \frac{4}{6}$$

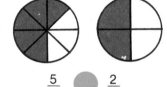

4.
$$\frac{5}{8} \bigcirc \frac{2}{4}$$

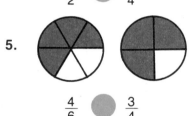

5.
$$\frac{4}{6} \bigcirc \frac{3}{4}$$

6.
$$\frac{4}{8} \bigcirc \frac{2}{6}$$

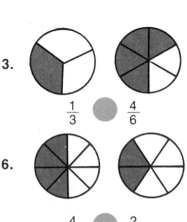

160

< or >? If you need to, use the number line.

7. $\frac{3}{8}$ ◯ $\frac{1}{2}$ 8. $\frac{5}{8}$ ◯ $\frac{1}{4}$ 9. $\frac{3}{4}$ ◯ $\frac{3}{8}$

10. $\frac{4}{4}$ ◯ $\frac{7}{8}$ 11. $\frac{11}{8}$ ◯ $\frac{2}{2}$ 12. $\frac{2}{4}$ ◯ $\frac{2}{2}$

13. $\frac{0}{4}$ ◯ $\frac{1}{2}$ 14. $\frac{9}{8}$ ◯ $\frac{3}{4}$ 15. $\frac{1}{2}$ ◯ $\frac{5}{8}$

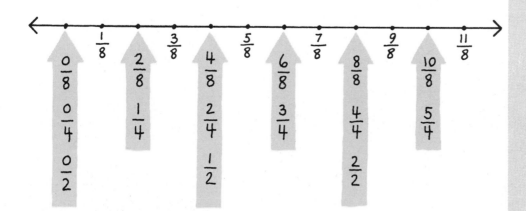

< or >?

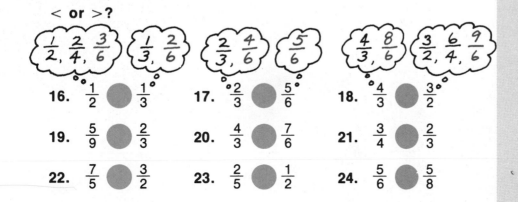

16. $\frac{1}{2}$ ◯ $\frac{1}{3}$ 17. $\frac{2}{3}$ ◯ $\frac{5}{6}$ 18. $\frac{4}{3}$ ◯ $\frac{3}{2}$

19. $\frac{5}{9}$ ◯ $\frac{2}{3}$ 20. $\frac{4}{3}$ ◯ $\frac{7}{6}$ 21. $\frac{3}{4}$ ◯ $\frac{2}{3}$

22. $\frac{7}{5}$ ◯ $\frac{3}{2}$ 23. $\frac{2}{5}$ ◯ $\frac{1}{2}$ 24. $\frac{5}{6}$ ◯ $\frac{5}{8}$

Which is more?

25. $\frac{1}{2}$ hour   26. $\frac{1}{4}$ of a pound   27. $\frac{3}{4}$ of a yard
    $\frac{3}{4}$ hour $\frac{3}{8}$ of a pound $\frac{2}{3}$ of a yard

28. $\frac{3}{2}$ of a foot 29. $\frac{2}{3}$ of a minute 30. $\frac{5}{16}$ of a mile
    $\frac{4}{3}$ of a foot $\frac{1}{2}$ of a minute $\frac{1}{4}$ of a mile

Adding fractions

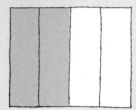

$$\frac{2}{4} + \frac{1}{4} = \frac{3}{4}$$

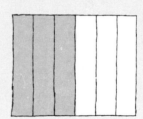

$$\begin{array}{r} \frac{3}{6} \\ + \frac{2}{6} \\ \hline \frac{5}{6} \end{array}$$

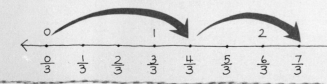

$$\frac{4}{3} + \frac{3}{3} = \frac{7}{3}$$

To add two fractions that have the same denominator:

Add the numerators to get the numerator of the sum.

Use the common denominator for the denominator of the sum.

EXERCISES

Give each sum.

1.

$$\frac{1}{6} + \frac{4}{6}$$

2.

$$\frac{1}{4} + \frac{2}{4}$$

3.

$$\frac{2}{5} + \frac{2}{5}$$

4.

$$\frac{3}{8} + \frac{4}{8}$$

5.

$$\frac{2}{6} + \frac{1}{6}$$

6.

$$\frac{3}{9} + \frac{2}{9}$$

Add.

7. $\frac{3}{5} + \frac{1}{5}$ 8. $\frac{2}{7} + \frac{2}{7}$ 9. $\frac{1}{4} + \frac{2}{4}$ 10. $\frac{1}{6} + \frac{4}{6}$

11. $\frac{4}{5} + \frac{2}{5}$ 12. $\frac{3}{8} + \frac{4}{8}$ 13. $\frac{2}{4} + \frac{3}{4}$ 14. $\frac{4}{3} + \frac{4}{3}$

15. $\frac{3}{4} + \frac{0}{4}$ 16. $\frac{1}{6} + \frac{5}{6}$ 17. $\frac{1}{2} + \frac{2}{2}$ 18. $\frac{5}{3} + \frac{2}{3}$

Add. Give each sum in lowest terms.

19. $\frac{3}{8}$ $+\frac{3}{8}$ 20. $\frac{5}{6}$ $+\frac{1}{6}$ 21. $\frac{5}{8}$ $+\frac{1}{8}$ 22. $\frac{1}{4}$ $+\frac{1}{4}$ 23. $\frac{2}{4}$ $+\frac{2}{4}$ 24. $\frac{3}{6}$ $+\frac{1}{6}$

25. $\frac{5}{8}$ $+\frac{7}{8}$ 26. $\frac{3}{6}$ $+\frac{5}{6}$ 27. $\frac{2}{8}$ $+\frac{4}{8}$ 28. $\frac{7}{4}$ $+\frac{3}{4}$ 29. $\frac{5}{4}$ $+\frac{5}{4}$ 30. $\frac{4}{8}$ $+\frac{2}{8}$

31. $\frac{2}{3}$ $+\frac{4}{3}$ 32. $\frac{1}{8}$ $+\frac{5}{8}$ 33. $\frac{3}{4}$ $+\frac{1}{4}$ 34. $\frac{1}{6}$ $+\frac{3}{6}$ 35. $\frac{2}{6}$ $+\frac{2}{6}$ 36. $\frac{0}{4}$ $+\frac{2}{4}$

37. $\frac{3}{8}$ $+\frac{7}{8}$ 38. $\frac{3}{4}$ $+\frac{3}{4}$ 39. $\frac{1}{4}$ $+\frac{5}{4}$ 40. $\frac{4}{6}$ $+\frac{5}{6}$ 41. $\frac{6}{5}$ $+\frac{4}{5}$ 42. $\frac{5}{9}$ $+\frac{7}{9}$

Solve.

43. Practiced $\frac{3}{4}$ hour on Monday. Practiced $\frac{2}{4}$ hour on Tuesday. How many hours in all?

44. Read $\frac{3}{8}$ of the book one night. Read $\frac{3}{8}$ of the book the next night. How much all together?

45. Hal is selling tickets for the school play. He sold $\frac{1}{5}$ of his tickets the first night and $\frac{2}{5}$ of his tickets the second night. What fraction of his tickets did he sell the first two nights?

46. Alice earned some money for raking leaves. She spent $\frac{1}{8}$ of it for a malt, and $\frac{3}{8}$ of it for a movie ticket. What fraction of the money did she spend?

Adding, unlike denominators

If fractions have the same denominator, adding them is easy. If the denominators are different, we use equivalent fractions that have the same denominator.

different denominators
$$\frac{3}{8} + \frac{1}{4} = \frac{3}{8} + \frac{2}{8}$$
same denominators

$$= \frac{5}{8}$$

8 is called a **common denominator**.

IMPORTANT NOTICE
If one denominator is a multiple of the other, the greater number can be used as a common denominator.

$$\frac{2}{3} = \frac{4}{6}$$
$$+ \frac{1}{6} = + \frac{1}{6}$$
$$\frac{5}{6}$$

EXERCISES
Give each sum in lowest terms.

1. $\frac{1}{4} + \frac{1}{2}$

2. $\frac{1}{6} + \frac{1}{2}$

3. $\frac{3}{8} + \frac{1}{4}$

4. $\frac{5}{9} + \frac{2}{3}$

5. $\frac{1}{3} + \frac{1}{6}$

6. $\frac{0}{8} + \frac{3}{4}$

7. $\frac{7}{8} + \frac{3}{4}$

8. $\frac{5}{6} + \frac{2}{3}$

9. $\frac{7}{3} + \frac{5}{6}$

10. $\frac{3}{4} + \frac{3}{8}$

11. $\frac{3}{8} + \frac{5}{16}$

12. $\frac{6}{5} + \frac{3}{10}$

164

Add. Give each sum in lowest terms.

13. $\dfrac{5}{6}$
    $+\dfrac{1}{3}$

14. $\dfrac{1}{4}$
    $+\dfrac{1}{8}$

15. $\dfrac{1}{9}$
    $+\dfrac{2}{3}$

16. $\dfrac{3}{8}$
    $+\dfrac{1}{2}$

17. $\dfrac{2}{3}$
    $+\dfrac{5}{6}$

18. $\dfrac{3}{10}$
    $+\dfrac{2}{5}$

19. $\dfrac{1}{2}$
    $+\dfrac{5}{4}$

20. $\dfrac{5}{16}$
    $+\dfrac{1}{2}$

21. $\dfrac{1}{8}$
    $+\dfrac{5}{16}$

22. $\dfrac{5}{4}$
    $+\dfrac{3}{8}$

23. $\dfrac{3}{8}$
    $+\dfrac{3}{4}$

24. $\dfrac{3}{4}$
    $+\dfrac{1}{2}$

25. $\dfrac{7}{8}$
    $+\dfrac{3}{16}$

26. $\dfrac{2}{9}$
    $+\dfrac{2}{3}$

27. $\dfrac{1}{2}$
    $+\dfrac{1}{4}$

28. $\dfrac{4}{3}$
    $+\dfrac{5}{6}$

29. $\dfrac{1}{2}$
    $+\dfrac{5}{8}$

30. $\dfrac{7}{3}$
    $+\dfrac{1}{9}$

31. $\dfrac{9}{16}$
    $+\dfrac{1}{2}$

32. $\dfrac{3}{8}$
    $+\dfrac{3}{4}$

33. $\dfrac{7}{2}$
    $+\dfrac{5}{14}$

34. $\dfrac{5}{6}$
    $+\dfrac{1}{3}$

35. $\dfrac{0}{8}$
    $+\dfrac{4}{4}$

36. $\dfrac{9}{16}$
    $+\dfrac{3}{8}$

Solve.

37. Jack spent $\dfrac{1}{2}$ of his allowance for a movie ticket and $\dfrac{1}{4}$ of his allowance for lunch. What fraction of his allowance did he spend?

38. Ralph painted $\dfrac{3}{8}$ of a fence the first day and $\dfrac{1}{4}$ of the fence the second day. How much of the fence did he paint during the two days?

Add across. Add down.

39.
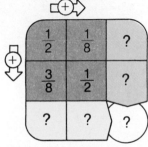

40.
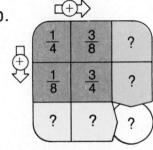

41.
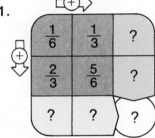

More about adding, unlike denominators

The least common multiple of the denominators is always the least common denominator.

EXAMPLE 1.

$$\frac{1}{2} + \frac{1}{3} = \frac{3}{6} + \frac{2}{6}$$

0, 2, 4, 6   0, 3, 6

$$= \frac{5}{6}$$

EXAMPLE 2.

$$\frac{3}{4} + \frac{1}{6} = \frac{9}{12} + \frac{2}{12}$$

0, 4, 8, 12   0, 6, 12

$$= \frac{11}{12}$$

$$\frac{3}{4} + \frac{1}{6} = \frac{18}{24} + \frac{4}{24}$$

$$= \frac{22}{24}$$

$$= \frac{11}{12}$$

The product of the denominators is always a common denominator.

SHORTCUT

Will the product of the denominators always be the least common denominator?

EXERCISES

Give each sum in lowest terms.

1. $\frac{1}{3} + \frac{1}{4}$
0, 3, 6, 9, 12 0, 4, 8, 12

2. $\frac{2}{3} + \frac{1}{4}$
0, 3, 6, 9, 12 0, 4, 8, 12

3. $\frac{1}{2} + \frac{2}{3}$
0, 2, 4, 6 0, 3, 6

4. $\frac{3}{4} + \frac{1}{5}$
20

5. $\frac{2}{3} + \frac{1}{8}$
24

6. $\frac{2}{3} + \frac{3}{4}$
12

7. $\frac{3}{4} + \frac{2}{5}$

8. $\frac{3}{5} + \frac{2}{3}$

9. $\frac{2}{5} + \frac{1}{3}$

10. $\frac{4}{5} + \frac{1}{2}$

11. $\frac{3}{5} + \frac{1}{2}$

12. $\frac{1}{5} + \frac{1}{2}$

13. $\frac{3}{2} + \frac{3}{4}$

14. $\frac{4}{3} + \frac{1}{8}$

15. $\frac{3}{8} + \frac{3}{5}$

Add. Give each sum in lowest terms.

16. $\frac{1}{3}$ $+\frac{1}{4}$

17. $\frac{4}{4}$ $+\frac{1}{6}$

18. $\frac{1}{2}$ $+\frac{3}{8}$

19. $\frac{3}{4}$ $+\frac{2}{3}$

20. $\frac{6}{5}$ $+\frac{3}{10}$

21. $\frac{1}{3}$ $+\frac{1}{5}$

22. $\frac{3}{8}$ $+\frac{2}{3}$

23. $\frac{2}{3}$ $+\frac{1}{2}$

24. $\frac{5}{12}$ $+\frac{1}{3}$

25. $\frac{3}{3}$ $+\frac{2}{2}$

26. $\frac{0}{5}$ $+\frac{3}{5}$

27. $\frac{7}{8}$ $+\frac{1}{3}$

28. $\frac{1}{4}$ $+\frac{3}{8}$

29. $\frac{5}{6}$ $+\frac{7}{10}$

30. $\frac{7}{5}$ $+\frac{1}{3}$

31. $\frac{7}{3}$ $+\frac{7}{4}$

32. $\frac{4}{3}$ $+\frac{3}{4}$

33. $\frac{11}{5}$ $+\frac{4}{5}$

34. $\frac{3}{2}$ $+\frac{2}{3}$

35. $\frac{5}{9}$ $+\frac{2}{3}$

36. $\frac{1}{2}$ $+\frac{5}{6}$

37. $\frac{3}{4}$ $+\frac{1}{8}$

38. $\frac{1}{5}$ $+\frac{2}{7}$

39. $\frac{4}{5}$ $+\frac{2}{3}$

This circle graph shows how James spent his allowance. What fraction of his allowance did he spend for

40. food?

41. a record?

42. a movie and food?

43. a record and clothes?

Find the missing digit.

44. $\frac{1}{3} + \frac{1}{\blacksquare} = \frac{5}{6}$

45. $\frac{1}{\blacksquare} + \frac{3}{4} = \frac{13}{12}$

46. $\frac{\blacksquare}{8} + \frac{1}{3} = \frac{17}{24}$

Subtracting fractions

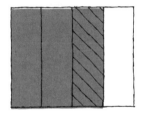

$$\frac{3}{4} - \frac{1}{4} = \frac{2}{4}$$

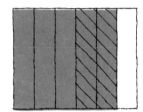

$$\begin{array}{r} \frac{5}{6} \\ - \frac{2}{6} \\ \hline \frac{3}{6} \end{array}$$

$$\frac{7}{4} - \frac{2}{4} = \frac{5}{4}$$

To subtract fractions that have the same denominator:

Subtract the numerators to get the numerator of the difference.

Use the common denominator for the denominator of the difference.

EXERCISES
Give each difference.

1.

$$\frac{3}{5} - \frac{1}{5}$$

2.

$$\frac{2}{4} - \frac{1}{4}$$

3.

$$\frac{6}{6} - \frac{1}{6}$$

4.

$$\frac{4}{6} - \frac{3}{6}$$

5.

$$\frac{5}{8} - \frac{2}{8}$$

6.

$$\frac{7}{8} - \frac{7}{8}$$

168

7. $\frac{5}{6} - \frac{4}{6}$ 8. $\frac{3}{2} - \frac{2}{2}$ 9. $\frac{4}{8} - \frac{1}{8}$ 10. $\frac{5}{9} - \frac{4}{9}$

11. $\frac{6}{7} - \frac{1}{7}$ 12. $\frac{5}{3} - \frac{1}{3}$ 13. $\frac{9}{4} - \frac{2}{4}$ 14. $\frac{1}{4} - \frac{1}{4}$

15. $\frac{3}{8} - \frac{3}{8}$ 16. $\frac{7}{8} - \frac{0}{8}$ 17. $\frac{11}{8} - \frac{6}{8}$ 18. $\frac{7}{6} - \frac{2}{6}$

Subtract. Give each difference in lowest terms.

19. $\frac{5}{6}$ 20. $\frac{6}{4}$ 21. $\frac{3}{5}$ 22. $\frac{5}{4}$ 23. $\frac{11}{8}$ 24. $\frac{5}{9}$
$-\frac{1}{6}$ $-\frac{2}{4}$ $-\frac{0}{5}$ $-\frac{1}{4}$ $-\frac{5}{8}$ $-\frac{2}{9}$

25. $\frac{12}{8}$ 26. $\frac{11}{4}$ 27. $\frac{2}{3}$ 28. $\frac{7}{4}$ 29. $\frac{7}{4}$ 30. $\frac{5}{8}$
$-\frac{6}{8}$ $-\frac{3}{4}$ $-\frac{2}{3}$ $-\frac{4}{4}$ $-\frac{3}{4}$ $-\frac{1}{8}$

31. $\frac{8}{6}$ 32. $\frac{5}{3}$ 33. $\frac{7}{6}$ 34. $\frac{5}{6}$ 35. $\frac{10}{9}$ 36. $\frac{12}{4}$
$-\frac{2}{6}$ $-\frac{2}{3}$ $-\frac{3}{6}$ $-\frac{5}{6}$ $-\frac{4}{9}$ $-\frac{4}{4}$

37. $\frac{7}{8}$ 38. $\frac{13}{4}$ 39. $\frac{10}{8}$ 40. $\frac{9}{6}$ 41. $\frac{10}{4}$ 42. $\frac{9}{6}$
$-\frac{3}{8}$ $-\frac{3}{4}$ $-\frac{2}{8}$ $-\frac{6}{6}$ $-\frac{2}{4}$ $-\frac{1}{6}$

Solve.

43. Bought $\frac{3}{4}$ dozen. Ate $\frac{1}{4}$ dozen. What fraction of a dozen was left?

44. Bought $\frac{7}{4}$ yards of yellow ribbon. Bought $\frac{2}{4}$ yards of red ribbon. How much more yellow ribbon was bought?

45. Marie jogged $\frac{12}{10}$ miles on Monday, and $\frac{8}{10}$ miles on Tuesday. How much farther did she jog on Monday?

46. Jill bought $\frac{11}{8}$ pounds of mixed nuts for a party. She ate $\frac{1}{8}$ pound. How many pounds were left?

Subtracting, unlike denominators

Remember:
If one denominator is a multiple of the other, the greater number can be used as a common denominator.

$$\frac{7}{8} - \frac{1}{4} = \frac{7}{8} - \frac{2}{8}$$
$$= \frac{5}{8}$$

Since 8 is a multiple of 4, 8 is a common denominator

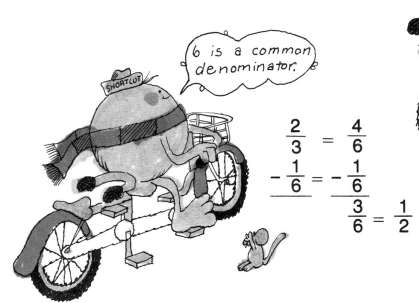

6 is a common denominator.

$$\frac{2}{3} = \frac{4}{6}$$
$$-\frac{1}{6} = -\frac{1}{6}$$
$$\frac{3}{6} = \frac{1}{2}$$

EXERCISES
Give each difference in lowest terms.

1. $\frac{1}{2} - \frac{1}{4}$

2. $\frac{3}{4} - \frac{1}{2}$

3. $\frac{3}{4} - \frac{3}{8}$

4. $\frac{1}{2} - \frac{1}{6}$

5. $\frac{3}{2} - \frac{0}{4}$

6. $\frac{7}{10} - \frac{1}{2}$

7. $\frac{5}{6} - \frac{2}{3}$

8. $\frac{3}{4} - \frac{1}{8}$

9. $\frac{9}{4} - \frac{3}{2}$

10. $\frac{5}{8} - \frac{1}{2}$

11. $\frac{5}{8} - \frac{1}{4}$

12. $\frac{7}{2} - \frac{5}{8}$

13. $\frac{3}{4} - \frac{5}{8}$

14. $\frac{9}{10} - \frac{3}{5}$

15. $\frac{5}{2} - \frac{3}{4}$

16. $\frac{4}{5} - \frac{4}{10}$

Give each difference in lowest terms.

17. $\dfrac{1}{2}$ $-\dfrac{1}{4}$
18. $\dfrac{5}{8}$ $-\dfrac{1}{4}$
19. $\dfrac{1}{3}$ $-\dfrac{1}{6}$
20. $\dfrac{1}{2}$ $-\dfrac{1}{8}$
21. $\dfrac{5}{6}$ $-\dfrac{1}{3}$
22. $\dfrac{3}{4}$ $-\dfrac{1}{8}$

23. $\dfrac{3}{2}$ $-\dfrac{5}{8}$
24. $\dfrac{3}{4}$ $-\dfrac{1}{2}$
25. $\dfrac{5}{9}$ $-\dfrac{1}{3}$
26. $\dfrac{8}{9}$ $-\dfrac{2}{3}$
27. $\dfrac{7}{6}$ $-\dfrac{2}{3}$
28. $\dfrac{5}{8}$ $-\dfrac{1}{2}$

29. $\dfrac{7}{4}$ $-\dfrac{0}{8}$
30. $\dfrac{5}{8}$ $-\dfrac{0}{2}$
31. $\dfrac{4}{3}$ $-\dfrac{5}{6}$
32. $\dfrac{3}{4}$ $-\dfrac{3}{8}$
33. $\dfrac{4}{4}$ $-\dfrac{1}{2}$
34. $\dfrac{7}{10}$ $-\dfrac{1}{5}$

35. $\dfrac{3}{4}$ $-\dfrac{5}{16}$
36. $\dfrac{9}{16}$ $-\dfrac{1}{4}$
37. $\dfrac{3}{4}$ $-\dfrac{9}{16}$
38. $\dfrac{3}{2}$ $-\dfrac{5}{6}$
39. $\dfrac{1}{2}$ $-\dfrac{3}{16}$
40. $\dfrac{9}{10}$ $-\dfrac{1}{2}$

Solve.

41.
a. How many pounds of candy?
b. How much more candy in the large box?

42. Terry swam $\dfrac{5}{8}$ of a mile in the morning and $\dfrac{1}{2}$ of a mile in the afternoon.

a. How far did she swim that day?

b. How much farther did she swim in the morning?

Who am I?

43. I am $\dfrac{2}{3}$ greater than $\dfrac{5}{6}$.

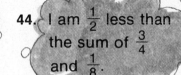

44. I am $\dfrac{1}{2}$ less than the sum of $\dfrac{3}{4}$ and $\dfrac{1}{8}$.

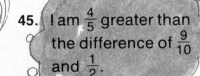

45. I am $\dfrac{4}{5}$ greater than the difference of $\dfrac{9}{10}$ and $\dfrac{1}{2}$.

More about subtracting, unlike denominators

Remember that the least common multiple of the denominators is the least common denominator.

Step 1. Choose a common denominator.

$$\frac{3}{2} - \frac{1}{3}$$

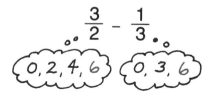 0, 2, 4, 6   0, 3, 6

Step 2. Change to equivalent fractions.

$$\frac{3}{2} - \frac{1}{3} = \frac{9}{6} - \frac{2}{6}$$

Step 3. Subtract.

$$\frac{3}{2} - \frac{1}{3} = \frac{9}{6} - \frac{2}{6}$$
$$= \frac{7}{6}$$

EXERCISES
Give each difference in lowest terms.

1. $\frac{1}{2} - \frac{1}{3}$ 0, 2, 4, 6   0, 3, 6

2. $\frac{3}{4} - \frac{1}{2}$ 0, 4   0, 2, 4

3. $\frac{3}{4} - \frac{2}{3}$ 0, 4, 8, 12   0, 3, 6, 9, 12

4. $\frac{2}{3} - \frac{1}{5}$

5. $\frac{7}{6} - \frac{3}{4}$

6. $\frac{5}{2} - \frac{4}{3}$

7. $\frac{2}{3} - \frac{1}{2}$

8. $\frac{1}{2} - \frac{1}{6}$

9. $\frac{3}{4} - \frac{1}{2}$

10. $\frac{3}{4} - \frac{1}{3}$

11. $\frac{5}{6} - \frac{2}{3}$

12. $\frac{5}{6} - \frac{1}{2}$

13. $\frac{7}{10} - \frac{2}{5}$

14. $\frac{2}{3} - \frac{1}{4}$

15. $\frac{3}{8} - \frac{1}{3}$

16. $\frac{5}{8}$
$-\frac{1}{4}$

17. $\frac{6}{8}$
$-\frac{1}{4}$

18. $\frac{5}{8}$
$-\frac{3}{8}$

19. $\frac{8}{9}$
$-\frac{1}{6}$

20. $\frac{3}{2}$
$-\frac{1}{5}$

21. $\frac{2}{3}$
$-\frac{4}{9}$

22. $\frac{3}{2}$
$-\frac{2}{3}$

23. $\frac{5}{6}$
$-\frac{2}{3}$

24. $\frac{4}{3}$
$-\frac{1}{3}$

25. $\frac{5}{12}$
$-\frac{2}{12}$

26. $\frac{2}{3}$
$-\frac{1}{2}$

27. $\frac{5}{8}$
$-\frac{0}{2}$

28. $\frac{7}{9}$
$-\frac{1}{3}$

29. $\frac{9}{2}$
$-\frac{3}{2}$

30. $\frac{5}{6}$
$-\frac{3}{4}$

31. $\frac{4}{3}$
$-\frac{3}{5}$

32. $\frac{3}{4}$
$-\frac{1}{2}$

33. $\frac{4}{3}$
$-\frac{3}{4}$

The table shows the rainfall each day for a week.

Day	Rainfall in inches
Sun.	$\frac{7}{10}$
Mon.	$\frac{1}{2}$
Tues	$\frac{1}{4}$
Weds.	none
Thurs.	none
Fri.	$\frac{3}{4}$
Sat.	none

34. How many days did it rain?
35. On which day did it rain the most?
36. What was the Sunday–Monday total?
37. How much more did it rain on Friday than on Sunday?
38. What was the total rainfall for the week?

Add across. Subtract down.

39.
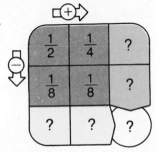

$\frac{1}{2}$	$\frac{1}{4}$	?
$\frac{1}{8}$	$\frac{1}{8}$	?
?	?	?

40.

$\frac{2}{3}$	$\frac{1}{2}$	?
$\frac{1}{4}$	$\frac{1}{6}$	?
?	?	?

41.

$\frac{5}{2}$	$\frac{4}{3}$	?
$\frac{5}{8}$	$\frac{1}{4}$	?
?	?	?

173

Problem solving

Mechanics often use fractions to select the right tool.
This wrench is called a $\frac{3}{8}$ wrench because the opening measures $\frac{3}{8}$ inches.

The size is given as a fraction in lowest terms.

1. Suppose that you are working with a set of wrenches that is graduated in sixteenths. What wrench would you select if you wanted the next larger wrench? [Remember: the size is given in lowest terms.]

   a. $\frac{1}{4}$ Answer: $\frac{5}{16}$

   b. $\frac{3}{8}$ **c.** $\frac{9}{16}$

   d. $\frac{3}{4}$ **e.** $\frac{1}{2}$

   f. $\frac{7}{8}$ **g.** $\frac{7}{16}$

2. Suppose that you are using a set of wrenches that is graduated in thirty-seconds. Give the next smaller wrench.

a. $\frac{1}{2}$ b. $\frac{9}{16}$

c. $\frac{3}{4}$ d. $\frac{3}{8}$

e. $\frac{5}{16}$ f. $\frac{7}{8}$

3. Which wrench is larger? (*Hint:* Use a common denominator.)

a. $\frac{9}{16}, \frac{5}{8}$ b. $\frac{1}{2}, \frac{15}{32}$

c. $\frac{13}{32}, \frac{7}{16}$ d. $\frac{3}{4}, \frac{7}{8}$

e. $\frac{5}{32}, \frac{1}{4}$ f. $\frac{5}{8}, \frac{19}{32}$

g. $\frac{13}{16}, \frac{3}{4}$ h. $\frac{15}{16}, \frac{7}{8}$

★ 4. What size wrench is halfway between these wrenches?

$\frac{4}{8}$ $\frac{6}{8}$

a. $\frac{1}{2}, \frac{3}{4}$ b. $\frac{5}{8}, \frac{3}{4}$

c. $\frac{3}{8}, \frac{1}{2}$ d. $\frac{3}{4}, \frac{7}{8}$

e. $\frac{5}{8}, \frac{11}{16}$ f. $\frac{1}{2}, \frac{9}{16}$

g. $\frac{9}{16}, \frac{5}{8}$ h. $\frac{13}{16}, \frac{7}{8}$

Whole numbers, mixed numbers, and fractions

There are 2 halves in 1.   There are 8 fourths in 2.

$$1 = \frac{2}{2}$$ $$2 = \frac{8}{4}$$

To write a whole number as a fraction, you can first write the whole number over a denominator of 1. Then you multiply both numerator and denominator by the same whole number.

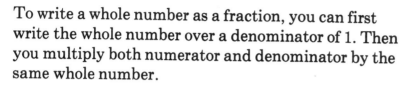

$$2 = \frac{2}{1} \underset{\times 3}{\overset{\times 3}{=}} \frac{6}{3}$$ $$5 = \frac{5}{1} \underset{\times 2}{\overset{\times 2}{=}} \frac{10}{2}$$

A **mixed number** has a whole number part and a fraction part:

$$1 + \frac{1}{4}$$

$$1\frac{1}{4} \leftarrow \text{mixed number}$$

You can change a mixed number to a fraction by adding.

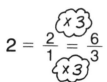

$$
\begin{aligned}
2\frac{1}{2} &= 2 + \frac{1}{2} \\
&= \frac{4}{2} + \frac{1}{2} \\
&= \frac{5}{2}
\end{aligned}
$$

EXERCISES
Give a mixed number for the red point.

1.

2.

3.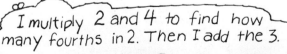

4.

Copy and complete.

5. $1 = \dfrac{\bullet}{2}$

6. $2 = \dfrac{\bullet}{2}$

7. $1 = \dfrac{\bullet}{3}$

8. $2 = \dfrac{\bullet}{3}$

9. $3 = \dfrac{\bullet}{2}$

10. $2 = \dfrac{\bullet}{4}$

11. $1 = \dfrac{\bullet}{4}$

12. $4 = \dfrac{\bullet}{2}$

Change to fractions. (*Hint:* Add.)

13. $1\frac{1}{2}$ 14. $1\frac{1}{3}$ 15. $2\frac{1}{2}$ 16. $3\frac{1}{4}$ 17. $1\frac{3}{4}$ 18. $2\frac{2}{3}$

19. $1\frac{1}{5}$ 20. $1\frac{2}{5}$ 21. $1\frac{3}{5}$ 22. $1\frac{4}{5}$ 23. $3\frac{1}{2}$ 24. $4\frac{1}{2}$

25. $2\frac{1}{3}$ 26. $2\frac{2}{3}$ 27. $1\frac{1}{8}$ 28. $1\frac{3}{8}$ 29. $1\frac{5}{8}$ 30. $2\frac{1}{8}$

I multiply 2 and 4 to find how many fourths in 2. Then I add the 3.

$2\frac{3}{4} = \frac{11}{4}$

SHORTCUT

Use the shortcut to change to fractions.

31. $1\frac{1}{2}$ 32. $3\frac{1}{3}$ 33. $2\frac{2}{3}$ 34. $2\frac{1}{2}$

35. $2\frac{2}{5}$ 36. $3\frac{1}{8}$ 37. $4\frac{2}{5}$ 38. $3\frac{1}{2}$

39. $2\frac{3}{5}$ 40. $5\frac{3}{8}$ 41. $4\frac{5}{8}$ 42. $3\frac{7}{8}$

Keeping Skills Sharp

1. $9\overline{)639}$

2. $8\overline{)736}$

3. $6\overline{)5658}$

4. $5\overline{)3640}$

5. $56\overline{)3210}$

6. $27\overline{)5963}$

7. $63\overline{)7000}$

8. $49\overline{)4297}$

Fractions, whole numbers, and mixed numbers

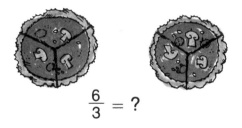

$$\frac{6}{3} = ?$$

Divide numerator by denominator

You can change a fraction to a whole number or a mixed number by dividing.

SHORTCUT

number of whole pizzas

$$\text{number of thirds in a whole pizza} \rightarrow 3\overline{)6} \leftarrow \text{number of thirds}$$

So, $\frac{6}{3} = 2$

$$\frac{11}{4} = ?$$

Divide numerator by denominator

number of whole pizzas

$$\text{number of fourths in a whole pizza} \rightarrow 4\overline{)11} \leftarrow \text{number of fourths}$$
$$\underline{8} $$
$$3 \leftarrow \text{number of fourths left over}$$

So, $\frac{11}{4} = 2\frac{3}{4}$

Other examples.

$$3\overline{)8}$$
$$\underline{-6}$$
$$2$$
$$\frac{8}{3} = 2\frac{2}{3}$$

$$2\overline{)7}$$
$$\underline{-6}$$
$$1$$
$$\frac{7}{2} = 3\frac{1}{2}$$

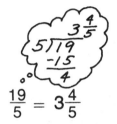
$$5\overline{)19}$$
$$\underline{-15}$$
$$4$$
$$\frac{19}{5} = 3\frac{4}{5}$$

EXERCISES

Change each fraction to a whole number or a mixed number.

1.

$$\frac{9}{4} = ?$$

2.

$$\frac{6}{2} = ?$$

3.

$$\frac{8}{3} = ?$$

4.

$$\frac{7}{4} = ?$$

5.

$$\frac{5}{2} = ?$$

6.

$$\frac{11}{4} = ?$$

Write as a whole number or a mixed number. Give the fraction part in lowest terms.

7. $\frac{3}{2}$ 8. $\frac{4}{3}$ 9. $\frac{6}{4}$ 10. $\frac{16}{8}$ 11. $\frac{6}{3}$ 12. $\frac{8}{2}$

13. $\frac{8}{3}$ 14. $\frac{8}{5}$ 15. $\frac{10}{3}$ 16. $\frac{4}{2}$ 17. $\frac{10}{4}$ 18. $\frac{13}{6}$

19. $\frac{7}{5}$ 20. $\frac{10}{2}$ 21. $\frac{15}{6}$ 22. $\frac{5}{4}$ 23. $\frac{5}{3}$ 24. $\frac{6}{2}$

25. $\frac{8}{4}$ 26. $\frac{7}{3}$ 27. $\frac{5}{2}$ 28. $\frac{11}{5}$ 29. $\frac{6}{5}$ 30. $\frac{7}{4}$

31. $\frac{7}{2}$ 32. $\frac{11}{8}$ 33. $\frac{20}{8}$ 34. $\frac{9}{4}$ 35. $\frac{9}{3}$ 36. $\frac{9}{2}$

Solve.

37. Each small pizza was cut into 3 equal parts. Hal ate 6 pieces. How many pizzas did he eat?

38. Joan jogged around a $\frac{1}{4}$-mile track 11 times. How many miles did she jog?

CHAPTER CHECKUP

Reduce to lowest terms. [pages 156–159]

1. $\frac{6}{8}$
2. $\frac{8}{10}$
3. $\frac{6}{9}$
4. $\frac{8}{6}$
5. $\frac{12}{8}$
6. $\frac{15}{10}$

< or >? [pages 160–161]

7. $\frac{5}{8}$ ⬤ $\frac{3}{4}$
8. $\frac{1}{2}$ ⬤ $\frac{5}{6}$
9. $\frac{3}{2}$ ⬤ $\frac{2}{3}$
10. $\frac{5}{2}$ ⬤ $\frac{2}{3}$

Add. Give each sum in lowest terms. [pages 162–167]

11. $\frac{2}{5}$ $+\frac{3}{5}$
12. $\frac{3}{4}$ $+\frac{1}{4}$
13. $\frac{1}{2}$ $+\frac{3}{8}$
14. $\frac{2}{3}$ $+\frac{5}{6}$
15. $\frac{3}{2}$ $+\frac{1}{3}$
16. $\frac{4}{3}$ $+\frac{4}{9}$

Subtract. Give each difference in lowest terms. [pages 168–173]

17. $\frac{5}{9}$ $-\frac{1}{9}$
18. $\frac{7}{8}$ $-\frac{3}{8}$
19. $\frac{5}{8}$ $-\frac{1}{4}$
20. $\frac{5}{6}$ $-\frac{2}{3}$
21. $\frac{3}{2}$ $-\frac{1}{3}$
22. $\frac{4}{3}$ $-\frac{3}{4}$

Change to a fraction in lowest terms. [pages 176–177]

23. $1\frac{1}{2}$
24. $1\frac{2}{3}$
25. $2\frac{1}{2}$
26. $2\frac{3}{4}$
27. $3\frac{1}{8}$
28. $3\frac{5}{8}$

Write as a whole number or a mixed number. [pages 178–179]

29. $\frac{8}{2}$
30. $\frac{5}{2}$
31. $\frac{4}{3}$
32. $\frac{12}{3}$
33. $\frac{7}{4}$
34. $\frac{13}{4}$

Solve. [pages 174–179]

35. Sarah climbed $\frac{3}{4}$ of a mile the first hour and $\frac{5}{8}$ of a mile the second hour.

a. How many miles did she climb during the first two hours?
b. How much farther did she climb the first hour?

Project

You may wish to work on this experiment in small groups.

1. Carry out the following experiment 50 times. For each toss, count the number of heads (H) and the number of tails (T). Record the results in a record like this:

Experiment : Tossing 10 pennies at once.										
Possible outcomes (H: heads; T: tails)	10H 0T	9H 1T	8H 2T	7H 3T	6H 4T	5H 5T	4H 6T	3H 7T	2H 8T	1H 9T	0H 10T
Tally of outcomes										
Fraction of outcomes										

2. Show your results on a bar graph.

3. Which outcome occurred most often? least often?

4. If you tossed 10 coins, would you have a better chance of getting the outcome | 10H 0T | or | 5H 5T | ?

CHAPTER REVIEW

Complete.

1.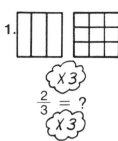

$$\frac{2}{3} = ?$$ (×3)

2.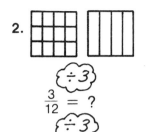

$$\frac{3}{12} = ?$$ (÷3)

3.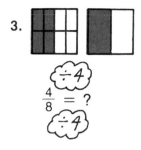

$$\frac{4}{8} = ?$$ (÷4)

Reduce to lowest terms.

4. $\frac{4}{6}$ (÷2)

5. $\frac{9}{6}$ (÷3)

6. $\frac{12}{4}$

7. $\frac{6}{8}$

8. $\frac{6}{4}$

9. $\frac{12}{8}$

< or >?

10. $\frac{1}{4}$ ⬤ $\frac{1}{2}$

11. $\frac{1}{2}$ ⬤ $\frac{3}{8}$

12. $\frac{1}{2}$ ⬤ $\frac{1}{3}$

13. $\frac{5}{8}$ ⬤ $\frac{3}{4}$

Add or subtract. Give each answer in lowest terms.

14. $\frac{1}{2} = \frac{2}{4}$
    $+ \frac{1}{4} = \frac{1}{4}$

15. $\frac{1}{3}$
    $+ \frac{5}{6}$

16. $\frac{1}{2}$
    $+ \frac{1}{3}$

17. $\frac{1}{2}$
    $- \frac{1}{3}$

18. $\frac{3}{2}$
    $- \frac{5}{6}$

19. $\frac{4}{5}$
    $- \frac{2}{3}$

Change to a fraction in lowest terms.

20.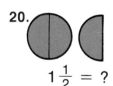

$$1\frac{1}{2} = ?$$

21.

$$2\frac{1}{3} = ?$$

22.

$$2\frac{3}{4} = ?$$

Change to a whole number or a mixed number.

23.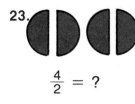

$$\frac{4}{2} = ?$$

24.

$$\frac{7}{4} = ?$$

25.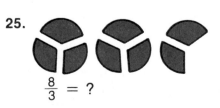

$$\frac{8}{3} = ?$$

182

1. Find the sum of the numbers in each row, column, and diagonal.

1	$\frac{1}{8}$	$\frac{3}{4}$
$\frac{3}{8}$	$\frac{5}{8}$	$\frac{7}{8}$
$\frac{1}{2}$	$\frac{9}{8}$	$\frac{1}{4}$

2. If all the sums are the same, the square is a magic square. Is it magic?

Complete these magic squares. Give fractions in lowest terms.

3.

	$\frac{1}{6}$	
$\frac{2}{3}$	$\frac{3}{2}$	$\frac{1}{3}$

4.

$\frac{2}{3}$		
	$\frac{5}{12}$	
$\frac{1}{3}$		$\frac{1}{6}$

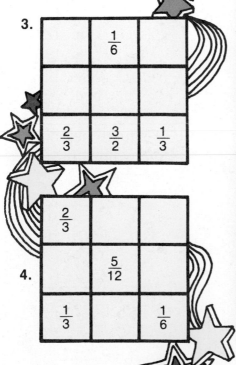

a b c d   a b c d   a b c d   a b c d   a b c d
14   34   14   4   30
a b c d   a b c d   c d   a b c d
15   31
a b c

MAJOR CHECKUP
Standardized Format

Choose the correct letter.

1. 783,463 rounded to the nearest hundred is:

    a. 783,000
    b. 783,460
    c. 783,500
    d. none of these

2. Which number is least?

    a. 6,983,425
    b. 6,894,715
    c. 6,099,098
    d. 6,243,527

3. Add.
$$3689 + 5747$$

    a. 8326
    b. 8436
    c. 9436
    d. none of these

4. Subtract.
$$6513 - 1844$$

    a. 4669
    b. 5331
    c. 5779
    d. none of these

5. Subtract.
$$8026 - 594$$

    a. 8572
    b. 8532
    c. 7532
    d. none of these

6. Multiply.
$$579 \times 6$$

    a. 3024
    b. 3074
    c. 3474
    d. none of these

7. Multiply.
$$384 \times 175$$

    a. 67,200
    b. 4992
    c. 61,580
    d. none of these

8. What is the remainder?
$$53\overline{)896}$$

    a. 16
    b. 48
    c. 53
    d. none of these

9. Divide.
$$39\overline{)4914}$$

    a. 126
    b. 136
    c. 125
    d. none of these

10. The measure of a right angle is

    a. 30°
    b. 60°
    c. 150°
    d. none of these

11. These triangles are congruent.

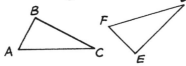

$\angle A$ corresponds to:

    a. $\angle D$
    b. $\angle E$
    c. $\angle F$
    d. none of these

12. A square has how many lines of symmetry?

    a. 1
    b. 2
    c. 4
    d. none of these

7
Fractions—
Multiplication
and
Division

Give the fraction of marbles that are

1.

   a. red.
   b. blue.

2.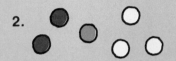

   a. red.
   b. blue.
   c. yellow.

3.

   a. red.
   b. green.
   c. blue.
   d. not blue.
   e. not green.

Fraction of a number

To find $\frac{1}{2}$ of a number you can divide by 2.

$$\frac{1}{2} \text{ of } 6 = 3$$

To find $\frac{1}{3}$ of a number you can divide by 3.

$$\frac{1}{3} \text{ of } 12 = 4$$

Divide by 4

$$\frac{1}{4} \text{ of } 20 = 5$$

EXERCISES

Complete.

1. $\frac{1}{2}$ of 12 = ?

2. $\frac{1}{3}$ of 12 = ?

3. $\frac{1}{4}$ of 8 = ?

4. $\frac{1}{5}$ of 10 = ?

5. $\frac{1}{8}$ of 8 = ?

6. $\frac{1}{6}$ of 12 = ?

7. $\frac{1}{3}$ of 18 = ?

8. $\frac{1}{2}$ of 18 = ?

9. $\frac{1}{3}$ of 30 = ?

10. $\frac{1}{8}$ of 24 = ?

11. $\frac{1}{4}$ of 16 = ?

12. $\frac{1}{3}$ of 15 = ?

13. $\frac{1}{2}$ of 20 = ?

14. $\frac{1}{5}$ of 15 = ?

15. $\frac{1}{4}$ of 36 = ?

16. $\frac{1}{6}$ of 18 = ?

17. $\frac{1}{6}$ of 36 = ?

18. $\frac{1}{4}$ of 32 = ?

1 dozen = 12

Complete.

19. $\frac{1}{2}$ of a dozen = ?

20. $\frac{1}{3}$ of a dozen = ?

21. $\frac{1}{4}$ of a dozen = ?

22. $\frac{1}{6}$ of a dozen = ?

1 hour = 60 minutes

How many minutes in

23. $\frac{1}{2}$ of an hour?

24. $\frac{1}{3}$ of an hour?

25. $\frac{1}{4}$ of an hour?

26. $\frac{1}{5}$ of an hour?

27. $\frac{1}{6}$ of an hour?

28. $\frac{1}{10}$ of an hour?

Solve.

29. Jerry had 48¢. He spent $\frac{1}{3}$ of it for a candy bar. How much did he spend? How much did he have left?

30. Donna has 436 stamps in her collection. $\frac{1}{4}$ of them are Canadian stamps. How many Canadian stamps does she have? How many non-Canadian stamps?

More about a fraction of a number

To find $\frac{2}{3}$ of a number, you can first find $\frac{1}{3}$ of the number and then multiply that by 2.

$$\frac{2}{3} \text{ of } 12 = 8$$

To find a fraction of a number:

(1) divide by the denominator and
(2) multiply that answer by the numerator.

$$\frac{3}{4} \text{ of } 20 = 15$$

EXERCISES

Complete.

1. $\frac{1}{6}$ of 24 = ___?___   2. $\frac{2}{6}$ of 24 = ___?___

3. $\frac{3}{6}$ of 24 = ___?___   4. $\frac{4}{6}$ of 24 = ___?___

5. $\frac{5}{6}$ of 24 = ___?___   6. $\frac{6}{6}$ of 24 = ___?___

188

Complete.

7. $\frac{2}{3}$ of 18 = _?_   8. $\frac{5}{6}$ of 12 = _?_   9. $\frac{3}{4}$ of 16 = _?_

10. $\frac{5}{8}$ of 24 = _?_   11. $\frac{1}{2}$ of 20 = _?_   12. $\frac{3}{2}$ of 12 = _?_

13. $\frac{3}{8}$ of 16 = _?_   14. $\frac{4}{4}$ of 20 = _?_   15. $\frac{4}{3}$ of 24 = _?_

16. $\frac{6}{5}$ of 25 = _?_   17. $\frac{3}{4}$ of 12 = _?_   18. $\frac{5}{6}$ of 18 = _?_

19. $\frac{1}{4}$ of 32 = _?_   20. $\frac{5}{2}$ of 14 = _?_   21. $\frac{2}{3}$ of 9 = _?_

22. $\frac{5}{3}$ of 21 = _?_   23. $\frac{1}{2}$ of 30 = _?_   24. $\frac{7}{8}$ of 24 = _?_

25. $\frac{4}{3}$ of 15 = _?_   26. $\frac{3}{3}$ of 15 = _?_   27. $\frac{3}{8}$ of 40 = _?_

Complete.

28. $\frac{2}{3}$ of a dozen = _?_   29. $\frac{3}{4}$ of a dozen = _?_   30. $\frac{4}{3}$ of a dozen = _?_

How many minutes?

31. $\frac{3}{4}$ of an hour   32. $\frac{5}{6}$ of an hour   33. $\frac{1}{10}$ of an hour

1 yard = 36 inches

1 pound = 16 ounces

1 foot = 12 inches

How many inches?

34. $\frac{2}{3}$ of a yard   35. $\frac{3}{4}$ of a yard

36. $\frac{5}{2}$ of a yard   37. $\frac{4}{9}$ of a yard

How many ounces?

38. $\frac{1}{2}$ of a pound 39. $\frac{3}{4}$ of a pound

40. $\frac{3}{8}$ of a pound 41. $\frac{5}{8}$ of a pound

How many inches?

42. $\frac{1}{2}$ of a foot   43. $\frac{2}{3}$ of a foot

44. $\frac{3}{4}$ of a foot   45. $\frac{5}{6}$ of a foot

189

Using mixed numbers

The Math Club needed $2\frac{1}{2}$ dozen doughnuts for their meeting.

To find the cost of $2\frac{1}{2}$ dozen doughnuts:

(1) Find the cost of 2 dozen.

(2) Find the cost of $\frac{1}{2}$ dozen.

(3) Add.

$$\$2.40 + \$.60 = \$3.00$$

The total cost is $3.00.

How many minutes?

7. 2 hours

8. $\frac{1}{2}$ hour

9. $2\frac{1}{2}$ hours

10. 1 hour

11. $\frac{2}{3}$ of an hour

12. $1\frac{2}{3}$ hours

13. 3 hours

14. $\frac{3}{4}$ hour

15. $3\frac{3}{4}$ hours

How many ounces?

16. 2 pounds

17. $\frac{1}{4}$ pound

18. $2\frac{1}{4}$ pounds

19. 1 pound

20. $\frac{3}{8}$ of a pound

21. $1\frac{3}{8}$ pounds

22. 3 pounds

23. $\frac{5}{8}$ pound

24. $3\frac{5}{8}$ pounds

EXERCISES

What is the cost?

1. 2 dozen

2. $\frac{1}{4}$ dozen

3. $2\frac{1}{4}$ dozen

4. 1 dozen

5. $\frac{3}{4}$ dozen

6. $1\frac{3}{4}$ dozen

How many inches?

25. 2 feet

26. $\frac{3}{4}$ of a foot

27. $2\frac{3}{4}$ feet

28. 3 feet

29. $\frac{2}{3}$ of a foot

30. $3\frac{2}{3}$ feet

How many feet?

31. 4 yards

32. $\frac{2}{3}$ of a yard

33. $4\frac{2}{3}$ yards

How many inches?

34. 2 yards

35. $\frac{5}{6}$ of a yard

36. $2\frac{5}{6}$ yards

37. There are 2 pints in a quart. How many pints in $7\frac{1}{2}$ quarts?

38. There are 4 quarts in a gallon. How many quarts in $3\frac{3}{4}$ gallons?

39. Linda earns $1.20 an hour for babysitting. How much does she earn for 2 hours and 15 minutes? *Hint:* 15 minutes $= \frac{1}{4}$ hour.

40. David rode his bicycle 8 miles in an hour. At that rate, how far could he ride his bicycle in $3\frac{3}{4}$ hours?

Keeping Skills Sharp

Give each sum in lowest terms.

1. $\frac{3}{8}$
$+\frac{1}{8}$

2. $\frac{3}{4}$
$+\frac{1}{2}$

3. $\frac{2}{3}$
$+\frac{5}{6}$

4. $\frac{1}{2}$
$+\frac{1}{3}$

5. $\frac{2}{3}$
$+\frac{1}{5}$

6. $\frac{3}{4}$
$+\frac{2}{3}$

Give each difference in lowest terms.

7. $\frac{5}{8}$
$-\frac{3}{8}$

8. $\frac{7}{8}$
$-\frac{3}{4}$

9. $\frac{4}{5}$
$-\frac{3}{10}$

10. $\frac{5}{6}$
$-\frac{2}{3}$

11. $\frac{2}{3}$
$-\frac{1}{4}$

12. $\frac{5}{6}$
$-\frac{3}{8}$

Multiplying fractions

Suppose that you were just learning to multiply whole numbers and that you had not memorized the basic facts yet. You could find the product of 2 and 3 this way.

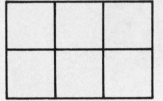

1. Pick a unit square.

2. Make a region that is as long as 3 squares and as wide as 2 squares.

3. Then count the total number of unit squares.

$$2 \times 3 = 6$$

You can do the same thing to find the product of $\frac{1}{2}$ and $\frac{1}{2}$.

1. Pick a unit square.

2. Make a region that is $\frac{1}{2}$ as long and $\frac{1}{2}$ as wide as the square.

3. Then find what fractional part of a square it is.

$$\frac{1}{2} \times \frac{1}{2} = \frac{1}{4}$$

Here are other examples.

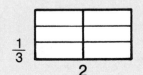

$$\frac{1}{3} \times 2 = \frac{2}{3}$$

$$\frac{2}{3} \times \frac{3}{4} = \frac{6}{12}$$

EXERCISES
Study the picture.
Then give the product.

1. 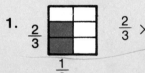 $\frac{2}{3} \times \frac{1}{2} = ?$

2. $\frac{3}{4} \times \frac{1}{2} = ?$

3. $\dfrac{3}{4}$ $\dfrac{2}{3}$ $\qquad$ $\dfrac{3}{4} \times \dfrac{2}{3} = \underline{?}$

4. $\dfrac{3}{4}$ $\dfrac{3}{3}$ $\qquad$ $\dfrac{3}{4} \times \dfrac{3}{3} = \underline{?}$

5. 2 $\dfrac{3}{5}$ $\qquad$ $2 \times \dfrac{3}{5} = \underline{?}$

6. 2 $\dfrac{3}{4}$ $\qquad$ $2 \times \dfrac{3}{4} = \underline{?}$

7. $\dfrac{2}{5}$ 2 $\qquad$ $\dfrac{2}{5} \times 2 = \underline{?}$

8. $\dfrac{2}{4}$ 3 $\qquad$ $\dfrac{2}{4} \times 3 = \underline{?}$

9. $\dfrac{1}{2}$ $\dfrac{3}{2}$ $\qquad$ $\dfrac{1}{2} \times \dfrac{3}{2} = \underline{?}$

10. $\dfrac{2}{3}$ $\dfrac{3}{2}$ $\qquad$ $\dfrac{2}{3} \times \dfrac{3}{2} = \underline{?}$

11. $\dfrac{4}{3}$ $\dfrac{3}{2}$ $\qquad$ $\dfrac{4}{3} \times \dfrac{3}{2} = \underline{?}$

12. $\dfrac{5}{3}$ $\dfrac{7}{4}$ 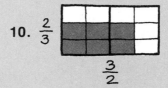 $\qquad$ $\dfrac{5}{3} \times \dfrac{7}{4} = \underline{?}$

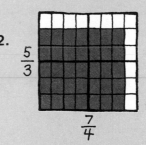

13. $\dfrac{2}{5}$ $\dfrac{2}{3}$

14. $\dfrac{4}{5}$ $\dfrac{1}{3}$

15. $\dfrac{3}{5}$ $\dfrac{1}{2}$

16. $\dfrac{2}{3}$ 2

More about multiplying fractions

To multiply fractional numbers:

1. Multiply the numerators to get the numerator of the product.

2. Multiply the denominators to get the denominator of the product.

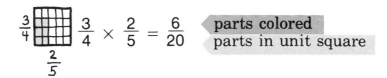

$\frac{3}{4} \times \frac{2}{5} = \frac{6}{20}$ parts colored / parts in unit square

$3 \times \frac{3}{4} = \frac{9}{4}$

$\frac{5}{2} \times \frac{4}{3} = \frac{20}{6}$

$= \frac{10}{3}$ lowest terms

Taking a fraction of a number is the same as multiplying by a fraction.

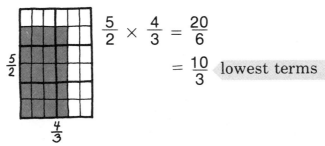

$15 \div 3 = 5$
$5 \times 2 = 10$

$\frac{2}{3}$ of \$15 = \$10

$\frac{2}{3} \times \$15 = \$\frac{30}{3} = \$10$

$\frac{1}{2}$ of $\frac{1}{3} = \frac{1}{2} \times \frac{1}{3}$

$= \frac{1}{6}$

194

EXERCISES

Give each product in lowest terms.

1. $\frac{1}{2} \times \frac{2}{3}$
2. $\frac{2}{5} \times \frac{3}{2}$
3. $4 \times \frac{3}{4}$
4. $\frac{2}{3} \times 2$

5. $\frac{1}{2} \times \frac{1}{3}$
6. $\frac{3}{2} \times \frac{3}{4}$
7. $\frac{4}{3} \times \frac{2}{5}$
8. $\frac{1}{4} \times \frac{5}{8}$

9. $\frac{2}{3} \times \frac{3}{4}$
10. $\frac{3}{8} \times \frac{2}{3}$
11. $4 \times \frac{2}{3}$
12. $\frac{5}{6} \times \frac{1}{3}$

13. $3 \times \frac{3}{4}$
14. $\frac{3}{5} \times \frac{2}{5}$
15. $\frac{4}{5} \times 2$
16. $\frac{3}{2} \times \frac{1}{4}$

17. $2 \times \frac{1}{2}$
18. $3 \times \frac{1}{3}$
19. $\frac{2}{3} \times \frac{3}{2}$
20. $\frac{3}{4} \times \frac{4}{3}$

> If the product of two numbers is 1, then the numbers are **reciprocals** of each other.

Give the reciprocal of

21. $\frac{1}{2}$ 2
22. $\frac{1}{3}$
23. 4

24. 3
25. $\frac{2}{3}$  $\frac{3}{2}$
26. $\frac{3}{4}$

Solve.

27. Baked 48 cookies. Ate $\frac{1}{6}$ of them. How many cookies were eaten?

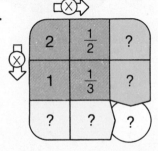

28. Live $\frac{5}{2}$ miles from school. Walk $\frac{1}{10}$ of this distance to get to the bus stop. How far to the bus stop?

29. $\frac{1}{2}$ of the garden is berries. $\frac{1}{3}$ of the berries are strawberrries. How much of the garden is strawberries?

30. $\frac{5}{8}$ of the class are girls. $\frac{1}{3}$ of the girls have blond hair. What fraction of the class are blond girls?

Copy and complete these multiplication boxes.

31.

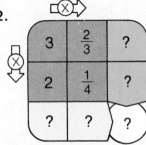

⊗		
2	$\frac{1}{2}$	?
1	$\frac{1}{3}$	?
?	?	?

32.

⊗		
3	$\frac{2}{3}$	?
2	$\frac{1}{4}$	?
?	?	?

33.

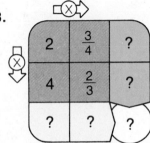

⊗		
2	$\frac{3}{4}$	?
4	$\frac{2}{3}$	?
?	?	?

Dividing fractions

How many $\frac{1}{2}$s in 3?

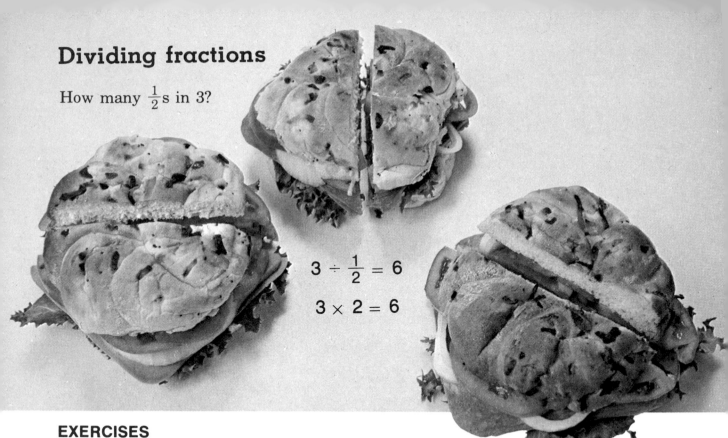

$$3 \div \frac{1}{2} = 6$$

$$3 \times 2 = 6$$

EXERCISES

First complete.

Then compare your answers in each exercise.

1.

   a. How many $\frac{1}{2}$s in 2?

   b. $2 \div \frac{1}{2} = \underline{?}$

   c. $2 \times 2 = \underline{?}$

2.

   a. How many $\frac{1}{4}$s in 2?

   b. $2 \div \frac{1}{4} = \underline{?}$

   c. $2 \times 4 = \underline{?}$

3.

   a. How many $\frac{1}{3}$s in 2?

   b. $2 \div \frac{1}{3} = \underline{?}$

   c. $2 \times 3 = \underline{?}$

4.

   a. How many $\frac{1}{4}$s in 3?

   b. $3 \div \frac{1}{4} = \underline{?}$

   c. $3 \times 4 = \underline{?}$

5. a. How many $\frac{2}{3}$s in 2?

b. $2 \div \frac{2}{3} = \underline{?}$

c. $2 \times \frac{3}{2} = \underline{?}$

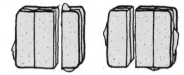

Change to a fraction.

1. $2\frac{1}{2}$ 2. $1\frac{1}{2}$

6. a. How many $\frac{3}{4}$s in 3?

b. $3 \div \frac{3}{4} = \underline{?}$

c. $3 \times \frac{4}{3} = \underline{?}$

3. $3\frac{1}{5}$ 4. $2\frac{1}{4}$

5. $1\frac{5}{8}$ 6. $1\frac{3}{4}$

7. a. How many $\frac{1}{4}$s in $\frac{3}{4}$?

b. $\frac{3}{4} \div \frac{1}{4} = \underline{?}$

c. $\frac{3}{4} \times 4 = \underline{?}$

7. $1\frac{1}{3}$ 8. $2\frac{3}{4}$

9. $1\frac{2}{3}$ 10. $2\frac{7}{8}$

11. $1\frac{5}{6}$ 12. $2\frac{3}{8}$

8. a. How many $\frac{2}{5}$s in $\frac{4}{5}$?

b. $\frac{4}{5} \div \frac{2}{5} = \underline{?}$

c. $\frac{4}{5} \times \frac{5}{2} = \underline{?}$

Change to a mixed number.

13. $\frac{3}{2}$ 14. $\frac{4}{3}$

15. $\frac{7}{4}$ 16. $\frac{5}{2}$

17. $\frac{9}{4}$ 18. $\frac{7}{3}$

Who am I?

9. Dividing by $\frac{1}{4}$ is the same as multiplying by me.

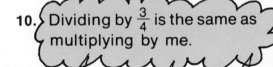

10. Dividing by $\frac{3}{4}$ is the same as multiplying by me.

19. $\frac{11}{4}$ 20. $\frac{7}{2}$

21. $\frac{5}{4}$ 22. $\frac{5}{3}$

23. $\frac{11}{8}$ 24. $\frac{11}{6}$

More about dividing fractions

Dividing by a number is the same as multiplying by the reciprocal of the number.

How many $\frac{3}{4}$s in $\frac{9}{2}$?

$$\frac{9}{2} \div \frac{3}{4} = ?$$

To answer the question, we first cut into fourths and arrange the pieces like this:

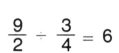

$$\frac{9}{2} \div \frac{3}{4} = 6$$

You get the same answer if you multiply by the reciprocal of $\frac{3}{4}$.

$$\frac{9}{2} \div \frac{3}{4} = \frac{9}{2} \times \frac{4}{3}$$
$$= \frac{36}{6}$$
$$= 6$$

The answer is 6.

EXERCISES
Complete.

1. $4 \div \frac{1}{2} = 4 \times \underline{2}$

2. $2 \div \frac{2}{3} = 2 \times \underline{?}$

3. $\frac{1}{2} \div 2 = \frac{1}{2} \times \underline{?}$

4. $\frac{2}{3} \div \frac{1}{3} = \frac{2}{3} \times \underline{?}$

5. $\frac{3}{4} \div \frac{1}{4} = \frac{3}{4} \times \underline{?}$

6. $\frac{4}{5} \div \frac{2}{5} = \frac{4}{5} \times \underline{?}$

7. $\frac{2}{3} \div \frac{3}{4} = \frac{2}{3} \times \underline{?}$

8. $\frac{5}{2} \div \frac{2}{3} = \frac{5}{2} \times \underline{?}$

9. $\frac{3}{8} \div \frac{3}{4} = \frac{3}{8} \times \underline{?}$

10. $\frac{5}{9} \div \frac{2}{3} = \frac{5}{9} \times \underline{?}$

11. $\frac{3}{4} \div \frac{7}{8} = \frac{3}{4} \times \underline{?}$

12. $\frac{5}{6} \div \frac{2}{3} = \frac{5}{6} \times \underline{?}$

Divide. Give answers in lowest terms.

13. $\dfrac{3}{4} \div \dfrac{5}{2} = \dfrac{3}{4} \times \dfrac{2}{5}$

$= \dfrac{6}{20}$

$= \dfrac{3}{10}$

14. $\dfrac{4}{5} \div \dfrac{2}{3}$

15. $9 \div \dfrac{3}{2}$

16. $\dfrac{5}{8} \div \dfrac{5}{7}$

17. $\dfrac{6}{5} \div 3$

18. $\dfrac{5}{4} \div \dfrac{1}{4}$

19. $\dfrac{5}{4} \div \dfrac{3}{4}$

20. $\dfrac{3}{5} \div \dfrac{2}{5}$

21. $\dfrac{4}{5} \div \dfrac{3}{4}$

22. $\dfrac{7}{8} \div \dfrac{3}{4}$

23. $\dfrac{3}{8} \div 2$

24. $\dfrac{4}{5} \div \dfrac{4}{3}$

25. $6 \div \dfrac{2}{3}$

26. $\dfrac{5}{6} \div \dfrac{5}{6}$

27. $\dfrac{6}{5} \div \dfrac{10}{3}$

28. $\dfrac{5}{9} \div \dfrac{2}{3}$

29. $\dfrac{3}{8} \div \dfrac{1}{2}$

30. $\dfrac{7}{8} \div \dfrac{5}{6}$

31. $\dfrac{3}{2} \div \dfrac{2}{3}$

32. $\dfrac{5}{9} \div \dfrac{3}{2}$

33. $\dfrac{7}{10} \div \dfrac{3}{5}$

34. $\dfrac{9}{4} \div \dfrac{3}{2}$

Solve.

35.

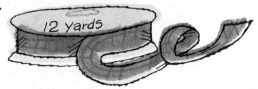

How many $\dfrac{3}{4}$-yard pieces can be cut from this ribbon?

36.

How many $\dfrac{5}{6}$-yard pieces can be cut from this roll? How much will be left over?

Follow the path and give the ending number.

37.

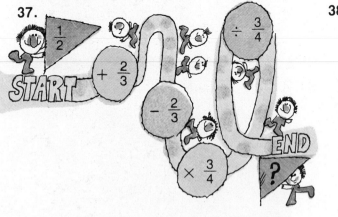

38.

Problem solving

GINGER SNAPS
MAKES 10 DOZEN

$\frac{3}{4}$ cup butter

2 cups sugar

2 eggs

$\frac{1}{2}$ cup molasses

2 teaspoons vinegar

4 cups flour

2 teaspoons soda

2 teaspoons ginger

$\frac{1}{2}$ teaspoon cinnamon

$\frac{1}{4}$ teaspoon cloves

1. **a.** How many cookies does a full recipe make?
   b. How many cookies in $\frac{1}{2}$ of a full recipe?

2. Find how much of each ingredient would be needed for $\frac{1}{2}$ of a recipe.

   a. butter **b.** sugar
   c. eggs **d.** molasses
   e. vinegar **f.** flour
   g. soda **h.** ginger
   i. cinnamon **j.** cloves

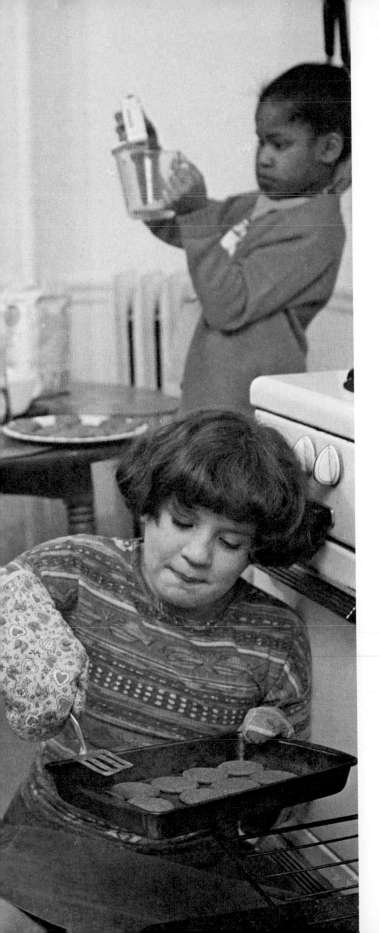

3. **a.** What fraction of a full recipe is 30 cookies?
   b. How much sugar would be needed for 30 cookies?
   c. How much cinnamon?

4. How much ginger would be needed for 40 cookies?

5. How much molasses would be needed for 80 cookies?

6. Suppose that you want to bake a full recipe of cookies and that you have $\frac{1}{4}$ cup of butter. How much more butter will you need?

7. How many teaspoons of spices (ginger, cinnamon, and cloves) are in the full recipe?

8. **a.** Suppose that you have only $\frac{3}{8}$ of a cup of molasses but plenty of the other ingredients. What fraction of a full recipe could you bake? *Hint:* How many $\frac{1}{2}$ cups in $\frac{3}{8}$ of a cup?
   b. How many cookies could you bake?

CHAPTER CHECKUP

Complete. [pages 186–189]

1. $\frac{1}{2}$ of 12 = _?_

2. $\frac{1}{4}$ of 20 = _?_

3. $\frac{1}{6}$ of 18 = _?_

4. $\frac{2}{3}$ of 24 = _?_

5. $\frac{3}{4}$ of 36 = _?_

6. $\frac{4}{3}$ of 48 = _?_

Give each product in lowest terms. [pages 192–195]

7. $\frac{1}{4} \times \frac{1}{3}$

8. $\frac{2}{3} \times \frac{1}{5}$

9. $\frac{3}{5} \times \frac{1}{2}$

10. $4 \times \frac{1}{2}$

11. $3 \times \frac{3}{4}$

12. $2 \times \frac{5}{6}$

13. $\frac{3}{4} \times \frac{2}{3}$

14. $\frac{2}{3} \times \frac{3}{2}$

15. $\frac{5}{4} \times \frac{8}{5}$

Give each quotient in lowest terms. [pages 196–199]

16. $\frac{1}{2} \div \frac{1}{3}$

17. $\frac{1}{2} \div \frac{1}{4}$

18. $\frac{1}{4} \div \frac{1}{2}$

19. $\frac{3}{5} \div 3$

20. $\frac{2}{3} \div 4$

21. $\frac{3}{8} \div 4$

22. $\frac{5}{9} \div \frac{3}{5}$

23. $\frac{2}{3} \div \frac{3}{4}$

24. $\frac{3}{4} \div \frac{2}{3}$

Solve. [pages 200–201]

25.

APPLES
96¢ a dozen

a. How much will $\frac{2}{3}$ dozen cost?

b. How much will $2\frac{3}{4}$ dozen cost?

26. Fred bought $\frac{3}{4}$ of a pound of mints. He ate $\frac{1}{2}$ of them. What fraction of a pound of mints did he eat?

27. Connie bought $\frac{5}{2}$ pounds of paraffin to make candles. If she used $\frac{1}{8}$ of a pound for each candle, how many candles could she make?

Project

How I spent yesterday

	hours
Sleeping	9
Eating	$1\frac{1}{2}$
In school	6
Play with friend after school	$2\frac{1}{2}$
Traveling to and from school	1
Homework	1
Practicing piano	$\frac{1}{2}$
Watching television	$1\frac{1}{2}$
Other	$1\frac{1}{2}$

1. The list shows how Alice spent her time during a 24-hour school day. Make a list of how you spent your time during a 24-hour school day.

2. Make a circle graph of how you spent your time. *Hint:* Draw a large circle and a radius. If you slept 8 hours, you will need to shade in $\frac{8}{24}$, or $\frac{1}{3}$, of the circle (360°) for sleeping.

   $\frac{1}{3}$ of 360° = 120°

   Measure off a 120° angle and label that part *Sleeping*.

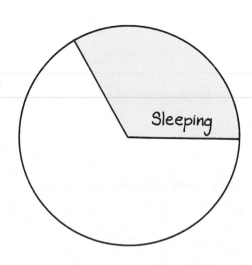

CHAPTER REVIEW

Complete.

1.

$\frac{1}{3}$ of 12 = $\underline{\ ?\ }$

2.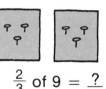

$\frac{2}{3}$ of 9 = $\underline{\ ?\ }$

3.

$\frac{3}{4}$ of 20 = $\underline{\ ?\ }$

Give each product in lowest terms.

4.

$\frac{1}{2} \times \frac{3}{4}$

5.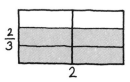

$2 \times \frac{2}{3}$

6.

$\frac{3}{5} \times \frac{3}{4}$

7. $\frac{2}{3} \times \frac{3}{4}$

8. $\frac{5}{8} \times \frac{2}{5}$

9. $\frac{1}{3} \times 3$

10. $\frac{7}{8} \times \frac{4}{3}$

11. $\frac{3}{2} \times \frac{2}{3}$

12. $\frac{4}{5} \times \frac{5}{2}$

Complete.

13. **a.** How many $\frac{1}{4}$s in 2?

   b. $2 \div \frac{1}{4} = \underline{\ ?\ }$

   c. $2 \times 4 = \underline{\ ?\ }$

14. **a.** How many $\frac{2}{3}$s in 2?

   b. $2 \div \frac{2}{3} = \underline{\ ?\ }$

   c. $2 \times \frac{3}{2} = \underline{\ ?\ }$

Give each quotient in lowest terms.

15. $\frac{3}{4} \div \frac{1}{2}$

16. $\frac{3}{5} \div 2$

17. $\frac{5}{9} \div \frac{2}{3}$

18. $\frac{3}{2} \div \frac{3}{4}$

19. $\frac{5}{6} \div \frac{4}{3}$

20. $\frac{3}{8} \div \frac{5}{2}$

21. $\frac{1}{3} \div \frac{5}{6}$

22. $\frac{3}{10} \div \frac{4}{5}$

CHAPTER CHALLENGE

1. Think about starting with a large unit square and folding it in half as shown above. You would end up with two thicknesses that are $\frac{1}{2}$ as large as the unit square.

   a. Suppose that you kept folding the paper. Complete this sequence of fractions for the size after each fold.

   $1, \frac{1}{2}, \frac{1}{4}, \underline{?}, \underline{?}, \underline{?}, \underline{?}, \underline{?}, \underline{?}, \underline{?}$

   b. Do the fractions in this sequence increase or decrease?

2. a. Suppose that the unit square described above is $\frac{1}{64}$ inch thick. Complete this sequence of fractions for the total thickness.

   $\frac{1}{64}, \frac{2}{64}, \frac{4}{64}, \underline{?}, \underline{?}, \underline{?}, \underline{?}, \underline{?}, \underline{?}, \underline{?}$

   b. Do the fractions in this sequence increase or decrease?

   c. How many folds would you have to make to have the total thickness of 8 inches?

3. Try this yourself.

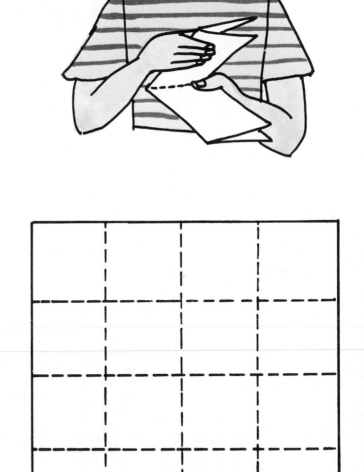

MAJOR CHECKUP
Standardized Format

Choose the correct letter.

1. 8,376,852 rounded to the nearest thousand is
   - a. 8,380,000
   - b. 8,376,000
   - c. 8,377,000
   - d. none of these

2. Add.
   7283
   5976
   187
   +2906
   - a. 14,132
   - b. 14,352
   - c. 15,352
   - d. none of these

3. Subtract.
   58307
   − 1659
   - a. 57,352
   - b. 56,748
   - c. 56,648
   - d. none of these

4. Multiply.
   682
   ×153
   - a. 104,346
   - b. 74,138
   - c. 100,046
   - d. none of these

5. Divide.
   $28\overline{)2893}$
   - a. 13
   - b. 13 R9
   - c. 103 R9
   - d. none of these

6. $\overline{AC}$ is called a

   - a. diameter
   - b. center
   - c. radius
   - d. none of these

7. The number pair for point A is

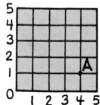

   - a. (1, 4)
   - b. (4, 0)
   - c. (4, 1)
   - d. none of these

8. Which is the greatest?
   - a. $\frac{1}{2}$
   - b. $\frac{3}{2}$
   - c. $\frac{2}{3}$
   - d. $\frac{5}{6}$

9. $\frac{1}{4} + \frac{2}{3} = \underline{?}$
   - a. $\frac{3}{7}$
   - b. $\frac{1}{4}$
   - c. $\frac{5}{6}$
   - d. none of these

10. $\frac{5}{6} - \frac{1}{2} = \underline{?}$
    - a. $\frac{1}{3}$
    - b. $\frac{2}{3}$
    - c. 1
    - d. none of these

11. $3\frac{2}{3}$ written as a fraction is
    - a. $\frac{10}{3}$
    - b. $\frac{8}{3}$
    - c. $\frac{11}{3}$
    - d. none of these

12. $\frac{5}{2}$ written as a mixed number is
    - a. $1\frac{1}{2}$
    - b. $2\frac{1}{2}$
    - c. $3\frac{1}{2}$
    - d. none of these

8
Decimals–
Addition and Subtraction

44.36

45.01

1.

2.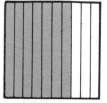

3.

4.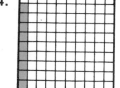

5.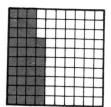

6.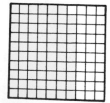

Tenths and hundredths

Below are 3 ways of writing about the number of shaded squares.

Ones	Tenths
1	7

$1\frac{7}{10}$ 1.7

The last numeral is called a **decimal fraction**, or just a **decimal**. "1.7" is read as "one and seven tenths." Study these examples.

EXAMPLE 1.

Ones	Tenths	Hundredths
1	0	6

1.06   (1 and 6 hundredths)

EXAMPLE 2.

Ones	Tenths	Hundredths
1	7	6

1.76   (1 and 76 hundredths)

Notice how the decimal is read. The picture shows that

7 tenths and **6** hundredths = **76** hundredths

EXERCISES

Give a decimal for the number of shaded squares.

1.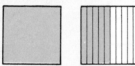

2.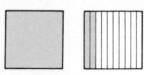

3.

4.

5.

6.

7.

8.

Read each decimal aloud.

9. 2.54	**10.** 25.4	**11.** 8.7	**12.** 8.07
13. 16.83	**14.** 9.40	**15.** 38.5	**16.** 4.9
17. 37.85	**18.** 62.5	**19.** 152.63	**20.** 48.75

Tell which number is greater.

21. .5, .6	**22.** .8, .2	**23.** .5, 1.5
24. 1.3, 1.8	**25.** 1.9, 1.6	**26.** 2.3, 2.7
27. 1.05, 1.06	**28.** 3.24, 3.21	**29.** 4.37, 4.39
30. 24.86, 24.93	**31.** 46.74, 46.52	**32.** 75.69, 75.48

Thousandths

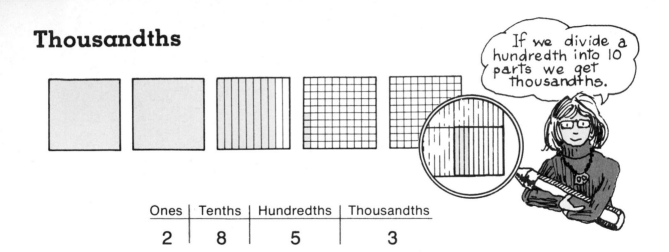

If we divide a hundredth into 10 parts we get thousandths.

Ones	Tenths	Hundredths	Thousandths
2	8	5	3

2.853

two and eight hundred fifty-three thousandths

Tens	Ones	Tenths	Hundredths	Thousandths
2	3	0	6	5

23.065

twenty-three and sixty-five thousandths

Tens	Ones	Tenths	Hundredths	Thousandths
5	8	0	0	9

58.009

fifty-eight and nine thousandths

EXERCISES
Read each decimal aloud.

1. 8.375
2. 691.8
3. 84.214
4. 65.017
5. 48.006
6. 523.74
7. 32.296
8. 7.063
9. 0.659
10. 0.003

Give the next three numbers.

11. 6.5, 6.6, 6.7, ?, ?, ?

12. 15.8, 15.9, 16.0, ?, ?, ?

13. 24.7, 24.8, 24.9, ?, ?, ?

14. 8.03, 8.04, 8.05, ?, ?, ?

15. 3.09, 3.10, 3.11, ?, ?, ?

16. 35.07, 35.08, 35.09, ?, ?, ?

17. 8.098, 8.099, 8.100, ?, ?, ?

18. 14.096, 14.097, 14.098, ?, ?, ?

Tell which digit is in the

19. tens place.

20. ones place.

21. hundredths place.

22. tenths place.

23. thousandths place.

24. hundreds place.

Copy each numeral and place a decimal point so that the statement makes sense.

25.

Ray Harroun averaged 12004 kilometers per hour when he won the first Indianapolis 500 race.

26.

Charles Lindbergh averaged 173468 kilometers per hour during his historic flight across the Atlantic.

Comparing and ordering decimals

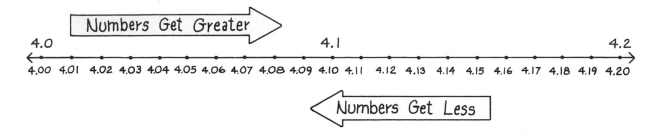

$$4.04 < 4.12$$

is less than

$$4.15 > 4.1$$

is greater than

EXERCISES

Give the number for each lettered point.

1.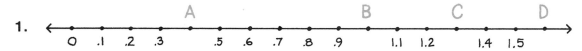

2.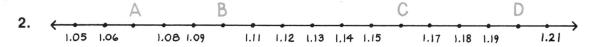

3.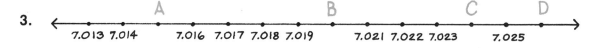

4.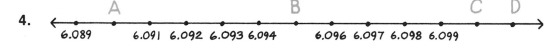

<, =, or >?

5. 3.1 ⬤ 3.4

6. 5.9 ⬤ 6.0

7. 12.0 ⬤ 12.1

8. 4.09 ⬤ 4.10

9. 4.00 ⬤ 4.0

10. 8.90 ⬤ 8.89

11. 3.784 ⬤ 3.782

12. 6.29 ⬤ 6.287

13. 12.080 ⬤ 12.08

14. Listed in the table are some states and their population density (the average number of people per square kilometer). Order the population densities from least to greatest.

State	Density of Population
Georgia	30.1
Kentucky	30.8
Louisiana	29.0
New Hampshire	30.7
Wisconsin	30.4

15. Listed are some past champions of the Professional Bowlers Association and their yearly averages. Order the averages from least to greatest.

Name	Year	Average
Don Carter	1962	212.844
Billy Hardwick	1963	210.346
Ray Bluth	1964	210.512
Dick Weber	1965	211.895
Wayne Zahn	1966	208.663
Wayne Zahn	1967	212.144

Multiply.

1. 48
   ×6

2. 93
   ×7

3. 152
   ×4

4. 293
   ×5

5. 614
   ×8

6. 921
   ×6

7. 352
   ×12

8. 406
   ×30

9. 527
   ×53

10. 283
    ×428

11. 921
    ×252

12. 742
    ×326

Rounding to the nearest whole number

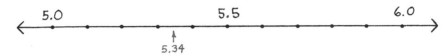

5.34 is between 5.0 and 6.0. It is nearer to 5.0.
5.34 rounded to the nearest whole number is 5.

Study these examples.

EXAMPLE 1.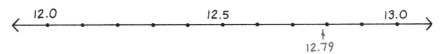

12.79 is nearer to 13.0 than to 12.0.
12.79 rounded to the nearest whole number is 13.

EXAMPLE 2.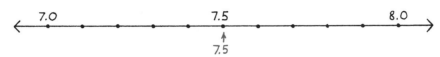

7.5 is exactly halfway between 7.0 and 8.0.
In this case we "round up."
7.5 rounded to the nearest whole number is 8.

EXERCISES
Round to the nearest whole number.

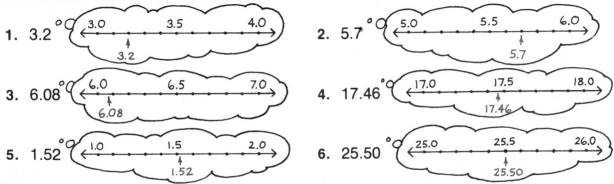

1. 3.2
2. 5.7
3. 6.08
4. 17.46
5. 1.52
6. 25.50

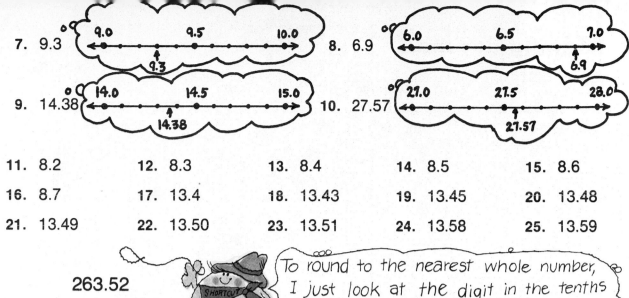

7. 9.3

8. 6.9

9. 14.38

10. 27.57

11. 8.2	12. 8.3	13. 8.4	14. 8.5	15. 8.6
16. 8.7	17. 13.4	18. 13.43	19. 13.45	20. 13.48
21. 13.49	22. 13.50	23. 13.51	24. 13.58	25. 13.59

263.52

To round to the nearest whole number, I just look at the digit in the tenths place. If it is less than 5, I round down. If it is 5 or greater, I round up.

263.52 rounded to the nearest whole number is **264**.

Round to the nearest whole number.

26. 5.73	27. 46.39	28. 85.46	29. 243.58
30. 49.674	31. 86.583	32. 42.486	33. 128.411
34. 96.514	35. 426.883	36. 2.488	37. 62.703

Round each price to the nearest dollar.

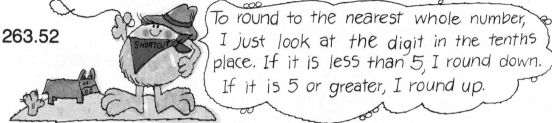

$43.95

$5.99

$16.23

$89.99

215

Adding decimals

You can find the sum of two decimals by lining up
the decimal points and adding in columns just as
you do with whole numbers.

EXAMPLE 1.   2.52 + 1.24 = ?

$$\begin{array}{r} 2.52 \\ +\ 1.24 \\ \hline 3.76 \end{array}$$

If a sum is 10 or greater, regroup!

EXAMPLE 2. $\begin{array}{r} 2.486 \\ +\ 3.592 \end{array}$

Step 1. Add thousandths.

$$\begin{array}{r} 2.486 \\ +\ 3.592 \\ \hline 8 \end{array}$$

Step 2. Add hundredths and regroup.

$$\begin{array}{r} {}^{1}\ \ \ \\ 2.486 \\ +\ 3.592 \\ \hline 78 \end{array}$$

Step 3. Add tenths and regroup.

$$\begin{array}{r} {}^{1}\ {}^{1}\ \ \\ 2.486 \\ +\ 3.592 \\ \hline .078 \end{array}$$

Step 4. Add ones.

$$\begin{array}{r} {}^{1}\ {}^{1}\ \ \\ 2.486 \\ +\ 3.592 \\ \hline 6.078 \end{array}$$

EXERCISES
Give each sum.

1. 43.6
    +21.0

2. 3.64
    +5.25

3. 7.08
    +2.10

4. 53.6
    +44.3

5. 0.638
    +0.211

6. 38.2
    +11.5

7. 4.78
    +3.19

8. 7.42
    +8.06

9. 5.431
    +2.081

10. 7.385
    +2.810

11. 633.4
    +683.3

12. 28.19
    +59.74

13. 7.416
    +3.829

14. 52.17
    +28.47

15. 8.382
    +3.695

16. 372.8
    +636.9

17. 33.96
    +97.49

18. 49.72
    +16.05

19. 65.03
    +8.29

20. 16.429
    +34.747

Solve.

21.
Wt. 2.79 kg
Cost $13.19
Wt. 3.08 kg
Cost $12.43

a. What is the total weight?
b. What is the total cost?

22. In 1920 the world land speed record was 249.522 kilometers per hour. Fifty years later the record was 752.145 kilometers per hour faster. What was the record then?

Add across. Add down.

23.

⊏+⊐⟩		
4.8	2.9	?
6.3	7.4	?
?	?	?

24.

⊏+⊐⟩		
.56	.39	?
.76	.84	?
?	?	?

25.

⊏+⊐⟩		
6.23	5.91	?
7.84	9.07	?
?	?	?

217

Subtracting decimals

You can find the difference of two decimals by lining up the decimal points and subtracting in columns just as you do with whole numbers.

EXAMPLE 1.   2.84 – 1.13 = ?

$$\begin{array}{r} 2.84 \\ -\ 1.13 \\ \hline 1.71 \end{array}$$

Sometimes you have to regroup before you can subtract.

EXAMPLE 2.

$$\begin{array}{r} 7.204 \\ -\ 1.265 \\ \hline \end{array}$$

Step 1. Regroup 1 tenth for 10 hundredths.

$$\begin{array}{r} 7.2\overset{1}{\cancel{2}}\overset{9}{0}4 \\ -\ 1.265 \\ \hline \end{array}$$

Step 2. Regroup 1 hundredth for 10 thousandths.

$$\begin{array}{r} 7.\overset{1}{\cancel{2}}\overset{9}{0}4 \\ -\ 1.265 \\ \hline \end{array}$$

Step 3. Subtract thousandths.

$$\begin{array}{r} 7.\overset{1}{\cancel{2}}\overset{9}{0}4 \\ -\ 1.265 \\ \hline 9 \end{array}$$

Step 4. Subtract hundredths.

$$\begin{array}{r} 7.\overset{1}{\cancel{2}}\overset{9}{0}4 \\ -\ 1.265 \\ \hline 39 \end{array}$$

Step 5. Regroup 1 one for 10 tenths.

$$\begin{array}{r} \overset{6}{\cancel{7}}.\overset{11}{\cancel{2}}\overset{9}{0}4 \\ -\ 1.265 \\ \hline 39 \end{array}$$

Step 6. Subtract tenths.

$$\begin{array}{r} \overset{6}{\cancel{7}}.\overset{11}{\cancel{2}}\overset{9}{0}4 \\ -\ 1.265 \\ \hline .939 \end{array}$$

Step 7. Subtract ones.

$$\begin{array}{r} \overset{6}{\cancel{7}}.\overset{11}{\cancel{2}}\overset{9}{0}4 \\ -\ 1.265 \\ \hline 5.939 \end{array}$$

218

EXERCISES
Give each difference.

1. 39.5 – 16.2	**2.** 5.98 – 2.46	**3.** 9.78 – 3.58	**4.** 68.67 – 24.35	**5.** 8.967 – 2.531
6. 75.2 – 38.9	**7.** 8.03 – 5.26	**8.** 4.16 – 2.57	**9.** 50.3 – 21.4	**10.** 3.00 – 1.86
11. 435.1 – 167.6	**12.** 2.060 – 1.784	**13.** 63.40 – 15.64	**14.** 40.35 – 21.84	**15.** 786.2 – 195.8
16. 6.756 – 5.851	**17.** 32.82 – 16.95	**18.** 892.4 – 365.9	**19.** 2.767 – 1.898	**20.** 7.631 – 4.594
21. 50.03 – 25.64	**22.** 230.0 – 137.8	**23.** 9.871 – 2.898	**24.** 5.242 – 3.557	**25.** 37.00 – 16.75

Solve.

26.

2.47 kg
$12.07

1.29 kg
$6.39

a. What is the total weight?

b. What is the total cost?

c. How much more does the larger sausage weigh?

d. How much less does the smaller sausage cost?

Copy and complete.

27. 5.63 – ■.8■ 2.79	**28.** 4.■69 – 1.7■■ 2.485	**29.** 7■.63■ – ■5.0■4 54.564	**30.** 4■.0■5 – ■2.84■ 35.193

219

More about adding and subtracting decimals

Remember to line up the decimal points when adding or subtracting decimals.

Write a "O" here and then add.

$5.38 + 0.496 = ?$

$$\begin{array}{r} 5.38\overset{1}{0} \\ +\ 0.496 \\ \hline 5.876 \end{array}$$

$28 + 15.84 + .73 = ?$

$$\begin{array}{r} \overset{1\,1}{28.00} \\ 15.84 \\ +\ .73 \\ \hline 44.57 \end{array}$$

$9.28 - 3.775 = ?$

$$\begin{array}{r} \overset{8}{9}.\overset{1}{2}\overset{7}{8}\overset{1}{0} \\ -\ 3.775 \\ \hline 5.505 \end{array}$$

$24 - 15.45 = ?$

$$\begin{array}{r} \overset{1\ \ 13\ \ 9}{2\!\!\!/4.\cancel{0}\cancel{0}} \\ -\ 15.45 \\ \hline 8.55 \end{array}$$

EXERCISES
Give each sum.

1. $\begin{array}{r} 3.684 \\ +2.85 \\ \hline \end{array}$
2. $\begin{array}{r} 0.430 \\ +6.597 \\ \hline \end{array}$
3. $\begin{array}{r} 4.963 \\ +2.84 \\ \hline \end{array}$
4. $\begin{array}{r} 6.00 \\ +3.25 \\ \hline \end{array}$
5. $\begin{array}{r} 112.625 \\ +\ 14. \\ \hline \end{array}$

6. $\begin{array}{r} 3.85 \\ 2.1 \\ +4.61 \\ \hline \end{array}$
7. $\begin{array}{r} 13.82 \\ 4.5 \\ +\ 6.3 \\ \hline \end{array}$
8. $\begin{array}{r} 8.375 \\ 14.5 \\ +\ 2.950 \\ \hline \end{array}$
9. $\begin{array}{r} 5 \\ 7.5 \\ +2.6 \\ \hline \end{array}$
10. $\begin{array}{r} 3.625 \\ 2 \\ +5.75 \\ \hline \end{array}$

11. 2.837 + 5.42   **12.** 39.7 + 16.985   **13.** 6.584 + 25.3

14. 16 + 3.8   **15.** 2.756 + 48.5   **16.** 63 + 58.275

Give each difference.

17. 52.68
  $-$ 5.4

18. 6.9
  $-$ 3.42

19. 9.36
  $-$ 4.8

20. 92.8
  $-$ 15.34

21. 32.
  $-$ 25.85

22. 4.385
  $-$ 2.63

23. 15
  $-$ 8.64

24. 9
  $-$ 3.625

25. 7.425
  $-$ 3.8

26. 734
  $-$ 16.85

27. 5.8 $-$ 4.25   **28.** 15.74 $-$ 3.618   **29.** 49.5 $-$ 37.837

30. 38 $-$ 3.65   **31.** 74 $-$ 52.8   **32.** 74.36 $-$ 36

Solve.

33. What is the total cost?

34. How much more is the lock than the chain?

35. Mary had a $20 bill. She bought both the lock and chain. How much money did she have left?

Addition and subtraction practice

Always remember to work inside the grouping symbols first.

The grouping symbols tell us to first add 14.8 and 15.2 and then subtract the sum from 35.2.

$$35.2 - (14.8 + 15.2) = 5.2$$

$$\begin{array}{r} \overset{1\ 1}{14.8} \\ +\ 15.2 \\ \hline 30.0 \end{array}$$

$$\begin{array}{r} 35.2 \\ -\ 30.0 \\ \hline 5.2 \end{array}$$

EXERCISES

Compute.

1. (25.6 − 11.8) + 9.4
2. 25.6 − (11.8 + 9.4)
3. (16.2 + 8.5) + 6.7
4. 16.2 + (8.5 + 6.7)
5. (9.74 + 3.61) − 2.86
6. 9.74 + (3.61 − 2.86)
7. (4.37 − 2.09) − 1.14
8. 4.37 − (2.09 − 1.14)
9. (8 − 3.82) + 1.4
10. 8 − (3.82 + 1.4)
11. (8.275 − 4.6) − 2
12. 8.275 − (4.6 − 2)

Solve.

13. In the 1924 Olympic games, John Weismuller swam the 100-meter freestyle in 59.0 seconds. In 1976, Jim Montgomery swam the 100 meters in 49.99 seconds. How much faster was his time than Weismuller's?

14. Dawn Fraser won the 100-meter freestyle in 1964. She set a new women's record, 59.9 seconds. In 1976, Kornelia Enders set a record that was 2.85 seconds less than Fraser's. What was Enders' time?

TARGET NUMBER

Kathy came within .016 of the target number, 10.

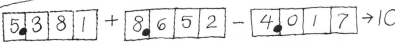

$$5.381 + 8.652 - 4.017 \rightarrow 10$$

$$\begin{array}{r} 5.381 \\ + 8.652 \\ \hline 14.033 \\ - 4.017 \\ \hline 10.016 \end{array}$$

How close did these players come to the target number?

1. $(3.486 + 9.059) - 3.742 \rightarrow 10$ 2. $(7.539 + 6.740) - 2.103 \rightarrow 10$

3. $(7.149 + 2.103) - 2.859 \rightarrow 10$ 4. $(6.328 + 9.417) - 5.918 \rightarrow 10$

Play the game.

1. Make a card for each of the digits 0 through 9.

2. Choose a leader.

3. Draw a table like this: $(\square\square\square\square + \square\square\square\square) - \square\square\square\square \rightarrow 10$

4. Without looking, the leader picks a card. Each player writes the digit in any square of the table.

5. The card is replaced in the deck and step 4 is repeated until all squares have been filled in.

6. The player who gets closest to the target number (10) wins the game.

223

Problem solving

Jane and Robert traveled in Canada with their parents. Here are some problems they solved during the trip.

1. Got Up
   Left 1 hour 35 minutes later.
   What time did they leave?

2. Stopped for Gasoline
   Tank holds 78 liters

   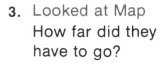
   Took **468** to fill.

   How much gasoline was in the tank before it was filled?

3. Looked at Map
   How far did they
   have to go?

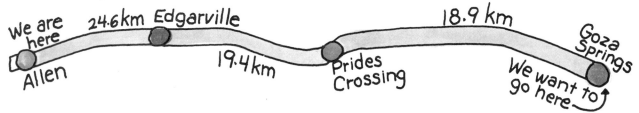

4. Stopped for Snack
   Robert had:

$1.25   95¢   49¢

Gave clerk:

How much change?

5. Checked Fuel Gauge
Tank holds 78 liters.
How much gasoline is in the tank?

6. Weighed Largest Fish
How much more did Jane's fish weigh?

JANE'S

2.76 kg

BILL'S

1.98 kg

7. Saw Road Sign
How far is it from Adams to Springville?

Adams   41.5 km

Springville 67.2 km

8. Checked Odometer

Before trip

582963

After trip

600849

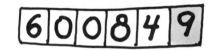

How many kilometers did they drive?

Make up a story.

PROBLEM SOLVING

★ NUMBER NEWS

46.3 + 28.6 + 12.7 = 62.2

CHAPTER CHECKUP

[pages 208–211]

In 159.378, which digit is in the

1. hundreds place?

2. hundredths place?

3. thousandths place?

4. tens place?

5. tenths place?

6. ones place?

<, =, or >? [pages 212–213]

7. 5.6 ◯ 6.5

8. 4.2 ◯ 4.20

9. 3.96 ◯ 3.9

10. 12.783 ◯ 12.738

11. 5.89 ◯ 5.9

12. 4.359 ◯ 4.36

Add. [pages 216–217, 220–221]

13. 5.4
    +2.3

14. 6.8
    +1.4

15. 7.03
    +6.59

16. 2.834
    +5.719

17. 35.26
     42.69
    +19.25

18. 36.8 + 29.25

19. 5.36 + 4

20. 74.296 + 3.1

Subtract. [pages 218–221]

21. 6.35
    − 3.12

22. 25.8
    − 16.3

23. 4.27
    − 1.89

24. 6.302
    − 1.748

25. 5.00
    − 3.72

26. 93.8 − 64.71

27. 73.5 − 29.678

28. 7 − 3.284

Solve. [pages 224–225]

CASHEWS 637.8 g $5.58

Peanuts 490.8 g $2.19

29. What is the total cost?

30. What is the total weight?

31. How much more do the cashews weigh?

32. How much less do the peanuts cost?

Project

Sarah and a friend decided to see how well they could estimate a minute. They got a stopwatch and Sarah told her friend when to start. When she thought that a minute had passed, Sarah said "Stop!" The actual time was 51.8 seconds. By how much did Sarah miss one minute?

1. Do this experiment in your class. Each student should have a turn estimating. Keep a record of your class results like this:

ONE MINUTE GUESSES			
NAME	TIME	ERROR IN SECONDS	ERROR ROUNDED TO NEAREST SECOND
SARAH	51.8	8.2	8

2. Make a bar graph of the errors rounded to the nearest second.

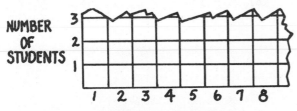

ERROR IN SECONDS

3. List some things that are shown on your graph.

4. If you have time, do the experiment for 30 seconds and compare your results.

CHAPTER REVIEW

Tell which digit is in the

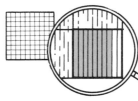

1. tenths place.

2. hundredths place.

3. ones place.

Ones	Tenths	Hundredths	Thousandths
1	3	5	8

4. thousandths place.

<, =, or >?

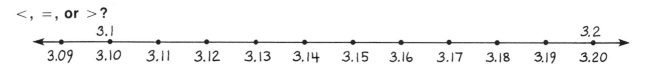

5. 3.2 ● 3.1   6. 3.11 ● 3.18   7. 3.2 ● 3.15

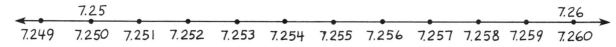

8. 7.25 ● 7.250   9. 7.256 ● 7.253   10. 7.257 ● 7.26

Add.

11. 5.68
    +3.59
    9.27

12. 3.058
    +6.749

13. 89.67
    +37.84

14. 42.9
    +5.78

15. 67.421
    +8.7

16. 5.893
    +2.70

17. 31.048
    +9.6

18. 59.831
    +74.665

19. 13.50
    +27.997

Subtract.

20. 59.14
    − 17.86
    41.28

21. 7.802
    − 3.194

22. 68.315
    − 9.527

23. 5
    − 2.84

24. 59.1
    − 28.426

25. 432.56
    − 18.3

26. 69.028
    − 18.655

27. 44.3
    − 18.57

28. 98.31
    − 17.485

I have two U.S. coins that total 30¢. One of the coins is not a nickel. What are the coins?

Use this decoder to find the answer:

A	C	D	E	I	K
78.24	27.6	6.095	18.375	6.95	6.102

L	N	Q	R	T	U
69.5	78.42	79.79	27.675	76.144	78.8

1. the sum of 36.83 and 42.96

2. the difference of 103.6 and 24.8

3. the difference of 128.1 and 49.86

4. the sum of 18.095 and 9.58

5. the sum of 15.8, 23.75, and 36.594

6. the difference of 35 and 16.625

7. the difference of 9.58 and 37.255

8. 26.5 greater than 51.74

9. equal to 78.420

10. 3.85 less than 9.945

11. 2 hundredths greater than 78.4

12. 4 hundredths less than 6.99

13. 5 tenths less than 28.1

14. 7 thousandths greater than 6.095

15. 75 thousandths greater than 18.3

16. ten times as great as 6.95

One coin is not a nickel!

| a | b | c | d | | a | b | c | d | | a | b | c | d | | a | b | c | d | | a | b | c | d |
14
34
14
4
30
| a | b | c | d | | a | b | c | d | | a | b | c | d | | | c | d | | a | b | c | d |
15
31
| a | b | c | | | | | a | b | c | | | | a | b | c | d |

MAJOR CHECKUP
Standardized Format

Choose the correct letter.

1. 195,832 rounded to the nearest ten thousand is

    a. 200,000
    b. 196,000
    c. 190,000
    d. none of these

2. In 182,659,034, which digit is in the ten millions place?

    a. 5
    b. 8
    c. 2
    d. none of these

3. Add.

$$\begin{array}{r} 3982 \\ 653 \\ 1859 \\ +74263 \\ \hline \end{array}$$

    a. 78,547
    b. 70,757
    c. 80,757
    d. none of these

4. Subtract.

$$\begin{array}{r} 83705 \\ -28659 \\ \hline \end{array}$$

    a. 55,146
    b. 55,046
    c. 65,154
    d. none of these

5. Multiply.

$$\begin{array}{r} 698 \\ \times 53 \\ \hline \end{array}$$

    a. 36,574
    b. 5584
    c. 31,874
    d. none of these

6. Divide.

$$49\overline{)10102}$$

    a. 26 R8
    b. 206 R8
    c. 260 R8
    d. none of these

7. The measure of $\angle AOC$ is

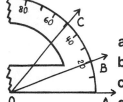

    a. 50°
    b. 120°
    c. 20°
    d. none of these

8. $\frac{3}{5} + \frac{1}{2} =$

    a. $\frac{4}{7}$
    b. $\frac{11}{10}$
    c. $\frac{2}{5}$
    d. none of these

9. $\frac{7}{8} - \frac{1}{3} =$

    a. $\frac{6}{5}$
    b. $\frac{6}{24}$
    c. $\frac{13}{24}$
    d. none of these

10. $2\frac{3}{4}$ written as a fraction is

    a. $\frac{9}{4}$
    b. $\frac{5}{2}$
    c. $\frac{11}{4}$
    d. none of these

11. $\frac{5}{8} \times \frac{2}{3} =$

    a. $\frac{5}{12}$
    b. $\frac{7}{24}$
    c. $\frac{10}{24}$
    d. none of these

12. $\frac{2}{3} \div \frac{3}{4} =$

    a. $\frac{1}{2}$
    b. $\frac{8}{9}$
    c. $\frac{9}{8}$
    d. none of these

9 Measurement

Time

We write: 7:15

We can say: seven fifteen
or, fifteen minutes after seven
or, quarter past seven

A.M. is used for times after 12:00
midnight and before 12:00 noon.

P.M. is used for times after 12:00 noon
and before 12:00 midnight.

If the time shown on the clock is in
the morning we write 7:15 A.M.

EXERCISES

Give the time. Be sure to write A.M. or P.M.

1.

Lunch time.

2.
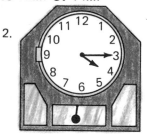

School's out.

3.

Time to get up.

4.

Time for bed.

5.
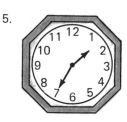

Let's watch the
football game.

6.

I'm getting up early
to go fishing.

Daylight or dark?

7. 2:06 A.M.   **8.** 12:00 noon   **9.** 3:15 P.M.   **10.** 12:00 midnight

EXAMPLE 1.

4 days 5 hours = $\underline{?}$ hours

To change days to hours, multiply by 24.

Solution:

$$\begin{array}{r} 24 \\ \times\ 4 \\ \hline 96 \\ +\ 5 \\ \hline 101 \end{array}$$

So, 4 days 5 hours = 101 hours

EXAMPLE 2.

582 minutes = $\underline{?}$ hours $\underline{?}$ minutes

To change minutes to hours, divide by 60.

Solution:

$$\begin{array}{r} 9 \\ 60\overline{)582} \\ -\ 540 \\ \hline 42 \end{array}$$

So, 582 minutes = 9 hours 42 minutes

Multiply or divide?

11. To change minutes to seconds, $\underline{?}$ by 60.

12. To change seconds to minutes, $\underline{?}$ by 60.

13. To change hours to days, $\underline{?}$ by 24.

14. To change days to hours, $\underline{?}$ by 24.

Rewrite each record setting time.

15. Rocking a chair

TIME: 336 hours
$\underline{?}$ days

16. Playing hopscotch

TIME: 36 hours 19 minutes
$\underline{?}$ minutes

17. Ferris-wheel riding
TIME: 22 days 4 hours 2 minutes
$\underline{?}$ weeks $\underline{?}$ days $\underline{?}$ hours
$\underline{?}$ minutes

18. Pogo-stick jumping
TIME: 8 hours 35 minutes
a. $\underline{?}$ minutes
b. If he jumped a total of 64,649 times, how many jumps did he average a minute?

More about time

A nature club started hiking at 8:40 A.M. They planned to hike for 1 hour and 30 minutes before taking their first break. Here is a way to find the time when they took their first break.

starting time

Add 1 hour

Add 30 minutes

Break time

8:40   9:40   10:10

> I first add 1 hour and then add 30 minutes to the answer.

The club started hiking again at 10:25. At 1:15 they stopped for lunch. Here is a way to find how long they hiked from the end of the break to lunch.

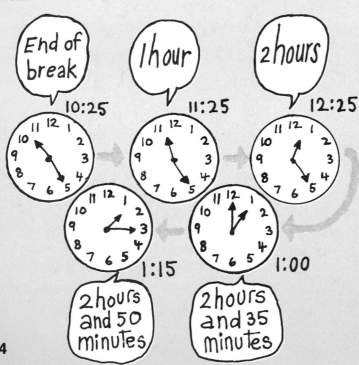

End of break   1 hour   2 hours

10:25   11:25   12:25

1:15   1:00

2 hours and 50 minutes

2 hours and 35 minutes

> I count ahead by hours and then by minutes.

234

EXERCISES

Give the time that is

1. 40 minutes later than 6:15.

2. 45 minutes later than 2:15.

3. 19 minutes later than 9:45.

4. 1 hour and 20 minutes later than 12:35.

5. 2 hours and 15 minutes later than 4:08.

6. 50 minutes earlier than 1:05.

7. 1 hour and 40 minutes earlier than 7:30.

8. 3 hours and 20 minutes earlier than 5:10.

How much time?

9. 5:30 to 6:15

10. 2:20 to 3:15

11. 4:45 to 6:30

12. 7:08 to 9:20

13. 10:45 to 1:30

14. 1:30 to 10:45

Solve.

15.

It is 6:50.
Show starts in 1 hour and 10 minutes.
What time does the show start?

16.

Started at 4:30.
Practiced for $1\frac{1}{4}$ hours.
What time did she finish?

17. Jan just missed the 9:07 train. The next train is at 10:48. How long will she have to wait?

18. On Saturday Dianne and her father spent $4\frac{1}{2}$ hours painting a fence. If they started at 9:20 A.M., what time did they finish?

19. John went to bed at 9:40 P.M. and got up at 7:20 A.M. How long did he sleep?

20. The time that Ms. Kelly works beyond 8 hours is considered overtime. One day she worked from 7:30 A.M. to 6:45 P.M. If she took $\frac{1}{2}$ hour for lunch, how much overtime did she work that day?

Millimeters and centimeters

The smaller unit marked on the ruler is a
millimeter and the larger unit is a **centimeter**.

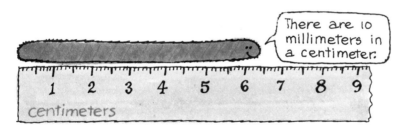

There are 10
millimeters in
a centimeter.

Measured to the nearest centimeter, the worm is
6 cm long.
Measured to the nearest millimeter, the worm is
64 mm long.

Instead of 64 mm, we can write 6.4 cm.

$$64 \text{ mm} = 6.4 \text{ cm}$$

EXERCISES
Measure to the nearest centimeter.

1.

2.

3.

4.

5.

6.

Measure to the nearest millimeter.
Give your answer in both millimeters and centimeters.

7.

8.

9.

10.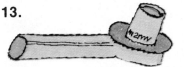

11.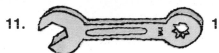

12.

13.

14.

15.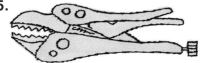

Measure to the nearest centimeter.

16. the length of your index finger

17. the width of your hand span

18. your height

19. the distance around your waist

Draw segments of

20. 8 cm   21. 8.2 cm   22. 7.4 cm   23. 6.3 cm   24. 63 mm

Complete.

25. 23 mm = _?_ cm   26. 40 mm = _?_ cm   27. 5 mm = _?_ cm

28. 3 cm = _?_ mm   29. 2.5 cm = _?_ mm   30. 12.6 cm = _?_ mm

Meters and kilometers

The basic unit for measuring length in the metric system is the **meter**.

The door is about 1 meter wide.

1 meter (m) = 100 cm

1 m = 1000 mm

The door is 106 cm wide.
We could also write the length as 1.06 m.

106 cm = 1.06 m

EXERCISES

Measure to the nearest hundredth of a meter.

1. the height of the door

2. the length of the chalkboard

3. the width of the hall

4. the distance between two opposite corners of your classroom

Complete. If you need to, look at a centimeter tape.

5. 125 cm = _?_ m

6. 150 cm = _?_ m

7. 200 cm = _?_ m

8. 1 m = _?_ cm

9. 1.4 m = _?_ cm

10. 2.34 m = _?_ cm

1 kilometer (km) = 1000 m

Utica - 145 km
Syracuse - 217 km
Rochester - 354 km
Niagara Falls - 475 km

11. How far is it to Niagara Falls?

12. How far is it from Utica to Rochester?

13. How far is it from Rochester to Niagara Falls?

Centimeter, meter, or kilometer?
Tell which unit you would use to measure

14. a pencil.

15. the distance to the moon.

16. a tall building.

17. the length of an airplane flight.

18. a city block.

19. the thickness of a dictionary.

Complete.

20. 2 km = _?_ m

21. 2.5 km = _?_ m

22. 3.48 km = _?_ m

Project

1. Estimate in meters a distance on the school grounds.

2. Keep a record of your classmates' estimates.

3. Measure the distance to see who had the closest estimate.

Perimeter

The distance around a figure is called the **perimeter** of the figure.

The perimeter of the picture is 99 cm.

The perimeter of a figure can be found by adding the lengths of its sides. The perimeter of the triangle is 14.4 cm.

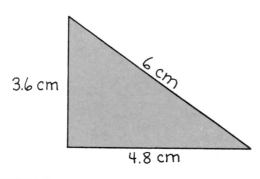

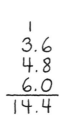

$$\begin{array}{r} \overset{1}{3.6} \\ 4.8 \\ 6.0 \\ \hline 14.4 \end{array}$$

WARNING! Make sure that the units are the same before you add the numbers.

EXERCISES
Give the perimeter of each figure.

1.
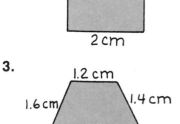

2.
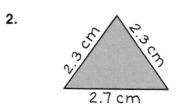

3.

4.
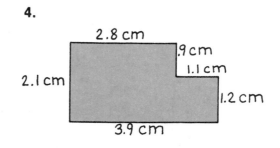

5.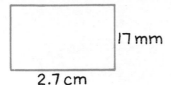

17 mm

2.7 cm

6.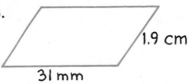

1.9 cm

31 mm

Copy and complete these tables.

7.

Squares	
Length of each side	Perimeter
32 mm	?
15 m	?
2.5 cm	?
5.25 m	?

8.

Rectangles		
Length	Width	Perimeter
4 cm	2 cm	?
18 mm	12 mm	?
12.4 m	7.6 m	?
24.3 m	18.7 m	?

9. Measure the length and width of a chalkboard to the nearest cm. Compute the perimeter.

10. Estimate the perimeter of your classroom to the nearest meter. Check your estimate by measuring.

11. The perimeter of a circle is called the **circumference** of the circle. Find a round object and measure its circumference.

Solve.

12. How much fencing is needed for a rectangular field that is 185 m long and 76 m wide?

13. A square park has a perimeter of 6812 meters. How long is each side?

Area

You can find the area of your desktop by first picking a unit—

1 square centimeter

—and then seeing how many square-centimeter tiles it takes to cover the desktop. Do you know a quicker way to find the area of the desktop? To find the area of a rectangle, you can multiply.

Area = length × width

Area = 2 cm × 4 cm

Area = 8 square centimeters

Notice that the area of the triangle below is $\frac{1}{2}$ the area of the rectangle. To find the area of a triangle, you can multiply, too.

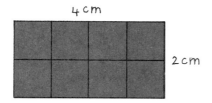

WARNING! Make sure that the units are the same before you multiply the numbers.

Area = $\frac{1}{2}$ × base × height

Area = $\frac{1}{2}$ × 5 cm × 2 cm

Area = 5 square centimeters

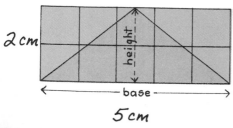

EXERCISES

Give each area.

1.

2.

3.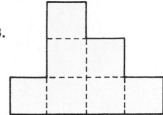

4.

5.

6.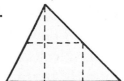

Give each area.

7.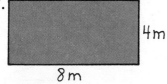

8.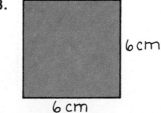

9.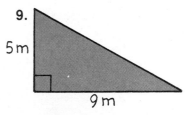

10.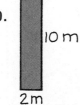

11.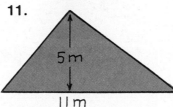

12.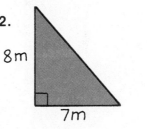

13. a. Measure to the nearest cm the length and width of your math book cover.
b. Compute the area.

14. a. Measure to the nearest meter the length and width of your classroom.
b. Compute the area.

Solve.

15. The base of a triangular piece of tile is 64 mm. Its height is 86 mm. What is its area?

16. The area of a rectangular piece of paper is 180 square centimeters. It is 15 cm long. What is its width?

Volume

To find the volume of the aquarium,
we first pick a unit:

 1 cubic centimeter

Then we see how many cubic-
centimeter blocks will fill the
aquarium. Is there a quicker way to
find the volume of the aquarium? To
find the volume of a rectangular
solid, you can multiply:

Volume = length × width × height

Volume = length × width × height
Volume = 5 cm × 3 cm × 2 cm
Volume = 30 cubic centimeters

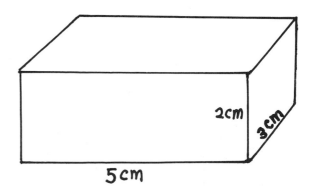

2cm

3cm

5cm

EXERCISES
Give each volume.

1.
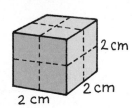
2 cm
2 cm
2 cm

2.
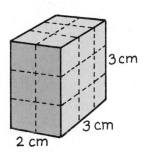
3 cm
3 cm
2 cm

3.
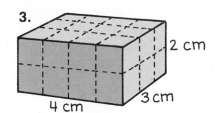
2 cm
4 cm
3 cm

4.
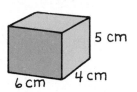
5 cm
6 cm
4 cm

5.
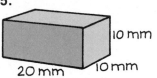
10 mm
20 mm
10 mm

6.
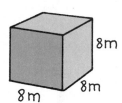
8 m
8 m
8 m

7.
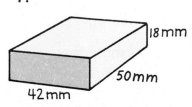
18 mm
50 mm
42 mm

8.
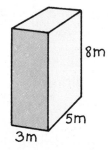
8 m
3 m
5 m

9.
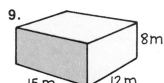
8 m
15 m
12 m

10. **a.** Measure to the nearest centimeter the length, width, and height of a desk drawer.
b. Compute its volume.

11. **a.** Measure to the nearest centimeter the length, width, and height of a bookcase.
b. Compute its volume.

Solve.

12. An aquarium is 42 cm long, 18 cm wide, and 20 cm high. How many cubic centimeters of water will it hold?

13. The volume of a sandbox is 3 cubic meters. The sandbox is 3 meters long and $\frac{1}{2}$ meter deep. How wide is the sandbox?

245

Liquid volume; weight

This box has a volume of 1 cubic centimeter:

It will hold 1 **milliliter** (mL) of liquid. The milliliter is used to measure small liquid volumes.

Since there are 1000 mL in a liter,

$$1 \text{ mL} = .001 \text{ liter}$$

The **liter** is used to measure larger liquid volumes.

$$1000 \text{ mL} = 1 \text{ liter(L)}$$

EXERCISES

Choose the correct liquid volume.

1.

4 milliliters
4 liters

2.

1 milliliter
1 liter

3.

200 milliliters
200 liters

4. **a.** Collect some containers and estimate the volume of each.
   b. Check your estimates by filling each container.

Complete.

5.

500 mL, or _?_ liter

6.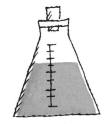

750 mL, or _?_ liter

7.

1.5 liters, or _?_ mL

8. 2000 mL = _?_ L

9. 375 mL = _?_ L

10. 2.4 L = _?_ mL

A cubic centimeter, or milliliter, of water weighs about 1 **gram** (g). The gram is used to measure small weights.

About 1 g

1000 g = 1 kilogram (kg)

The **kilogram** is used to measure heavier weights.

About 1 kg

Since there are 1000 g in 1 kg,

1 g = .001 kg

Choose the correct weight.

11.

5 g
5 kg

12.

5 g
5 kg

13.

200 g
200 kg

14. Weigh yourself in kilograms.

15. **a.** Estimate the weight of some objects.
    b. Check your estimates by weighing.

Complete.

16.

550 g, or _?_ kg

17.

1250 g, or _?_ kg

18.

3.4 kg, or _?_ g

19. 1500 g = _?_ kg

20. 248 g = _?_ kg

21. 43 g = _?_ kg

22. 3.2 kg = _?_ g

23. .5 kg = _?_ g

24. .03 kg = _?_ g

Inch

Now we will measure length using the customary system. The **inch** (in.) is a unit in the customary system for measuring length.

The ruler is marked in $\frac{1}{16}$ inches. It can be used to measure the length of the needle to the nearest inch, $\frac{1}{2}$ inch, $\frac{1}{4}$ inch, $\frac{1}{8}$ inch, or $\frac{1}{16}$ inch.

The length of the needle measured to the nearest:

inch is 4 in. (4").

$\frac{1}{2}$" is $4\frac{1}{2}$".

$\frac{1}{4}$" is $4\frac{1}{4}$".

$\frac{1}{8}$" is $4\frac{3}{8}$".

$\frac{1}{16}$" is $4\frac{5}{16}$".

EXERCISES

Draw segments of these lengths.

1. $2\frac{1}{2}$ in.

2. 3 in.

3. $1\frac{3}{4}$ in.

4. $2\frac{5}{8}$ in.

5. $3\frac{1}{4}$ in.

6. $1\frac{1}{16}$ in.

7. $2\frac{3}{16}$ in.

8. $\frac{7}{8}$ in.

9. $1\frac{3}{8}$ in.

10. $3\frac{5}{16}$ in.

11. $2\frac{15}{16}$ in.

12. $\frac{11}{16}$ in.

Measure the length of each object to the nearest
$\frac{1}{4}$ in., $\frac{1}{8}$ in., and $\frac{1}{16}$ in.

13.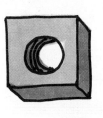

14.

15.

Measure.

16. the length of your pencil to the nearest $\frac{1}{8}$"

17. the width of your math book to the nearest $\frac{1}{4}$"

18. the diameter of (distance across) a penny to the nearest $\frac{1}{16}$"

Which is longer?

19. $1\frac{1}{2}$" or $1\frac{1}{4}$"

20. $2\frac{1}{4}$" or $2\frac{3}{8}$"

21. $4\frac{1}{2}$" or $4\frac{7}{16}$"

22. $3\frac{7}{8}$" or $3\frac{9}{16}$"

23. $5\frac{13}{16}$" or $5\frac{3}{4}$"

24. $6\frac{5}{8}$" or $5\frac{11}{16}$"

Solve.

25. The thickness of a certain book is $\frac{7}{8}$". How high would a stack of 12 of these books be?

26. A rectangular picture is $7\frac{1}{2}$" wide and 5" high. What is its perimeter?

Keeping Skills Sharp

1. $\frac{3}{8} \times \frac{1}{2}$

2. $\frac{1}{2} \times \frac{1}{3}$

3. $\frac{3}{4} \times \frac{1}{5}$

4. $\frac{5}{6} \times \frac{3}{4}$

5. $\frac{7}{8} \times 4$

6. $\frac{4}{3} \times \frac{3}{4}$

7. $\frac{3}{4} \div \frac{1}{4}$

8. $\frac{9}{2} \div \frac{3}{4}$

9. $3 \div \frac{2}{3}$

10. $\frac{1}{2} \div \frac{3}{8}$

11. $\frac{7}{4} \div \frac{3}{2}$

12. $\frac{7}{6} \div \frac{2}{3}$

Inch, foot, yard, and mile

12 in. = 1 foot (ft)
3 ft (') = 1 yard (yd)
or
36 in. = 1 yd

5280 ft = 1 mile (mi)
or
1760 yd = 1 mi

Sometimes you will need to change from one unit
to another. Study these examples.

EXAMPLE 1.

5 ft 4 in. = _?_ in.

To change feet to inches,
multiply by 12.

Solution:
```
   12
 × 5
 ────
   60
 + 4
 ────
   64
```

So, 5 ft 4 in. = 64 in.

EXAMPLE 2.

196 ft = _?_ yd _?_ ft

To change feet to yards,
divide by 3.

Solution:
```
        65
    3 ) 196
     - 18
     ────
       16
     - 15
     ────
        1
```

So, 196 ft = 65 yd 1 ft.

EXERCISES

Multiply or divide?

1. To change from feet to inches, _?_ by 12.

2. To change from inches to feet, _?_ by 12.

3. To change from feet to yards, _?_ by 3.

4. To change from yards to feet, _?_ by 3.

5. To change from inches to yards, _?_ by 36.

6. To change from yards to inches, _?_ by 36.

Complete.

7. 8 ft = _?_ in.

8. 48 ft = _?_ yd

9. 132 in. = _?_ ft

10. 13 in. = _?_ ft _?_ in.

11. 15 yd = _?_ ft

12. 79 ft = _?_ yd _?_ ft

13. 2 mi = _?_ ft

14. 5 mi = _?_ yd

15. Blue Whale

Largest ever measured
Length: 110 '

_?_ yd _?_ ft

16. African Bush Elephant

Largest ever measured
Length: 33' 2 "

_?_ in.

Make the measurement. Then copy and complete the sentence.

17. Your height
_?_ in. = _?_ ft _?_ in.

18. Your waist
_?_ in. = _?_ ft _?_ in.

19. The height of your classroom
_?_ ft = _?_ yd _?_ ft

20. The length of your classroom
_?_ ft = _?_ yd _?_ ft

Add. (Regroup 12 in. for 1 ft)

21. 5 ft 9 in.
+3 ft 6 in.
_____
3 in.

22. 7 ft 8 in.
+6 ft 6 in.

(Regroup 3 ft for 1 yd)

23. 9 yd 2 ft
+3 yd 2 ft

24. 8 yd
+15 yd 2 ft

Subtract. (Regroup 1 ft for 12 in.)

25. 7 14
    8 ft 2 in.
  – 2 ft 5 in.
  _____
    9 in.

26. 6 ft
– 2 ft 7 in.

27. 5 yd 1 ft
– 1 yd 2 ft

28. 6 yd
– 4 yd 1 ft

Perimeter, area, and volume

You can add to find the perimeter.

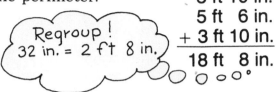

Regroup! 32 in. = 2 ft 8 in.

```
          2
     5 ft  6 in.
     3 ft 10 in.
     5 ft  6 in.
  +  3 ft 10 in.
    18 ft  8 in.
```

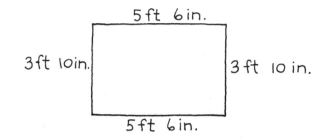

5 ft 6 in.

3 ft 10 in.

3 ft 10 in.

5 ft 6 in.

You can multiply to find the area.

Area = length × width
Area = 12 yd × 3 yd
Area = 36 square yards

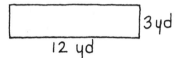

3 yd

12 yd

You can multiply to find the volume.

Volume = length × width × height
Volume = 5 yd × 6 yd × 4 yd
Volume = 120 cubic yards

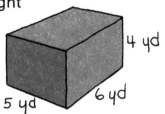

4 yd

5 yd   6 yd

EXERCISES

Give the perimeter of each rectangle.

1.
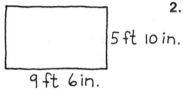
5 ft 10 in.
9 ft 6 in.

2.
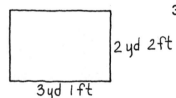
2 yd 2 ft
3 yd 1 ft

3.
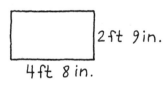
2 ft 9 in.
4 ft 8 in.

Give the area of each rectangle.

4.
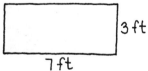
3 ft
7 ft

5.
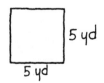
5 yd
5 yd

6.
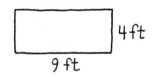
4 ft
9 ft

Give the volume of each rectangular solid.

7.
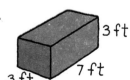
3 ft
3 ft   7 ft

8.
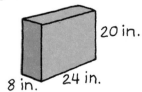
20 in.
8 in.   24 in.

9.
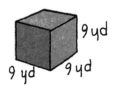
9 yd
9 yd   9 yd

252

Is the question about length, area, or volume?

10. How much sand?

11. How much string?

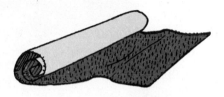

12. How much carpet?

Solve.

13. A rectangular floor is 20 feet long and 13 feet wide. What is its perimeter? Its area?

14. The area of a rectangular patio is 72 square feet. Its length is 9 feet. What is its width?

15. How many square inches in a square foot? In a square yard?

16. How many cubic inches in a cubic foot? In a cubic yard?

17. The perimeter of a square garden is 40 feet. What is its area?

18. The area of a square is 49 square feet. What is its perimeter?

19. The area of a rectangular carpet is 54 square yards. Its width is 6 yards. What is its perimeter?

20. The width of a rectangle is 5 yards. Its length is twice its width. What is its area?

Each figure is made from rectangles. Find each area.

21.
8 in.
8 in.
4 in.
2 in.
4 in.
6 in.

22.
6 ft
6 ft
2 ft
2 ft 2 ft

23.
2 in.
2 in.
8 in.
6 in.
4 in.
2 in.

Each solid is made from rectangular solids. Find each volume.

24.
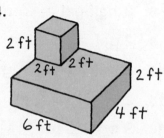
2 ft
2 ft 2 ft
2 ft
4 ft
6 ft

25.
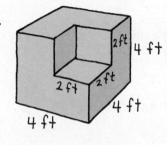
2ft 4 ft
2 ft 2 ft
4 ft
4 ft

★26.
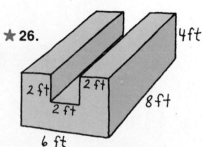
4ft
2 ft 2 ft
2 ft
8 ft
6 ft

Liquid volume; weight

Here are some customary units for measuring liquid volumes.

1 cup (c)

2 c = 1 pint (pt)

2 pt = 1 quart (qt)

2 qt = 1 half-gallon ($\frac{1}{2}$-gal)

4 qt = 1 gallon (gal)

EXERCISES
Complete.

1.

_?_ qt

2.

_?_ pt

3.

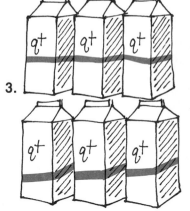

_?_ gal

4. 2 qt = _?_ pt

5. 6 c = _?_ pt

6. 3 half-gal = _?_ qt

7. 6 qt = _?_ half-gal

8. 8 pt = _?_ qt

9. 2 gal = _?_ qt

10. 10 pt = _?_ c

11. 12 qt = _?_ gal

12. 8 half-gal = _?_ gal

13. $2\frac{1}{2}$ qt = _?_ pt

14. $3\frac{1}{2}$ qt = _?_ pt

15. $2\frac{3}{4}$ gal = _?_ qt

16. 9 qt = _?_ gal

17. 11 pt = _?_ qt

18. 9 c = _?_ pt

Here are some units for measuring weight.

The **ounce** (oz) is used to measure small weights.

about 1 oz

16 oz = 1 pound (lb)
The **pound** is used to measure heavier weights.

about 1 lb

2000 lb = 1 ton
The **ton** is used to measure quite heavy objects.

about 1 ton

Choose the correct weight.

19.

72 oz
72 lb
72 tons

20.

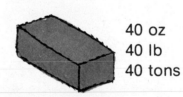

40 oz
40 lb
40 tons

21. **a.** Weigh yourself in pounds.
b. Is the combined weight of all the students in your class less than or greater than a ton?

Complete.

22. 9 lb = _?_ oz

23. 192 oz = _?_ lb

24. 200 oz = _?_ lb _?_ oz

25. 498 oz = _?_ lb _?_ oz

Problem solving

Architects design buildings where
people work and live. One of the
things that an architect considers
when designing a building is the
floor plan. Here is the floor plan of a
three-bedroom house.

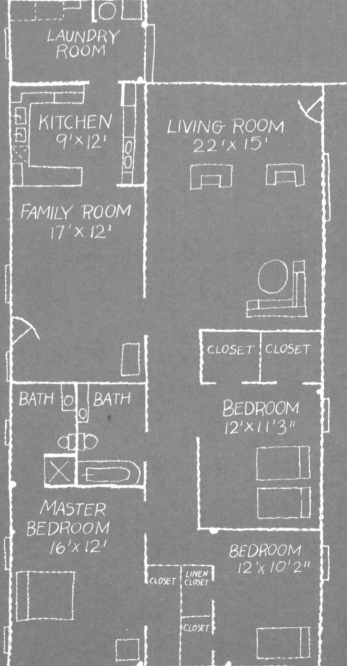

GARAGE
21' 7" x 21' 2"

LAUNDRY
ROOM

KITCHEN
9' x 12'

LIVING ROOM
22' x 15'

FAMILY ROOM
17' x 12'

CLOSET   CLOSET

BEDROOM
12' x 11' 3"

BATH   BATH

MASTER
BEDROOM
16' x 12'

CLOSET   LINEN
CLOSET

BEDROOM
12' x 10' 2"

CLOSET

UP, DOWN, & FORWARD

ARCHITECTS

1. What is the length of the family room?

2. What is the width of the smallest bedroom?

3. a. A carpenter wants to put a molding around the ceiling of the smallest bedroom. How much molding is needed?
   b. If the molding comes in 5-foot lengths, how many lengths should the carpenter order?

4. a. The living room floor is to be carpeted. How many square feet of carpeting are needed?
   b. How many square yards of carpeting are needed? Round your answer up to the next yard.
   c. If the carpet costs $9.50 a square yard, what will the total cost be?

5. The floor in the master bedroom is to be covered with carpet tiles that are 1 foot square. How many tiles will it take?

6. The family room floor is to be covered with square tiles that measure 8 inches on a side. How many tiles are needed?

7. A heating and cooling contractor needs to find the volume of the house. If the ceilings are 8 feet high, what is the volume of the living room?

8. The walls and ceiling of the largest bedroom are going to be painted. How many square feet are to be painted? (Don't consider doors and windows.)

CHAPTER CHECKUP

Give the time. Be sure to write A.M. or P.M. [pages 232–235]

1.

2.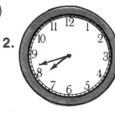

Complete. [pages 236–239, 246–251, 254–255]

3. 4 days 7 hours = ? hours

4. 8 hours 5 minutes = ? minutes

5. 3 minutes = ? seconds

6. 253 minutes = ? hours ? minutes

7. 1 m = ? cm

8. 1 cm = ? mm

9. 3 km = ? m

10. 3.8 km = ? m

11. 1 liter = ? mL

12. 425 mL = ? liter

13. 1.2 kg = ? g

14. .45 kg = ? g

15. 500 g = ? kg

16. 3 ft = ? in.

17. 1 mi = ? ft

18. 3 mi = ? yd

19. 18 yd = ? ft

20. 18 ft = ? yd

21. 3 c = ? pt

22. 8 qt = ? gal

23. 5 lb = ? oz

24. 4 tons = ? lb

Measure the rectangle with a centimeter ruler.
Complete. [pages 240–245]

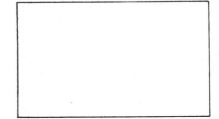

25. The length of the rectangle is = ? cm.

26. The width is = ? cm.

27. The perimeter is = ? cm.

28. The area is ? square cm.

29. The volume is ? cubic cm.

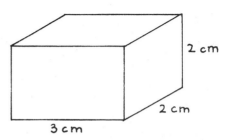

[pages 248–249]

Measure the length of the ribbon to the nearest

30. $\frac{1}{4}$ inch.   31. $\frac{1}{8}$ inch.   32. $\frac{1}{16}$ inch.

Project

How much water would be wasted if you left the drinking fountain on all night?

1. Find out how many seconds you have to leave the fountain on to collect a liter of water.

2. How long is it from the time your school ends one day to the time it begins the next day? How many seconds is that?

3. How many liters of water would be wasted?

4. If the same amount of water were in your classroom, how deep would it be?

CHAPTER REVIEW

Complete.

1. The length is _?_ centimeters.

2. The width is _?_ centimeters.

3. The perimeter is _?_ centimeters.

4. The area is _?_ square centimeters.

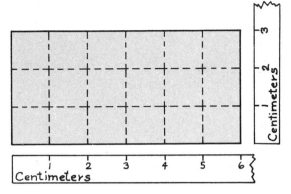

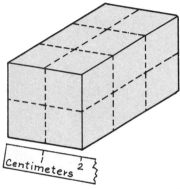

5. The volume is _?_ cubic centimeters.

Complete.

6. 1 centimeter = _?_ millimeters

7. 1 meter = _?_ centimeters

8. 1 kilometer = _?_ meters

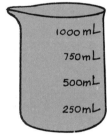

9. 1 liter = _?_ milliliters

10. 1 kilogram = _?_ grams

Measure the length of the pen to the nearest

11. $\frac{1}{4}$ inch.

12. $\frac{1}{8}$ inch.

13. $\frac{1}{16}$ inch.

Complete.

14. 1 foot = _?_ inches

15. 1 yard = _?_ feet

CHAPTER CHALLENGE

If the vertices of a figure are on the crossing points of graph paper, you can find the area (*A*) of the figure by knowing the number of boundary points (*B*) and the number of interior points (*I*).

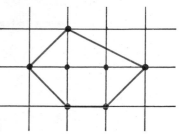

Boundary points (*B*): 5

Interior points (*I*): 2

Area (*A*): $3\frac{1}{2}$

Complete.

1.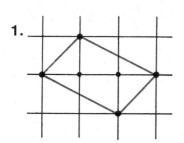

B: ?
I: ?
A: ?

2.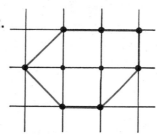

B: ?
I: ?
A: ?

3.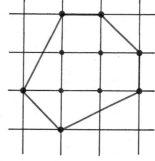

B: ?
I: ?
A: ?

4. **a.** Copy and complete this table for the figure above.

	B	$\frac{1}{2} \times B$	$\frac{1}{2} \times B + I$	$\frac{1}{2} \times B + I - 1$	A
Figure 1					
Figure 2					
Figure 3					

b. Compare the last two columns of your completed table.

5. You can find the area by using this formula:

$$A = \frac{1}{2} \times B + I - 1$$

Get some graph paper, draw some figures, and use the formula to find their area.

MAJOR CHECKUP
Standardized Format

Choose the correct letter.

1. Multiply.

386
× 147

    a. 56,742
    b. 56,502
    c. 4632
    d. none of these

2. Divide.

65)7839

    a. 12 R39
    b. 120 R39
    c. 102 R39
    d. none of these

3. $\overleftrightarrow{CD}$ is parallel to ?

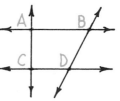

    a. $\overleftrightarrow{AC}$
    b. $\overleftrightarrow{BD}$
    c. $\overleftrightarrow{AB}$
    d. none of these

4. The two triangles are congruent. ∠BAC is congruent to:

    a. ∠TRS
    b. ∠TSR
    c. ∠STR
    d. none of these

5. $\frac{3}{2} + \frac{4}{3} =$

    a. $\frac{7}{5}$
    b. $\frac{17}{6}$
    c. 3
    d. none of these

6. $\frac{5}{6} - \frac{1}{4} =$

    a. $\frac{15}{4}$
    b. 2
    c. $\frac{1}{6}$
    d. none of these

7. $3\frac{2}{3} =$

    a. $\frac{8}{3}$
    b. $\frac{10}{3}$
    c. $\frac{11}{3}$
    d. none of these

8. $\frac{17}{3} =$

    a. $5\frac{1}{3}$
    b. $6\frac{1}{3}$
    c. $5\frac{2}{3}$
    d. none of these

9. Multiply.

$\frac{3}{8} \times \frac{5}{6}$

    a. $\frac{15}{48}$
    b. $\frac{1}{6}$
    c. $\frac{15}{24}$
    d. none of these

10. Divide.

$\frac{2}{9} \div \frac{3}{4}$

    a. $\frac{27}{8}$
    b. $\frac{1}{6}$
    c. $\frac{8}{27}$
    d. none of these

11. Add.

85.92 + 6.849

    a. 154.41
    b. 92.769
    c. 81.769
    d. none of these

12. Subtract.

50.6 − 3.94

    a. 11.2
    b. 46.66
    c. 47.66
    d. none of these

10
Consumer
Mathematics

Making change

Mary bought this record for $3.44.

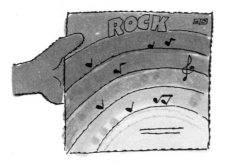

She gave the clerk a ten-dollar bill.

Here is how the clerk counted out Mary's change.

three forty-four
three forty-five
three fifty
three seventy-five
4 dollars
5 dollars
10 dollars

Notice that the clerk didn't always say *dollars* and *cents*. How much change did Mary get back?

EXERCISES

How much money?

1.

2.

The total cost is shown on the sales slip. You give the clerk the money shown. List the change that the clerk might count out.

3. total $ .79

4. total $ .38

5. total $ 5.16

6. total $ 2.75

7. total $ 6.46

8. total $ 8.15

Solve.

9. Robert bought a book for $3.29. He gave the clerk $5. How much change did he get back?

10. Donna bought 2 packages of notebook paper for $1.69 each. She gave the clerk $10. How much change did she get back?

★11. David has 2 coins in his pocket. Neither coin is a silver dollar. How much money might he have?

Computing prices

Suppose that you want to buy 1 ball of twine. Here is how to compute the price.

$$
\begin{array}{r}
29\frac{2}{3}\ ¢\ \text{each} \\
3\overline{)89¢} \\
\underline{-6} \\
29 \\
\underline{-27} \\
2
\end{array}
$$

The exact price is $29\frac{2}{3}$¢. However, you do not have a fraction of a cent. Fractional prices are *rounded up to the next cent.* So the price of 1 ball of twine is 30¢.

EXERCISES

Find the price of one item.

1. 2 for $1.89

2. 3 for $1.79

3. 4 for 98¢

4. 2 for 97¢

Give the total price.

5.

6.

7.

8.

Hint: Add the prices of
2 packages and 1 package.

Solve.

9. Find the total price of 2 feathers,
1 package of large beads, and 3
tubes of glue.

10. Find the price of 9 packages of
small beads and 4 shells.

11. Which costs more, 3 tubes of
glue or 2 packages of large
beads? How much more?

12. **a.** If you bought 1 of each item,
what would be the total price?
b. If you gave the clerk a
five-dollar bill, how much
change would you get?

small beads
4 for 35¢

shells
3 for 47¢

2 for 69¢
GLUE
GLUE

feathers
28¢ each

large beads
2 for $1.29

More about computing prices

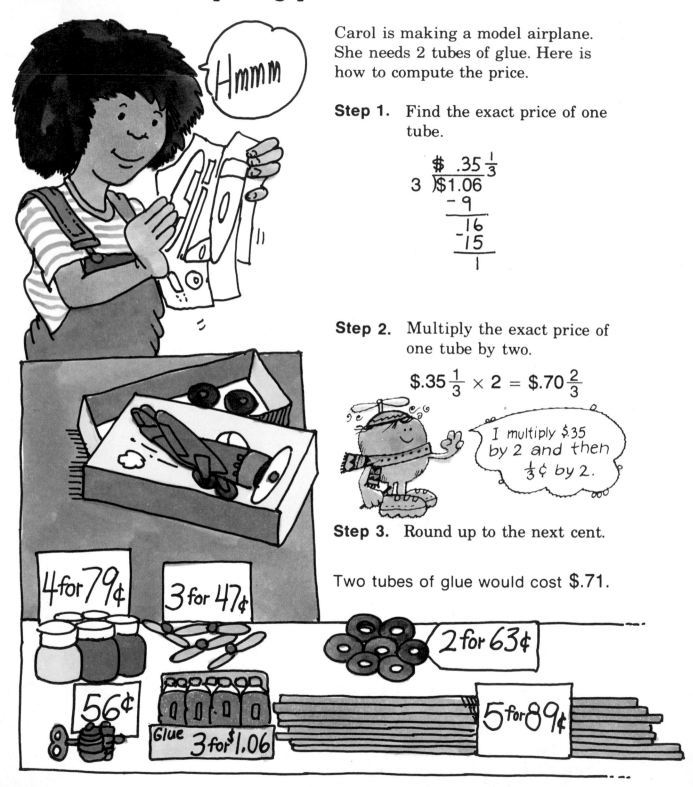

Carol is making a model airplane. She needs 2 tubes of glue. Here is how to compute the price.

Step 1. Find the exact price of one tube.

$$3 \overline{)\$1.06} \quad \$.35\tfrac{1}{3}$$

$$
\begin{array}{r}
\$.35\tfrac{1}{3} \\
3\overline{)\$1.06} \\
-9 \\
\hline
16 \\
-15 \\
\hline
1
\end{array}
$$

Step 2. Multiply the exact price of one tube by two.

$$\$.35\tfrac{1}{3} \times 2 = \$.70\tfrac{2}{3}$$

I multiply $.35 by 2 and then $\tfrac{1}{3}$¢ by 2.

Step 3. Round up to the next cent.

Two tubes of glue would cost $.71.

4 for 79¢

3 for 47¢

2 for 63¢

56¢

Glue 3 for $1.06

5 for 89¢

EXERCISES

Compute the total price.

1.

2.

3.

4.

5.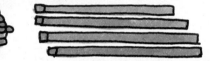

6.

7.

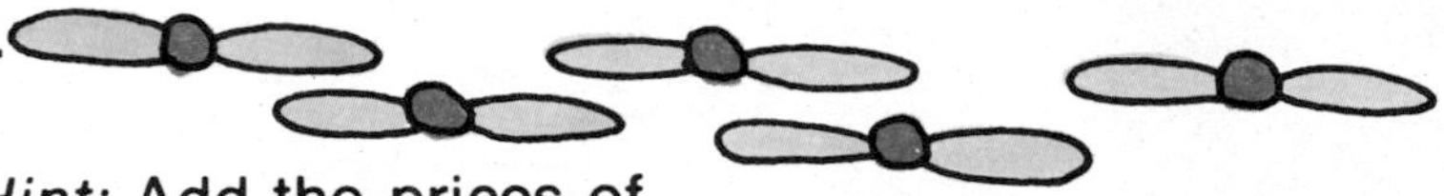

Hint: Add the prices of
3  ✈ and 2 ✈.

8.

Solve.

9. Model airplane kits are on sale for 3 for $5.
Al has $4 and wants to buy 2 kits. How
much money will he have left?

10. Randy wants to buy 3 packages of tiles. They
are on sale for 2 packages for 79¢. She has
94¢. How much more money does she need?

1. 125
    ×3

2. 245
    ×7

3. 318
    ×6

4. 729
    ×8

5. 502
    ×9

6. 635
    ×5

7. 423
    ×12

8. 896
    ×22

9. 527
    ×40

10. 744
    ×57

11. 529
    ×92

Computing discounts

You have often seen advertisements like these. They are designed to get the customer's attention. It is a good idea to take advantage of sales. However, you shouldn't buy an item just because it is on sale. You should have a use for it.

Here is how to compute the sale price (discount price).

Step 1. Divide regular price by 3.

$$
3 \overline{)\begin{array}{l} \$1.82\frac{2}{3} \\ \$5.48 \\ -3 \\ \overline{24} \\ -24 \\ \overline{8} \\ -6 \\ \overline{2} \end{array}}
$$

Step 2. Round to the nearest cent.

$1.83 discount.

Step 3. Subtract discount from regular price.

$$
\begin{array}{r} \$5.48 \\ -\ 1.83 \\ \hline \$\ 3.65 \end{array}
$$
← Sale Price

EXERCISES
Compute the amount of discount and the sale price.

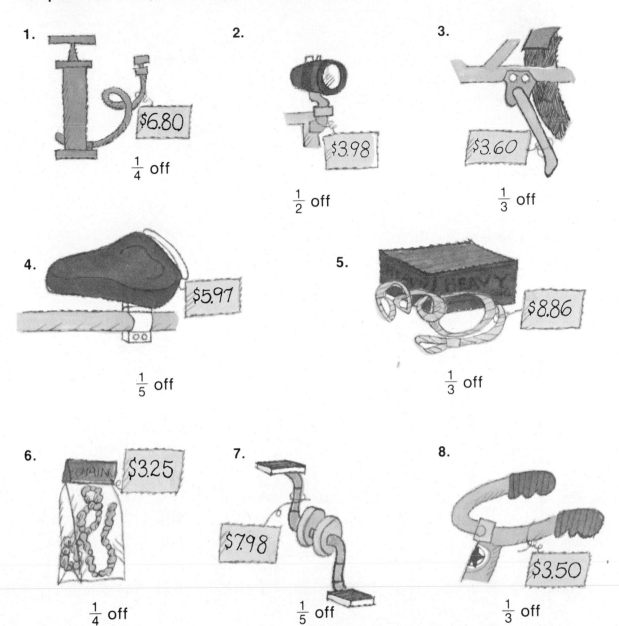

1. $6.80
$\frac{1}{4}$ off

2. $3.98
$\frac{1}{2}$ off

3. $3.60
$\frac{1}{3}$ off

4. $5.97
$\frac{1}{5}$ off

5. $8.86
$\frac{1}{3}$ off

6. $3.25
$\frac{1}{4}$ off

7. $7.98
$\frac{1}{5}$ off

8. $3.50
$\frac{1}{3}$ off

Solve.

9. A bicycle is on sale for $\frac{1}{4}$ off the regular price of $126.75. What is the sale price?

10. A bicycle that regularly sells for $162.95 is on sale for $\frac{1}{5}$ off. Mel has $118.50. How much more does he need to buy the bicycle?

Sales tax

In most states you pay the merchant a tax (a sales tax) when you buy goods. The merchant then gives the tax to the state. The rate of sales tax depends on the state in which you live.

There are sales-tax tables which a clerk uses to find the amount of tax to charge a customer. The table shown is based on the rate of 5 cents per $1.00 (a rate of 5%, "five percent"). Study this sales receipt.

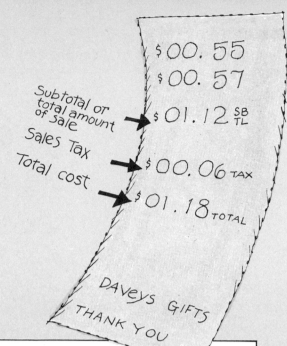

Subtotal or total amount of sale → $00.55 / $00.57 / $01.12 SB TL

Sales Tax → $00.06 TAX

Total cost → $01.18 TOTAL

DAVEYS GIFTS
THANK YOU

Sales Tax Table (5%)							
Sale	Tax	Sale	Tax	Sale	Tax	Sale	Tax
.01 – .10	.00	7.90 – 8.09	.40	15.90 – 16.09	.80	23.90 – 24.09	1.20
.11 – .27	.01	8.10 – 8.29	.41	16.10 – 16.29	.81	24.10 – 24.29	1.21
.28 – .47	.02	8.30 – 8.49	.42	16.30 – 16.49	.82	24.30 – 24.49	1.22
.48 – .68	.03	8.50 – 8.69	.43	16.50 – 16.69	.83	24.50 – 24.69	1.23
.69 – .89	.04	8.70 – 8.89	.44	16.70 – 16.89	.84	24.70 – 24.89	1.24
.90 – 1.09	.05	8.90 – 9.09	.45	16.90 – 17.09	.85	24.90 – 25.09	1.25
1.10 – 1.29	.06	9.10 – 9.29	.46	17.10 – 17.29	.86	25.10 – 25.29	1.26
1.30 – 1.49	.07	9.30 – 9.49	.47	17.30 – 17.49	.87	25.30 – 25.49	1.27
1.50 – 1.69	.08	9.50 – 9.69	.48	17.50 – 17.69	.88	25.50 – 25.69	1.28
1.70 – 1.89	.09	9.70 – 9.89	.49	17.70 – 17.89	.89	25.70 – 25.89	1.29
1.90 – 2.09	.10	9.90 – 10.09	.50	17.90 – 18.09	.90	25.90 – 26.09	1.30
2.10 – 2.29	.11	10.10 – 10.29	.51	18.10 – 18.29	.91	26.10 – 26.29	1.31
2.30 – 2.49	.12	10.30 – 10.49	.52	18.30 – 18.49	.92	26.30 – 26.49	1.32
2.50 – 2.69	.13	10.50 – 10.69	.53	18.50 – 18.69	.93	26.50 – 26.69	1.33
2.70 – 2.89	.14	10.70 – 10.89	.54	18.70 – 18.89	.94	26.70 – 26.89	1.34
2.90 – 3.09	.15	10.90 – 11.09	.55	18.90 – 19.09	.95	26.90 – 27.09	1.35
3.10 – 3.29	.16	11.10 – 11.29	.56	19.10 – 19.29	.96	27.10 – 27.29	1.36
3.30 – 3.49	.17	11.30 – 11.49	.57	19.30 – 19.49	.97	27.30 – 27.49	1.37
3.50 – 3.69	.18	11.50 – 11.69	.58	19.50 – 19.69	.98	27.50 – 27.69	1.38
3.70 – 3.89	.19	11.70 – 11.89	.59	19.70 – 19.89	.99	27.70 – 27.89	1.39
3.90 – 4.09	.20	11.90 – 12.09	.60	19.90 – 20.09	1.00	27.90 – 28.09	1.40
4.10 – 4.29	.21	12.10 – 12.29	.61	20.10 – 20.29	1.01	28.10 – 28.29	1.41
4.30 – 4.49	.22	12.30 – 12.49	.62	20.30 – 20.49	1.02	28.30 – 28.49	1.42
4.50 – 4.69	.23	12.50 – 12.69	.63	20.50 – 20.69	1.03	28.50 – 28.69	1.43
4.70 – 4.89	.24	12.70 – 12.89	.64	20.70 – 20.89	1.04	28.70 – 28.89	1.44
4.90 – 5.09	.25	12.90 – 13.09	.65	20.90 – 21.09	1.05	28.90 – 29.09	1.45
5.10 – 5.29	.26	13.10 – 13.29	.66	21.10 – 21.29	1.06	29.10 – 29.29	1.46
5.30 – 5.49	.27	13.30 – 13.49	.67	21.30 – 21.49	1.07	29.30 – 29.49	1.47
5.50 – 5.69	.28	13.50 – 13.69	.68	21.50 – 21.69	1.08	29.50 – 29.69	1.48
5.70 – 5.89	.29	13.70 – 13.89	.69	21.70 – 21.89	1.09	29.70 – 29.89	1.49
5.90 – 6.09	.30	13.90 – 14.09	.70	21.90 – 22.09	1.10	29.90 – 30.09	1.50
6.10 – 6.29	.31	14.10 – 14.29	.71	22.10 – 22.29	1.11	30.10 – 30.29	1.51
6.30 – 6.49	.32	14.30 – 14.49	.72	22.30 – 22.49	1.12	30.30 – 30.49	1.52
6.50 – 6.69	.33	14.50 – 14.69	.73	22.50 – 22.69	1.13	30.50 – 30.69	1.53
6.70 – 6.89	.34	14.70 – 14.89	.74	22.70 – 22.89	1.14	30.70 – 30.89	1.54
6.90 – 7.09	.35	14.90 – 15.09	.75	22.90 – 23.09	1.15		
7.10 – 7.29	.36	15.10 – 15.29	.76	23.10 – 23.29	1.16		
7.30 – 7.49	.37	15.30 – 15.49	.77	23.30 – 23.49	1.17		
7.50 – 7.69	.38	15.50 – 15.69	.78	23.50 – 23.69	1.18		
7.70 – 7.89	.39	15.70 – 15.89	.79	23.70 – 23.89	1.19		

EXERCISES

Give the amount of the sale, the sales tax, and the total cost.

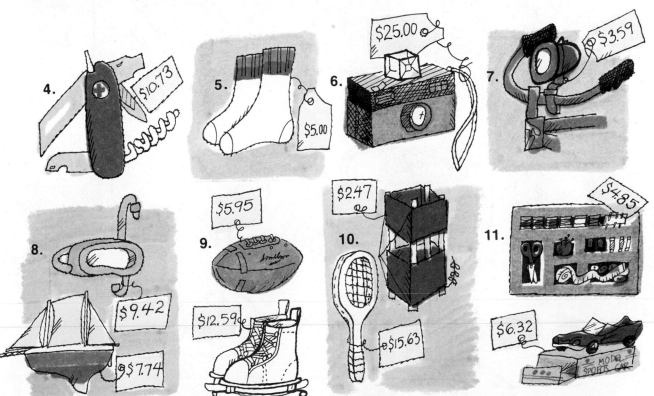

1. **SPORTS CENTER**

SOLD TO: Ruth Charles INVOICE 100

Quan.	Description	Price	Amount
1	shoes	$17.95	
1	socks	$1.89	
		$19.84	
	tax	.99	
	total		

orignal invoice

2. **artisans shop**

Customer Louis David
Date August Address 7618 Brookline

Quan.	Description	Price	Amount
2	Bracelets	$3.95	$7.90
1	Earrings	$2.90	$2.90
			10.80
	tax		.54
	total		

NO. 6134

3. **COOKWARES** 71946

SOLD TO: Lynn ? DATE July

Quan.	Description	Price
1	pan	$7.25
1	spoon	$.69
1	strainer	$1.39
		$9.33
	tax	.47
	total	

If the sales tax is 5%, what would the sales tax be for these sales? (*Hint:* Use the table.)

4. $10.73

5. $5.00

6. $25.00

7. $3.59

8. $9.42 / $7.74

9. $5.95

10. $2.47 / $15.63

11. $4.85 / $6.32

12. John bought a $15.60 tennis racket that was on sale for $\frac{1}{4}$ off. If he paid a 5% sales tax, what was the total price?

13. Anne bought 2 pairs of tennis socks that were on sale at 3 pairs for $5. She also bought a can of balls for $2.69. What was the total cost if she paid a 5% sales tax?

273

Practice exercises

Compute the total cost. Use the sales tax table on page 272 to include a 5% sales tax.

1.  $3.48 $4.44

2. 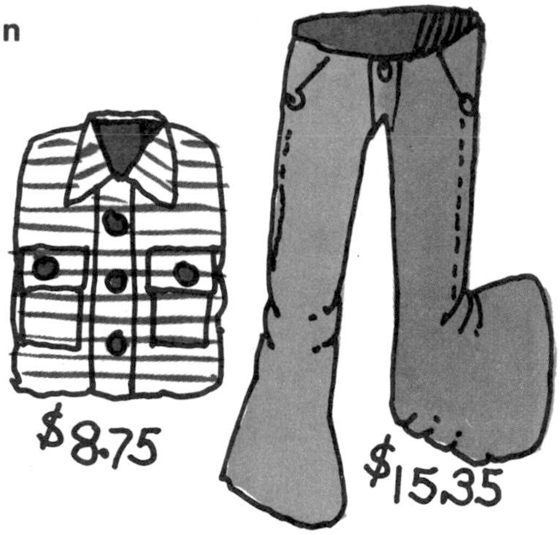 $8.75 $15.35

3.  $12.79 $1.75 $6.47

4. 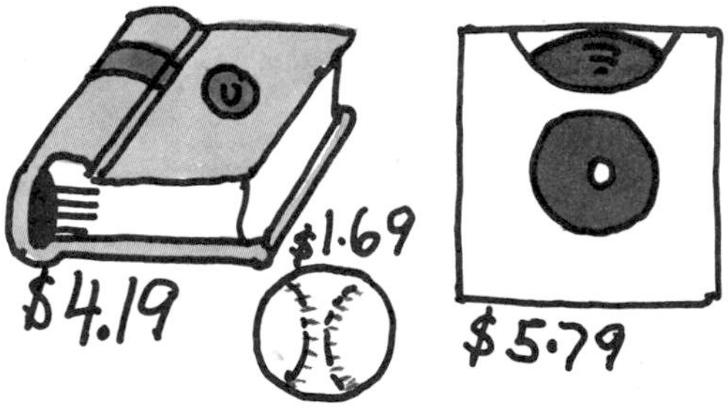 $4.19 $1.69 $5.79

5. 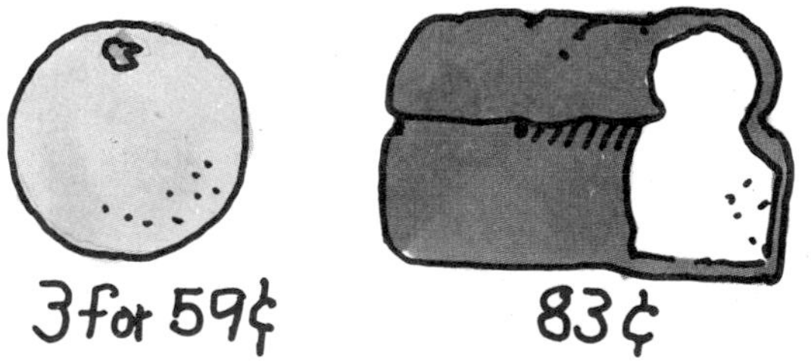 3 for 59¢   83¢

6.  3 for 59¢   95¢

7. 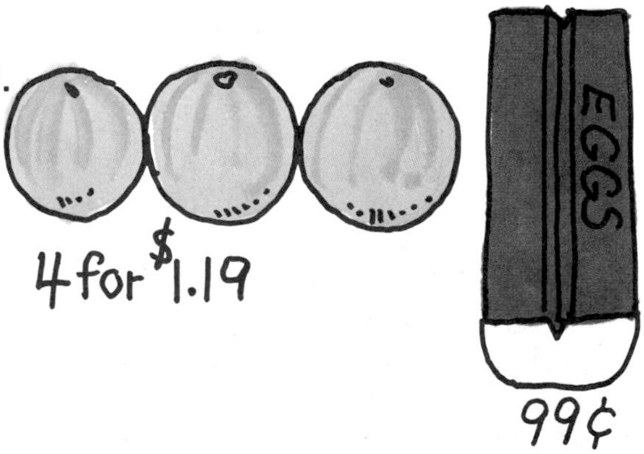 4 for $1.19   99¢

8. 3 for 59¢   2 for $1.35

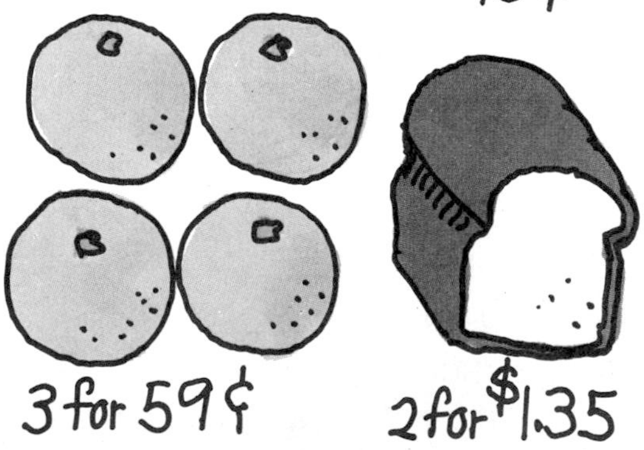

Solve. Do not include a sales tax.

9. You have:

You buy:

3 for $4.00

How much money do you have left?

10. You have:

You want to buy:

$42.75   ⅓ off

How much more money do you need?

11. Andrea had $4.05. She bought a notebook for $2.89 and 1 package of paper for $.97. How much money did she have left?

12. John has $5.75. He returned 54 soda bottles for 3¢ each. He bought a camping knife for $5.19. How much money did he have left?

13. The backpack that Sarah wants costs $12.50. If she waits two weeks, it will be on sale for $\frac{1}{3}$ off. She now has $6.30. How much more money will she need if she buys the pack on sale?

14. Terry wants some $21.95 ice skates. The skates are now marked down $\frac{1}{4}$ ($\frac{1}{4}$ off). He can earn $1.75 an hour raking leaves. He plans to work 6 hours. How much more money will he need?

Keeping Skills Sharp

1. $4\overline{)284}$ 2. $8\overline{)392}$ 3. $7\overline{)588}$ 4. $6\overline{)906}$ 5. $9\overline{)477}$

6. $12\overline{)348}$ 7. $23\overline{)596}$ 8. $40\overline{)748}$ 9. $52\overline{)925}$ 10. $63\overline{)896}$

11. $71\overline{)3784}$ 12. $85\overline{)9516}$ 13. $79\overline{)8342}$ 14. $68\overline{)5974}$ 15. $46\overline{)6835}$

Sales

Have you noticed that you always get a sales slip when you buy something? The slip gives you a record of the sale. Also, if you should decide to return something, most merchants ask that you return the sales slip with the item.

EXERCISES

Look at the sales slip to answer each question.

1. Where was the purchase made?

2. What was the date of the purchase?

3. How many grocery (GR) items were bought?

4. How much tax was charged?

5. What was the total cost?

6. How much money did the clerk receive?

7. How much change did the clerk give back?

Al's Supermarket
10-08-81

$	4.50	MT
$	1.22	MT
$	.49	GR
$	.99	GR TX
$	.39	GR
$	.30	PR
$	.69	GR TX
$	.25	GR
$	.79	PR
$	9.62	SUB
$	.09	TAX
$	9.71	TOTL
$	20.00	CASH
$	10.29	CHANGE

A clerk at Richard's Paint Store filled out this sales slip. The "Amount" column has not yet been completed.

8. How many gallons of latex paint were ordered? What should be the amount charged for the latex paint?

RICHARD'S PAINTS
235 Central St
Salem, Ill
59836

DATE: August 11, 1981
NAME: Davey D. Rizzotto
ADDRESS: 149 Leavitt St, Salem

Quantity	Description	Price each	Amount
2 gal	Latex - hot pink	10.59	
3 qt	Enamel - purple	4.69	
2	5" Brush - nylon	5.75	
1	2" Sable brush	3.93	
1	7" Roller Set	8.25	
5	Drop Cloths	.89	
		Subtotal	
		Tax	
		Total	

Returned Items Must be Accompanied by this sales slip.

What should be the amount charged for these items?

9. 3 qt of enamel   10. 2 5" brushes   11. 5 drop cloths

12. What is the total price?

13. If the sales tax is 5%, how much should be charged for sales tax? (Use the table on page 272.)

14. What is the total cost?

15. Mr. Rizzotto returned 1 quart of the enamel and 2 drop cloths. How much was his refund? (Don't forget the sales tax!)

277

1. What is the total price of the boots and stove? [pages 266–267]

2. What is the price of 1 candle? of two candles? [pages 266–269]

3. What is the price of 3 packages of freeze-dried food? of 5 packages? [pages 266–269]

4. The camping store is going to sell the boots for $\frac{1}{3}$ off. How much will the discount be? What will be the sale price? [pages 270–271]

5. A hiking club wants to buy a compass, 2 knives, 1 dozen candles, and 2 packages of freeze-dried foods. What is the total price? If they are charged a 5% sales tax, what will be the total cost? (Use the table on page 272.) [pages 272–278]

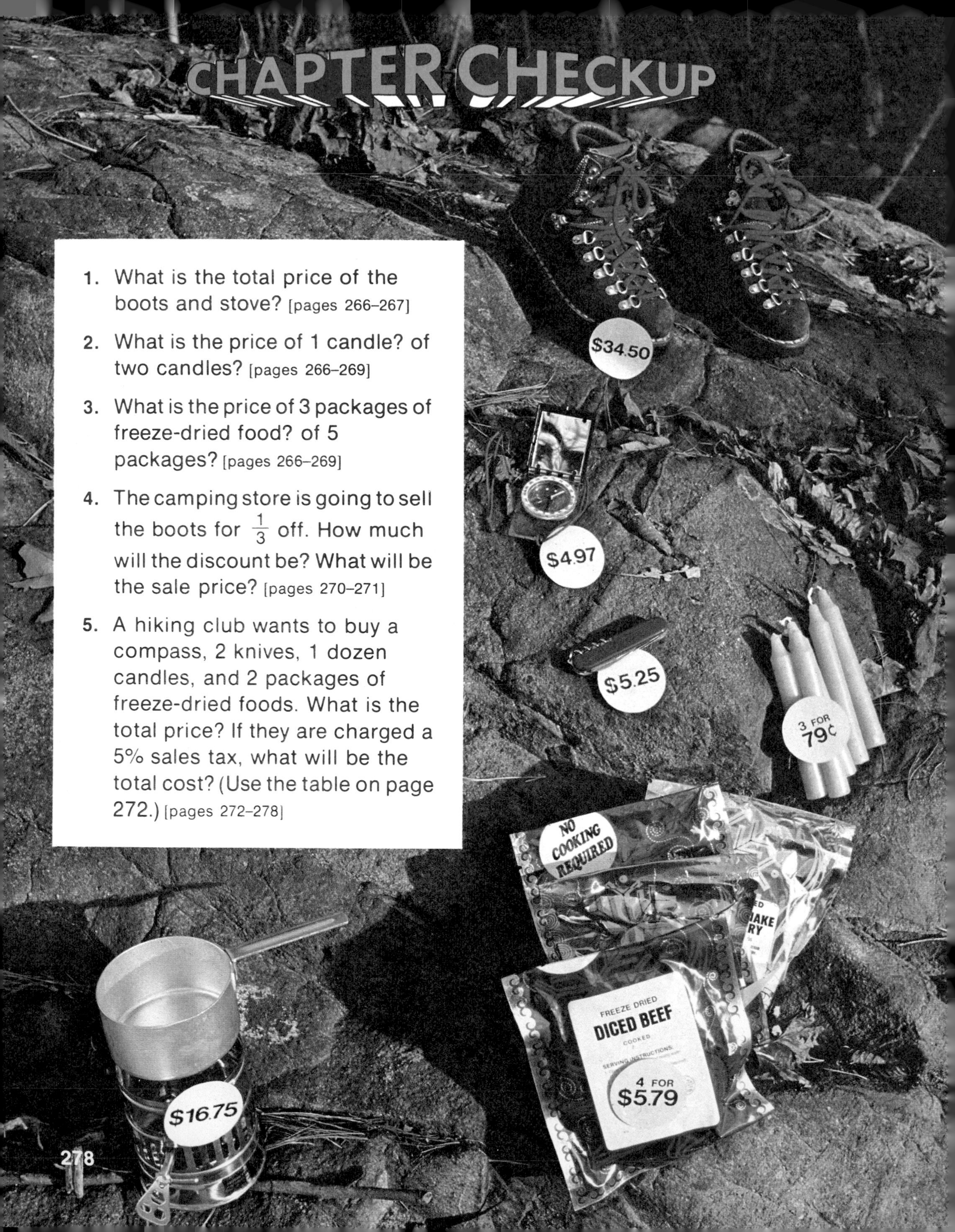

$34.50

$4.97

$5.25

3 FOR 79¢

NO COOKING REQUIRED

FREEZE DRIED DICED BEEF COOKED
SERVING INSTRUCTIONS
4 FOR $5.79

$16.75

Project

1. Get a catalog that has an order form in it.

2. Pretend that a rich relative gave you $100. Pick out from the catalog the things you would buy with the $100.

3. Fill out an order form.

CHAPTER REVIEW

1. What is the price of 1 sign? (Remember to round *up*.)

6 for 50¢

2. What is the price of 2 decals? (*Hint:* Double the price for 1 decal.)

3 for 49¢

3. a. What is the discount?

SALE! $\frac{1}{3}$ OFF

906

(Remember to round to the nearest cent.)

   b. What is the sale price?

$24.79

4. a. What is the total price?
   b. How much is a 5% sales tax on the total price? (Use the table on page 272.)

   c. What would the total cost be, including the 5% sales tax?

$7.79

$15.47

You may have a savings account. The most common kind of savings account is called a *passbook account.* A record of all the transactions is kept in the passbook. The bank (or savings and loan company) pays you *interest* (like rent) for the use of your money.

No. 72357

	Date	Withdrawal	Deposit	Interest	Balance
1 2 3 4	1/2/79		5.00		88.47
5 6 7	3/20/79			1.02	89.49
8 9 10	4/18/79	15.00			74.49
11 12 13 14	5/3/79	23.00			51.49
15 16	5/19/79		11.50		
17 18 19 20					

VILLAGE SAVINGS BANK

VILLAGE SAVINGS BANK founded in 1880

Look at the passbook above to answer the following questions.

1. How much was deposited on 1/2/79 (January 2, 1979)?

2. On what date was interest added (credited) to the account?

3. What was the balance of the account on 4/18/79?

4. How much was taken out of the account on 5/3/79?

5. What transaction took place on 4/18/79?

6. How much was in the savings account after the deposit on 5/19/79?

7. If possible, study savings-account passbooks from some local banks.

281

MAJOR CHECKUP
Standardized Format

Choose the correct letter.

1. Multiply.
586
×304

a. 19,924
b. 19,804
c. 178,144
d. none of these

2. Divide.
36)8,489

a. 235 R29
b. 225 R29
c. 236 R29
d. none of these

3. How many lines of symmetry does a parallelogram have?

a. 1
b. 2
c. 4
d. none of these

4. $\frac{5}{4} + \frac{1}{2} = \underline{?}$

a. 1
b. $\frac{7}{4}$
c. $\frac{3}{2}$
d. none of these

5. $\frac{5}{9} - \frac{1}{3} = \underline{?}$

a. $\frac{2}{3}$
b. $\frac{2}{9}$
c. $\frac{4}{9}$
d. none of these

6. $\frac{3}{8} \times \frac{2}{3} = \underline{?}$

a. $\frac{5}{24}$
b. $\frac{9}{16}$
c. $\frac{1}{4}$
d. none of these

7. $\frac{4}{5} \div \frac{2}{3} = \underline{?}$

a. $\frac{5}{6}$
b. $\frac{6}{5}$
c. $\frac{2}{15}$
d. none of these

8. $5.6 + 3.78 = \underline{?}$

a. 9.38
b. 4.34
c. 43.4
d. none of these

9. $315.6 - 24.83 = \underline{?}$

a. 6.73
b. 380.77
c. 67.3
d. none of these

10. How much time from 11:20 A.M. to 1:45 P.M.?

a. $2\frac{1}{2}$ hr
b. 1 hr 25 min
c. 2 hr 25 min
d. none of these

11.

Volume = $\underline{?}$

a. 10 cm
b. 36 square cm
c. 36 cubic cm
d. none of these

12. 875 mL = $\underline{?}$

a. 87.5 liters
b. 8.75 liters
c. .875 liter
d. none of these

282

11
Mixed
Numbers—
Addition
and
Subtraction

Give each answer as both a mixed number and a fraction.

1. How many tomatoes?

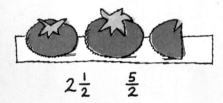

$2\frac{1}{2}$ $\frac{5}{2}$

2. How many sandwiches?

3. How many pizzas?

4. How many candy bars?

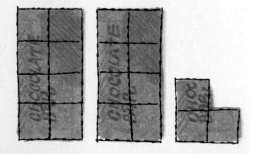

Fractions and mixed numbers

Here is a way to change a mixed number to a fraction.

$2\frac{3}{4} = \frac{11}{4}$

I first multiply these red numbers to find how many fourths in 2. Then I add the 3.

Here is a way to change a fraction to a mixed number.

$\frac{11}{4} = 2\frac{3}{4}$

Divide the numerator by the denominator.

Number of whole cookies → Remainder / Divisor

Number of fourths in a whole cookie → $4\overline{)11}$

$2\frac{3}{4}$

-8

3

Number of fourths left over

EXERCISES

Give each length as a mixed number and a fraction in lowest terms.

1.

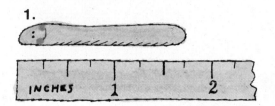

2.

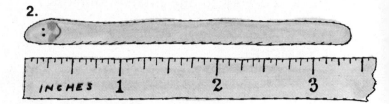

Change to fractions in lowest terms.

3. $1\frac{1}{3}$ **4.** $1\frac{1}{2}$ **5.** $2\frac{1}{4}$ **6.** $3\frac{1}{5}$ **7.** $2\frac{1}{6}$ **8.** $3\frac{1}{8}$

9. $3\frac{1}{4}$ **10.** $2\frac{3}{4}$ **11.** $2\frac{1}{3}$ **12.** $2\frac{1}{2}$ **13.** $4\frac{2}{3}$ **14.** $2\frac{3}{8}$

15. $1\frac{7}{8}$ **16.** $3\frac{1}{2}$ **17.** $3\frac{3}{4}$ **18.** $3\frac{5}{8}$ **19.** $3\frac{1}{3}$ **20.** $4\frac{1}{2}$

21. $5\frac{3}{8}$ **22.** $8\frac{5}{6}$ **23.** $9\frac{3}{10}$ **24.** $12\frac{1}{2}$ **25.** $15\frac{2}{3}$ **26.** $20\frac{3}{4}$

Change each fraction to a mixed number.

27. $\frac{3}{2}$ **28.** $\frac{4}{3}$ **29.** $\frac{5}{2}$ **30.** $\frac{9}{4}$ **31.** $\frac{6}{5}$ **32.** $\frac{9}{5}$

33. $\frac{9}{8}$ **34.** $\frac{11}{4}$ **35.** $\frac{11}{8}$ **36.** $\frac{11}{6}$ **37.** $\frac{5}{3}$ **38.** $\frac{15}{4}$

39. $\frac{13}{8}$ **40.** $\frac{7}{3}$ **41.** $\frac{9}{5}$ **42.** $\frac{13}{4}$ **43.** $\frac{11}{5}$ **44.** $\frac{11}{3}$

45. $\frac{12}{5}$ **46.** $\frac{26}{3}$ **47.** $\frac{39}{4}$ **48.** $\frac{43}{8}$ **49.** $\frac{61}{2}$ **50.** $\frac{73}{5}$

Keeping Skills Sharp

Give each product in lowest terms.

1. $\frac{3}{5} \times \frac{2}{1}$ **2.** $\frac{3}{4} \times \frac{2}{5}$ **3.** $\frac{5}{8} \times \frac{4}{3}$ **4.** $\frac{2}{3} \times \frac{3}{2}$

5. $5 \times \frac{3}{4}$ **6.** $4 \times \frac{2}{3}$ **7.** $\frac{7}{8} \times 2$ **8.** $\frac{5}{9} \times 3$

9. $\frac{5}{9} \times \frac{3}{5}$ **10.** $\frac{5}{8} \times \frac{8}{5}$ **11.** $\frac{2}{5} \times \frac{10}{3}$ **12.** $\frac{3}{2} \times \frac{7}{9}$

285

Adding and subtracting mixed numbers

Here is a way to add mixed numbers.

EXAMPLE.

$2\frac{1}{4}$

$+1\frac{1}{2}$

Step 1.
Change to fractions
with a common denominator.

$2\frac{1}{4} = 2\frac{1}{4}$

$+1\frac{1}{2} = 1\frac{2}{4}$

Step 2.
Add fractions.

$2\frac{1}{4} = 2\frac{1}{4}$

$+1\frac{1}{2} = 1\frac{2}{4}$

$\frac{3}{4}$

Step 3.
Add whole numbers.

$2\frac{1}{4} = 2\frac{1}{4}$

$+1\frac{1}{2} = 1\frac{2}{4}$

$3\frac{3}{4}$

You can subtract "in columns" too.

EXAMPLE.

$3\frac{5}{6}$

$-2\frac{1}{6}$

Step 1.
Subtract
fractions.

$3\frac{5}{6}$

$-2\frac{1}{6}$

$\frac{4}{6}$

Step 2.
Subtract whole
numbers.

$3\frac{5}{6}$

$-2\frac{1}{6}$

$1\frac{4}{6}$

Step 3.
Reduce fraction to
lowest terms.

$3\frac{5}{6}$

$-2\frac{1}{6}$

$1\frac{4}{6} = 1\frac{2}{3}$

286

EXERCISES

Add. Give the fraction in lowest terms.

1. $3\frac{1}{3}$
    $+2\frac{1}{3}$

2. $4\frac{1}{8}$
    $+1\frac{3}{8}$

3. $5\frac{1}{4}$
    $+2\frac{1}{4}$

4. $2\frac{1}{6}$
    $+2\frac{1}{6}$

5. $2\frac{1}{2} = 2\frac{2}{4}$
    $+3\frac{1}{4} = 3\frac{1}{4}$

6. $4\frac{1}{3}$
    $+5\frac{1}{2}$

7. $3\frac{1}{2}$
    $+4\frac{1}{8}$

8. $4\frac{1}{3}$
    $+5\frac{1}{6}$

9. $6\frac{1}{2}$
    $+5$

10. $7\frac{1}{2}$
    $+8\frac{1}{3}$

11. $9\frac{5}{9}$
    $+6\frac{1}{9}$

12. $42\frac{1}{6}$
    $+19\frac{2}{3}$

Subtract. Give the fraction in lowest terms.

13. $8\frac{2}{3}$
    -5

14. $9\frac{5}{8}$
    $-3\frac{3}{8}$

15. $8\frac{5}{6}$
    $-4\frac{1}{6}$

16. $5\frac{5}{8}$
    $-1\frac{1}{8}$

17. $7\frac{5}{6} = 7\frac{5}{6}$
    $-2\frac{1}{3} = 2\frac{2}{6}$

18. $5\frac{5}{8}$
    $-2\frac{1}{4}$

19. $8\frac{5}{6}$
    $-4\frac{1}{2}$

20. $8\frac{5}{6}$
    $-\frac{1}{4}$

21. $18\frac{7}{10}$
    $-6\frac{1}{5}$

22. $48\frac{5}{6}$
    $-34\frac{1}{4}$

23. $22\frac{2}{3}$
    $-7\frac{2}{5}$

24. $19\frac{4}{5}$
    $-12\frac{3}{10}$

Solve.

25. Need: $4\frac{3}{4}$ cups of flour

    Have: $1\frac{1}{8}$ cups of flour
    How much more flour is needed?

26. Bought: $2\frac{1}{2}$ pounds of peanuts

    Bought: $1\frac{3}{8}$ pounds of cashews
    How many pounds of nuts were bought?

More about adding mixed numbers

When the sum of the fractions is greater than 1, you will need to regroup.

$$2\frac{3}{4}$$
$$+1\frac{1}{2}$$

Step 1.
Change to a common denominator.

$$2\frac{3}{4} = 2\frac{3}{4}$$
$$+1\frac{1}{2} = 1\frac{2}{4}$$

Step 2.
Add fractions.

$$2\frac{3}{4} = 2\frac{3}{4}$$
$$+1\frac{1}{2} = 1\frac{2}{4}$$
$$\frac{5}{4}$$

Step 3.
Add whole numbers.

$$2\frac{3}{4} = 2\frac{3}{4}$$
$$+1\frac{1}{2} = 1\frac{2}{4}$$
$$3\frac{5}{4}$$

Step 4.
Regroup.

$$2\frac{3}{4} = 2\frac{3}{4}$$
$$+1\frac{1}{2} = 1\frac{2}{4}$$
$$3\frac{5}{4} = 4\frac{1}{4}$$

I find the sum in two steps.

Step 1.
Add and regroup.

$$2\frac{3}{4} \quad \frac{3}{4}$$
$$+1\frac{1}{2} \quad +\frac{2}{4}$$
$$\frac{1}{4} \quad \frac{5}{4}$$

Step 2.
Add.

$$2\frac{3}{4}$$
$$+1\frac{1}{2}$$
$$4\frac{1}{4}$$

EXERCISES
Regroup the sum.

1. $$2\frac{2}{3}$$
    $$+1\frac{1}{3}$$
    $$3\frac{3}{3} = 4$$

2. $$5\frac{1}{2} = 5\frac{2}{4}$$
    $$+2\frac{3}{4} = 2\frac{3}{4}$$
    $$7\frac{5}{4} =$$

3. $$4\frac{3}{4} = 4\frac{6}{8}$$
    $$+2\frac{3}{8} = 2\frac{3}{8}$$
    $$6\frac{9}{8} =$$

Add.

4. $3\frac{1}{9}$
$+5\frac{4}{9}$

5. $1\frac{3}{5}$
$+6\frac{2}{5}$

6. $4\frac{3}{8}$
$+3\frac{1}{4}$

7. $3\frac{2}{3}$
$+3\frac{1}{6}$

8. $6\frac{1}{2}$
$+2\frac{1}{3}$

9. $5\frac{1}{10}$
$+4\frac{7}{10}$

10. $4\frac{1}{2}$
$+6\frac{1}{2}$

11. $3\frac{1}{4}$
$+8\frac{3}{4}$

12. $8\frac{3}{4}$
$+4\frac{5}{8}$

13. $4\frac{2}{3}$
$+9\frac{1}{2}$

14. $7\frac{3}{4}$
$+7\frac{2}{3}$

15. $9\frac{7}{8}$
$+8\frac{1}{4}$

16. $7\frac{5}{9}$
$+8\frac{2}{3}$

17. $8\frac{2}{3}$
$+9\frac{5}{6}$

18. $5\frac{3}{4}$
$+8\frac{3}{8}$

19. $5\frac{7}{10}$
$+5\frac{9}{10}$

20. $9\frac{7}{8}$
$+6\frac{3}{4}$

21. $9\frac{5}{6}$
$+9\frac{2}{3}$

22. $10\frac{2}{3}$
$+8\frac{3}{4}$

23. $12\frac{1}{2}$
$+7\frac{2}{3}$

24. $15\frac{1}{4}$
$+14\frac{7}{8}$

25. $26\frac{5}{8}$
$+18\frac{3}{4}$

26. $39\frac{5}{6}$
$+15\frac{3}{8}$

27. $43\frac{5}{6}$
$+38\frac{3}{4}$

Find the perimeter of each figure.

28.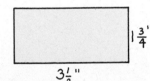

29.

30.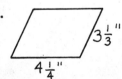

Solve.

31. Alison bought $5\frac{2}{3}$ yards of red ribbon and $4\frac{1}{2}$ yards of blue ribbon. How many yards of ribbon did she buy?

32. Cindy rode her bicycle $6\frac{7}{10}$ miles the first hour and $5\frac{1}{2}$ miles the second hour. How many miles did she ride altogether?

33. To get to school, Samuel walks $3\frac{3}{4}$ blocks to the bus stop and then rides the bus $18\frac{1}{2}$ blocks. How far does he travel to get to school?

34. John is $59\frac{3}{4}$ inches tall. Kay is $2\frac{3}{4}$ inches taller than John. How tall is Kay?

More about subtracting mixed numbers

Sometimes you have to regroup before you subtract.

EXAMPLE. $8\frac{1}{4}$

$\qquad -\ 3\frac{3}{8}$

Step 1.

Change to a common denominator.

$8\frac{1}{4} = 8\frac{2}{8}$

$-\ 3\frac{3}{8} = 3\frac{3}{8}$

Step 2.

Since $\frac{2}{8}$ is less than $\frac{3}{8}$, regroup 1 for $\frac{8}{8}$.

$8\frac{1}{4} = 8\frac{2}{8} = 7\frac{10}{8}$

$-\ 3\frac{3}{8} = 3\frac{3}{8} = 3\frac{3}{8}$

Step 3.

Subtract.

$8\frac{1}{4} = 8\frac{2}{8} = 7\frac{10}{8}$

$-\ 3\frac{3}{8} = 3\frac{3}{8} = 3\frac{3}{8}$

$\qquad\qquad\qquad\qquad\ 4\frac{7}{8}$

Here is how I find the difference.

$8\frac{1}{4} = 8\frac{2}{8}\ \ ^{7\frac{10}{8}}$

$-\ 3\frac{3}{8} = 3\frac{3}{8}$

$\qquad\qquad\ 4\frac{7}{8}$

EXERCISES

Subtract.

1. $5\frac{1}{4} = 5\frac{1}{4} = 4\frac{5}{4}$

   $-\ 2\frac{1}{2} = 2\frac{2}{4} = 2\frac{2}{4}$

2. $6\frac{1}{8} = 6\frac{1}{8} = 5\frac{9}{8}$

   $-\ 3\frac{3}{4} = 3\frac{6}{8} = 3\frac{6}{8}$

3. $7\frac{2}{3} = 7\frac{8}{12} = 6\frac{20}{12}$

   $-\ 4\frac{3}{4} = 4\frac{9}{12} = 4\frac{9}{12}$

4. $6\ \ = 5\frac{4}{4}$

   $-\ 2\frac{1}{4} = 2\frac{1}{4}$

5. $9\ \ = 8\frac{3}{3}$

   $-\ 5\frac{2}{3} = 5\frac{2}{3}$

6. $7\ \ = 6\frac{8}{8}$

   $-\ 3\frac{5}{8} = 3\frac{5}{8}$

290

7. $9\frac{5}{9}$
$-4\frac{1}{9}$

8. $8\frac{4}{5}$
$-2\frac{3}{5}$

9. $5\frac{3}{4}$
$-1\frac{1}{2}$

10. $9\frac{5}{6}$
$-4\frac{2}{3}$

11. $7\frac{1}{2}$
$-2\frac{1}{3}$

12. $9\frac{3}{4}$
$-4\frac{2}{3}$

13. 8
$-3\frac{1}{2}$

14. 6
$-4\frac{3}{5}$

15. 12
$-3\frac{7}{10}$

16. 11
$-5\frac{3}{4}$

17. 15
$-6\frac{3}{8}$

18. 16
$-9\frac{4}{5}$

19. $9\frac{1}{4}$
$-3\frac{1}{2}$

20. $8\frac{1}{2}$
$-4\frac{3}{4}$

21. $7\frac{3}{8}$
$-2\frac{3}{4}$

22. $10\frac{2}{3}$
$-8\frac{5}{6}$

23. $11\frac{1}{8}$
$-6\frac{3}{4}$

24. $12\frac{2}{3}$
$-8\frac{5}{6}$

Solve.

25. Diane is $8\frac{3}{4}$ inches taller than her little brother. If Diane is $58\frac{1}{2}$ inches tall, how tall is her brother?

26. One week, David watched $6\frac{1}{4}$ hours of television. The next week he watched 8 hours of television. How much more did he watch the second week?

27. In basketball, the rim of the basket is 10 feet above the floor. Stan can jump up and reach $7\frac{1}{4}$ feet above the floor. How much higher must he jump to touch the basket rim?

28. A share of certain stock sold for $32\frac{5}{8}$ dollars. Two weeks later it sold for $34\frac{1}{8}$ dollars a share. How much did the value of the stock increase?

Keeping Skills Sharp

Give the quotients in lowest terms.

1. $\frac{2}{3} \div \frac{3}{4}$

2. $\frac{3}{4} \div \frac{2}{3}$

3. $\frac{5}{6} \div \frac{1}{4}$

4. $\frac{1}{4} \div \frac{5}{6}$

5. $\frac{5}{9} \div 3$

6. $\frac{7}{8} \div 2$

7. $4 \div \frac{3}{5}$

8. $7 \div \frac{3}{4}$

9. $\frac{7}{8} \div \frac{5}{2}$

10. $\frac{6}{5} \div \frac{3}{8}$

11. $\frac{5}{6} \div \frac{3}{2}$

12. $\frac{4}{5} \div \frac{5}{3}$

Practice

Add.

$O\ \ 3\frac{2}{5}+1\frac{1}{4}=3\frac{8}{20}+1\frac{5}{20}$
$=4\frac{13}{20}$

1. $5\frac{1}{3} + 2\frac{1}{3}$ **2.** $8\frac{1}{9} + 2\frac{1}{9}$ **3.** $4\frac{1}{3} + 3\frac{1}{3}$

4. $8\frac{1}{4} + 2\frac{1}{2}$ **5.** $3\frac{1}{8} + 6\frac{1}{4}$ **6.** $9\frac{2}{5} + 4\frac{1}{10}$

7. $8\frac{2}{3} + 4\frac{1}{2}$ **8.** $6\frac{4}{5} + 9\frac{1}{2}$ **9.** $7\frac{2}{3} + 7\frac{5}{6}$

10. $5\frac{2}{3} + 6\frac{3}{4}$ **11.** $9\frac{4}{5} + 8\frac{9}{10}$ **12.** $6\frac{5}{8} + 4\frac{3}{4}$

Subtract.

13. $8\frac{5}{6} - 3\frac{1}{6}$ **14.** $4\frac{1}{2} - 2\frac{1}{2}$ **15.** $7\frac{3}{4} - 5$ **16.** $9\frac{5}{6} - 4\frac{2}{3}$

17. $9 - 3\frac{1}{2}$ **18.** $12 - 4\frac{5}{8}$ **19.** $10 - 5\frac{3}{4}$ **20.** $12 - 6\frac{3}{5}$

21. $12 - 9\frac{1}{2}$ **22.** $13\frac{3}{8} - 6\frac{3}{4}$ **23.** $16\frac{4}{9} - 12\frac{2}{3}$ **24.** $18\frac{1}{8} - 4\frac{5}{6}$

Solve.

25.

How many dozen doughnuts?

26.

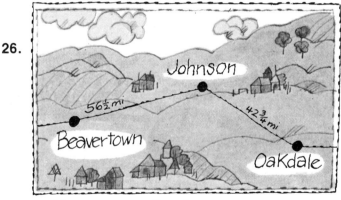

a. How many miles from Beavertown to Oakdale?

b. Johnson is how much farther from Beavertown than from Oakdale?

27. On her first try, Mary long-jumped $12\frac{5}{6}$ feet. On her second try, she jumped $13\frac{1}{4}$ feet. How much farther was her second jump?

28. A rectangular garden is $10\frac{1}{2}$ feet wide and $14\frac{1}{4}$ feet long. How much fencing is needed to go around the garden?

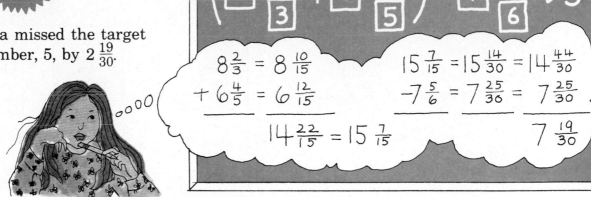

$$\left(8\frac{2}{3}+6\frac{4}{5}\right)-7\frac{5}{6}\Rightarrow 5$$

Lisa missed the target number, 5, by $2\frac{19}{30}$.

$$8\frac{2}{3}=8\frac{10}{15}$$
$$+6\frac{4}{5}=6\frac{12}{15}$$
$$\overline{\quad\quad 14\frac{22}{15}=15\frac{7}{15}}$$

$$15\frac{7}{15}=15\frac{14}{30}=14\frac{44}{30}$$
$$-7\frac{5}{6}=7\frac{25}{36}=7\frac{25}{30}$$
$$\overline{\quad\quad\quad\quad 7\frac{19}{30}}$$

How close did these players come to the target number?

1. $\left(3\frac{2}{5}+4\frac{4}{6}\right)-2\frac{1}{8}\Rightarrow 5$

2. $\left(2\frac{4}{5}+4\frac{3}{6}\right)-1\frac{2}{8}\Rightarrow 5$

3. $\left(5\frac{2}{4}+8\frac{6}{2}\right)-3\frac{1}{4}\Rightarrow 5$

4. $\left(8\frac{6}{4}+3\frac{2}{2}\right)-5\frac{1}{4}\Rightarrow 5$

Play the game.

1. Make a digit card for each of the digits 1 through 9.

2. Choose a game leader.

3. Draw a table like this: $\left(\square\frac{\square}{\square}+\square\frac{\square}{\square}\right)-\square\frac{\square}{\square}\Rightarrow 5$

4. Without looking, the leader picks a card. Each player writes the digit in his or her table.

5. The leader replaces the card in the deck and step 4 is repeated until the tables have been filled in.

6. The player who gets closest to the target number, 5, wins the game.

293

Problem solving

A bird-watching club decided to make some bluebird houses from the plan shown. Here are some problems that they solved.

1. The club ordered a 4' × 8' piece of plywood. The plywood was 62¢ per square foot. What was the total price?

2. Some fronts were cut from a piece that was $6\frac{3}{8}$ inches wide. How much was cut from the width of the piece?

3. One club member drilled a hole in each front. How far from the top was the center of the hole? How far from the side?

4. Two sides were to be cut from a rectangular piece $5\frac{1}{2}$" wide. How long must the piece be if a saw cut (kerf) uses $\frac{1}{8}$"?

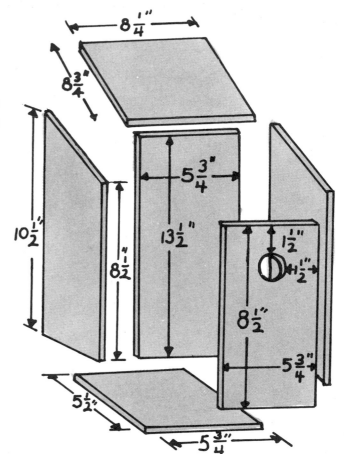

Material: $\frac{1}{2}$" exterior plywood

5. The club bought $2\frac{1}{4}$ pounds of number 4 common nails and $1\frac{3}{4}$ pounds of number 6 common nails. How many pounds of nails did they buy? If nails cost 60¢ a pound, what was the total price of the nails?

6. They bought $3\frac{1}{2}$ dozen screws for 28¢ a dozen. What was the total price of the screws? (*Hint:* Find the price of 3 dozen and of $\frac{1}{2}$ dozen.)

7. Each birdhouse was to be placed on a wooden post $4\frac{3}{4}$ feet above the ground. If the posts were $7\frac{1}{2}$ feet long, how deep did the holes have to be?

8. This record was kept of the number of hours that each member worked on the project.

Name	Hours
Bill	$3\frac{1}{2}$
Carla	4
Dennis	$2\frac{3}{4}$
Howie	$4\frac{1}{2}$
John	$3\frac{1}{4}$
Sue	5

How many hours were spent on the project?

CHAPTER CHECKUP

Change to a fraction in lowest terms. [pages 284–285]

1. $2\frac{1}{2}$
2. $4\frac{1}{3}$
3. $2\frac{2}{3}$
4. $1\frac{3}{4}$
5. $5\frac{5}{6}$
6. $4\frac{5}{8}$

Change to a mixed number. [pages 284–285]

7. $\frac{9}{2}$
8. $\frac{10}{3}$
9. $\frac{11}{4}$
10. $\frac{12}{5}$
11. $\frac{15}{8}$
12. $\frac{15}{6}$

Add. [pages 286–289]

13. $4\frac{1}{2}$
    $+3$

14. $6\frac{2}{3}$
    $+2$

15. $5\frac{1}{4}$
    $+2\frac{1}{4}$

16. $7\frac{3}{4}$
    $+8\frac{1}{8}$

17. $9\frac{1}{2}$
    $+3\frac{1}{3}$

18. $4\frac{2}{3}$
    $+6\frac{1}{4}$

19. $8\frac{2}{3}$
    $+7\frac{1}{2}$

20. $9\frac{3}{8}$
    $+6\frac{3}{4}$

21. $15\frac{5}{9}$
    $+8\frac{2}{3}$

22. $23\frac{7}{8}$
    $+17\frac{3}{4}$

23. $35\frac{5}{6}$
    $+9\frac{5}{8}$

24. $38\frac{7}{10}$
    $+26\frac{9}{10}$

Subtract. [pages 286–287, 290–291]

25. $9\frac{5}{8}$
    -2

26. $6\frac{3}{5}$
    -4

27. $10\frac{5}{9}$
    $-2\frac{2}{9}$

28. $12\frac{5}{8}$
    $-5\frac{1}{4}$

29. $13\frac{2}{3}$
    $-6\frac{1}{2}$

30. $15\frac{3}{4}$
    $-7\frac{2}{3}$

31. 6
    $-4\frac{2}{3}$

32. 5
    $-3\frac{7}{8}$

33. $18\frac{1}{4}$
    $-9\frac{3}{5}$

34. $26\frac{1}{3}$
    $-8\frac{5}{6}$

35. $19\frac{3}{8}$
    $-7\frac{2}{3}$

36. $34\frac{1}{6}$
    $-17\frac{5}{8}$

Solve. [pages 294–295]

Name	Denise	Ella	Frank	George
Pounds Collected	$10\frac{3}{4}$	$8\frac{1}{8}$	$7\frac{1}{2}$	$12\frac{5}{8}$

37. Together Denise and Ella collected how many pounds?

38. Who collected $3\frac{1}{4}$ pounds less than Denise?

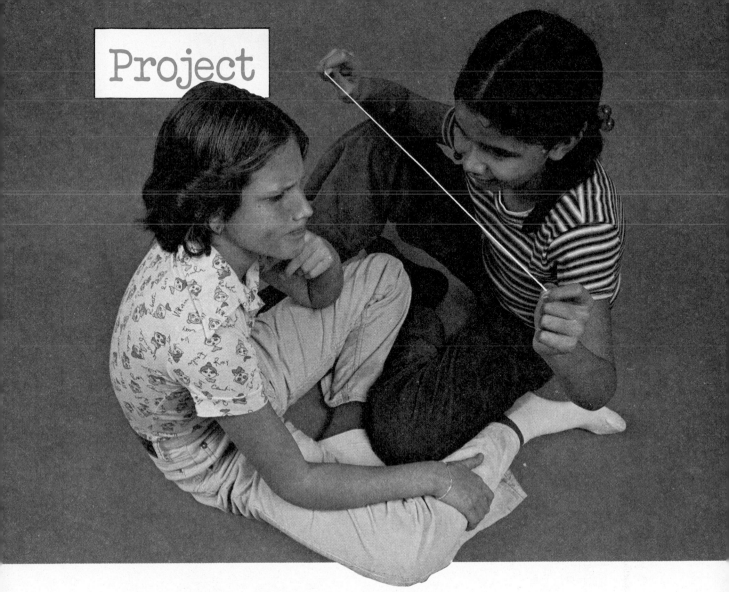

Project

1. *Without measuring,* cut off a piece of string that is somewhere between 10 and 20 inches long.

2. Ask your classmates to estimate the length of the string and keep a record of the estimates like this:

Name	Estimate of Length	Actual Length	Error
Denise	16 ½ "		

3. Measure the string to the nearest $\frac{1}{4}$ inch and compute the error of each estimate.

4. Who had the least error? the greatest error?

5. Make a bar graph of the errors.

CHAPTER REVIEW

Change to a fraction in lowest terms.

$3\frac{2}{5} = \frac{17}{5}$

1. $1\frac{1}{2}$ 2. $2\frac{1}{3}$ 3. $2\frac{3}{4}$ 4. $5\frac{2}{3}$

5. $6\frac{1}{4}$ 6. $3\frac{1}{7}$ 7. $9\frac{2}{5}$ 8. $4\frac{3}{8}$

Change to a mixed number.

$\frac{9}{2} = 4\frac{1}{2}$ $2\overline{)9} \begin{array}{c} 4\frac{1}{2} \\ \underline{-8} \\ 1 \end{array}$

9. $\frac{7}{2}$ 10. $\frac{7}{4}$ 11. $\frac{14}{3}$ 12. $\frac{18}{5}$

13. $\frac{16}{3}$ 14. $\frac{27}{8}$ 15. $\frac{33}{4}$ 16. $\frac{68}{9}$

Add.

$\begin{array}{r} 4\frac{1}{3} = 4\frac{4}{12} \\ +2\frac{1}{4} = 2\frac{3}{12} \\ \hline 6\frac{7}{12} \end{array}$

17. $\begin{array}{r} 2\frac{1}{5} \\ +1 \\ \hline \end{array}$ 18. $\begin{array}{r} 5\frac{5}{9} \\ +2\frac{2}{9} \\ \hline \end{array}$ 19. $\begin{array}{r} 6\frac{3}{4} \\ +3\frac{1}{2} \\ \hline \end{array}$ 20. $\begin{array}{r} 8\frac{3}{5} \\ +6\frac{1}{4} \\ \hline \end{array}$

$\begin{array}{r} 8\frac{3}{4} = 8\frac{3}{4} \\ +2\frac{1}{2} = 2\frac{2}{4} \\ \hline 10\frac{5}{4} = 11\frac{1}{4} \end{array}$

21. $\begin{array}{r} 5\frac{1}{2} \\ +8\frac{1}{2} \\ \hline \end{array}$ 22. $\begin{array}{r} 7\frac{3}{4} \\ +9\frac{5}{8} \\ \hline \end{array}$ 23. $\begin{array}{r} 12\frac{2}{3} \\ +5\frac{5}{6} \\ \hline \end{array}$ 24. $\begin{array}{r} 9\frac{3}{10} \\ +14\frac{4}{5} \\ \hline \end{array}$

Subtract.

$\begin{array}{r} 5\frac{2}{3} = 5\frac{4}{6} \\ -1\frac{1}{2} = 1\frac{3}{6} \\ \hline 4\frac{1}{6} \end{array}$

25. $\begin{array}{r} 7\frac{1}{3} \\ -3 \\ \hline \end{array}$ 26. $\begin{array}{r} 5\frac{3}{4} \\ -1\frac{1}{4} \\ \hline \end{array}$ 27. $\begin{array}{r} 8\frac{5}{6} \\ -4\frac{2}{3} \\ \hline \end{array}$ 28. $\begin{array}{r} 12\frac{5}{8} \\ -3\frac{1}{2} \\ \hline \end{array}$

$\begin{array}{r} 9\frac{1}{4} = 9\frac{3}{12} = 8\frac{15}{12} \\ -2\frac{2}{3} = 2\frac{8}{12} = 2\frac{8}{12} \\ \hline 6\frac{7}{12} \end{array}$

29. $\begin{array}{r} 12 \\ -8\frac{5}{8} \\ \hline \end{array}$ 30. $\begin{array}{r} 15\frac{1}{4} \\ -6\frac{1}{2} \\ \hline \end{array}$ 31. $\begin{array}{r} 17\frac{3}{8} \\ -8\frac{2}{3} \\ \hline \end{array}$ 32. $\begin{array}{r} 13\frac{1}{6} \\ -5\frac{3}{4} \\ \hline \end{array}$

CHAPTER CHALLENGE

Work through each path to find the missing number.

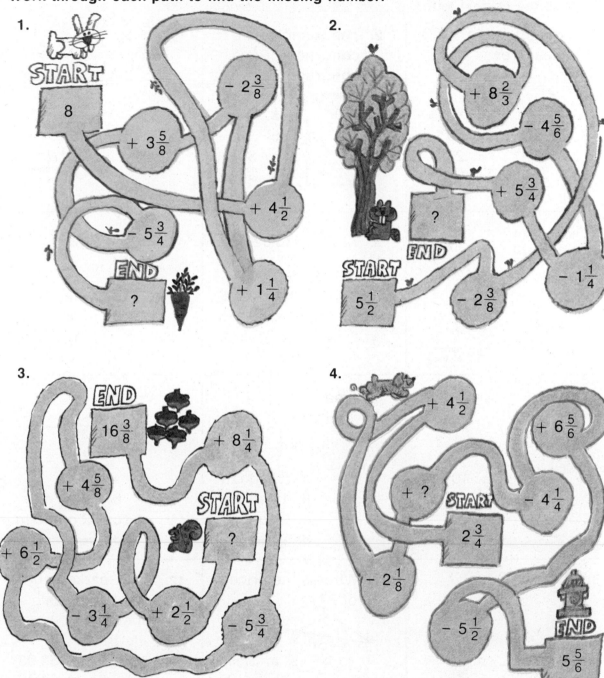

1.

START

8

$+ 3\frac{5}{8}$

$- 2\frac{3}{8}$

$+ 4\frac{1}{2}$

$- 5\frac{3}{4}$

END

?

$+ 1\frac{1}{4}$

2.

$+ 8\frac{2}{3}$

$- 4\frac{5}{6}$

$+ 5\frac{3}{4}$

?

END

START

$5\frac{1}{2}$

$- 2\frac{3}{8}$

$- 1\frac{1}{4}$

3.

END

$16\frac{3}{8}$

$+ 4\frac{5}{8}$

$+ 8\frac{1}{4}$

START

?

$+ 6\frac{1}{2}$

$- 3\frac{1}{4}$

$+ 2\frac{1}{2}$

$- 5\frac{3}{4}$

4.

$+ 4\frac{1}{2}$

$+ 6\frac{5}{6}$

$+ ?$

START

$2\frac{3}{4}$

$- 4\frac{1}{4}$

$- 2\frac{1}{8}$

$- 5\frac{1}{2}$

END

$5\frac{5}{6}$

Form W

| a | b | c | d | | a | b | c | d | | a | b | c | d | | a | b | c | d | | a | b | c | d |
14 | | | | | 34 | | | | | 14 | | | | | 4 | | | | | 30 | | | |
| a | b | c | d | | | | | | | | | | | | c | d | | a | b | c | d |
15 | | | | | | | | | | | | | | | | | | | 31 | | | |
| | | | a | b | c | Standardized Format | | | | a | b | c | | a | b | c | d |

MAJOR CHECKUP
Standardized Format

Choose the correct letter.

---

1. A right angle measures

    a. 100°
    b. 50°
    c. 25°
    d. none of these

2. The triangles are congruent. $\overline{BC}$ is congruent to

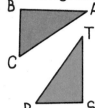

    a. $\overline{RT}$
    b. $\overline{SR}$
    c. $\overline{ST}$
    d. none of these

3. $\frac{5}{6} \times \frac{2}{9} =$

    a. $\frac{5}{27}$
    b. $\frac{5}{9}$
    c. $\frac{5}{18}$
    d. none of these

---

4. $\frac{4}{9} \div \frac{4}{3} =$

    a. $\overline{27}$
    b. $\frac{1}{3}$
    c. 3
    d. none of these

5. 74.3 + 113.82 =

    a. 121.25
    b. 1212.5
    c. 188.12
    d. none of these

6. 56.4 − 4.35 =

    a. 52.05
    b. 1.29
    c. 12.9
    d. none of these

---

7. 1 km = <u>?</u> m

    a. 10
    b. 1000
    c. 100
    d. none of these

8. Area =

5 cm   4 cm

    a. 20 sq cm
    b. 18 sq cm
    c. 9 sq cm
    d. none of these

9. Volume =

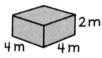

2m   4 m   4 m

    a. 32 m
    b. 32 sq m
    c. 32 cubic m
    d. none of these

---

10. 1 lb = <u>?</u> oz

    a. 12
    b. 16
    c. 24
    d. none of these

11. What is the price of 2?

3 for $1.49

    a. $.50
    b. $1.00
    c. $.99
    d. none of these

12. $\frac{1}{3}$ off marked price What is the sale price?

$13.39

    a. $8.93
    b. $4.46
    c. $17.85
    d. none of these

12
Decimals– Multiplication and Division

1.  .30

2.

3.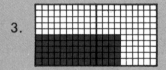

4.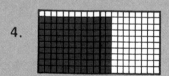

5.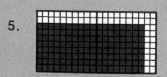

Multiplying decimals

If we multiply, we get the number of unit squares that are yellow.

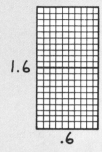

.96 of a unit square is yellow.

$$\begin{array}{r} 1.6 \\ \times\ .6 \\ \hline .96 \end{array}$$

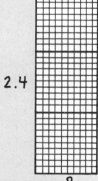

1.92 unit squares are yellow.

$$\begin{array}{r} 2.4 \\ \times\ .8 \\ \hline 1.92 \end{array}$$

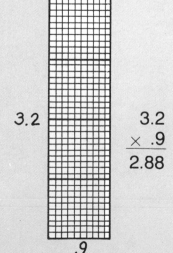

$$\begin{array}{r} 3.2 \\ \times\ .9 \\ \hline 2.88 \end{array}$$

EXERCISES

First study the picture. Then give the product.

1.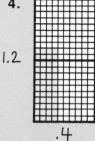
.8
.2
$$\begin{array}{r} .8 \\ \times .2 \\ \hline \end{array}$$

2.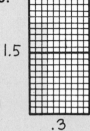
.9
.4
$$\begin{array}{r} .9 \\ \times .4 \\ \hline \end{array}$$

3.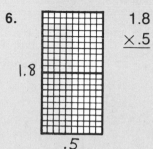
.7
.6
$$\begin{array}{r} .7 \\ \times .6 \\ \hline \end{array}$$

4.
1.2
.4
$$\begin{array}{r} 1.2 \\ \times .4 \\ \hline \end{array}$$

5.
1.5
.3
$$\begin{array}{r} 1.5 \\ \times .3 \\ \hline \end{array}$$

6.
1.8
.5
$$\begin{array}{r} 1.8 \\ \times .5 \\ \hline \end{array}$$

Give the product. Then check your answer by looking at the picture.

7.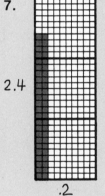
2.4
.2
$$\begin{array}{r} 2.4 \\ \times .2 \\ \hline \end{array}$$

8.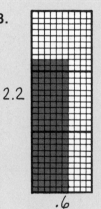
2.2
.6
$$\begin{array}{r} 2.2 \\ \times .6 \\ \hline \end{array}$$

9.
2.8
.4
$$\begin{array}{r} 2.8 \\ \times .4 \\ \hline \end{array}$$

Keeping Skills Sharp

Give each sum in lowest terms.

1. $\dfrac{2}{3}$
$+\dfrac{2}{3}$

2. $\dfrac{3}{8}$
$+\dfrac{1}{8}$

3. $\dfrac{1}{6}$
$+\dfrac{5}{6}$

4. $\dfrac{3}{8}$
$+\dfrac{1}{4}$

5. $\dfrac{0}{4}$
$+\dfrac{1}{2}$

6. $\dfrac{5}{3}$
$+\dfrac{5}{6}$

7. $\dfrac{2}{3}$
$+\dfrac{1}{2}$

8. $\dfrac{5}{8}$
$+\dfrac{3}{4}$

9. $\dfrac{3}{2}$
$+\dfrac{2}{3}$

10. $\dfrac{3}{4}$
$+\dfrac{2}{3}$

11. $\dfrac{5}{6}$
$+\dfrac{3}{8}$

12. $\dfrac{3}{5}$
$+\dfrac{3}{4}$

Multiplying decimals—a shortcut

You can find the product by looking at the picture. You can also use this shortcut to find the product.

$$\begin{array}{r} 1.8 \\ \times\ .6 \\ \hline \end{array}$$

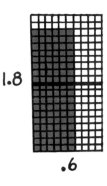

1.8

.6

Step 1. Multiply the numbers as whole numbers.

$$\begin{array}{r} 1.8 \\ \times\ .6 \\ \hline 108 \end{array}$$

Step 2. Count the digits to the right of the decimal points in the factors.

$$\begin{array}{r} 1.8 \leftarrow 1\ digit \\ \times\ .6 \leftarrow 1\ digit \\ \hline 2\ digits \end{array}$$

Step 3. Count off the same number of digits to place the decimal point in the product.

$$\begin{array}{r} 1.8 \\ \times\ .6 \\ \hline 1.08 \end{array}$$

This is the number of unit squares that are red

Study these examples.

$$\begin{array}{r} 3.25 \leftarrow 2 \\ \times\ .6 \leftarrow 1 \\ \hline 1.950\quad 3 \end{array}$$

$$\begin{array}{r} 25.2 \\ \times\ 6.4 \\ \hline 1008 \\ 15120 \\ \hline 161.28 \end{array}$$

$$\begin{array}{r} 53.8 \\ \times\ 2.14 \\ \hline 2152 \\ 5380 \\ 107600 \\ \hline 115.132 \end{array}$$

EXERCISES

Multiply.

1. 28 $\times\,.5$	2. 56 $\times\,.3$	3. 135 $\times\,.6$	4. 2.78 $\times\,8$	5. 39.5 $\times\,3$
6. 32.1 $\times\,.3$	7. 72.4 $\times\,.8$	8. 2.95 $\times\,.6$	9. 6.08 $\times\,.4$	10. 59.9 $\times\,.7$
11. 8.21 $\times\,1.5$	12. 74.8 $\times\,.08$	13. 5.93 $\times\,3.7$	14. 36.9 $\times\,.09$	15. 57.4 $\times\,8.5$
16. 42.6 $\times\,16.2$	17. 3.78 $\times\,2.57$	18. 29.7 $\times\,34.8$	19. 54.6 $\times\,5.62$	20. 97.8 $\times\,2.09$

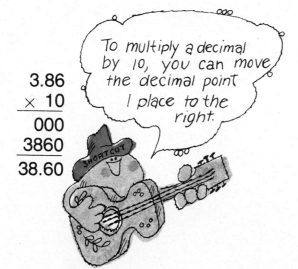

$$
\begin{array}{r}
3.86 \\
\times\ 10 \\
\hline
000 \\
3860 \\
\hline
38.60
\end{array}
$$

To multiply a decimal by 10, you can move the decimal point 1 place to the right.

Use the shortcut to find these products.

21. 35.2×10 22. 2.96×10

23. $.789 \times 10$ 24. 74.1×10

See if you can find a shortcut for multiplying by 100.

25. 1.56×100 26. $.65 \times 100$

27. 9.34×100 28. $.878 \times 100$

Solve.

29.

symphony $7.49

What is the price of 10 records?

30. What is the area of a rectangular garden that measures 8.3 m by 5.6 m?

31. What is the volume of a rectangular box that measures 9.5 cm by 4.8 cm by 3.6 cm?

More about multiplying decimals

Sometimes you will need to write one or more zeros in the product before you can place the decimal point.

$$\begin{array}{r} .3 \\ \times\ .2 \\ \hline .06 \end{array}$$ 2 digits

$$\begin{array}{r} .04 \\ \times\ .2 \\ \hline .008 \end{array}$$ 3 digits

EXERCISES
Multiply.

1. $\begin{array}{r}.2\\ \times 3\\ \hline\end{array}$	2. $\begin{array}{r}.2\\ \times .3\\ \hline\end{array}$	3. $\begin{array}{r}.02\\ \times 3\\ \hline\end{array}$	4. $\begin{array}{r}.4\\ \times .2\\ \hline\end{array}$	5. $\begin{array}{r}.3\\ \times .1\\ \hline\end{array}$
6. $\begin{array}{r}.5\\ \times .3\\ \hline\end{array}$	7. $\begin{array}{r}.02\\ \times .4\\ \hline\end{array}$	8. $\begin{array}{r}.02\\ \times .1\\ \hline\end{array}$	9. $\begin{array}{r}23\\ \times .02\\ \hline\end{array}$	10. $\begin{array}{r}4\\ \times .2\\ \hline\end{array}$
11. $\begin{array}{r}13.2\\ \times .06\\ \hline\end{array}$	12. $\begin{array}{r}24.3\\ \times .05\\ \hline\end{array}$	13. $\begin{array}{r}1.14\\ \times 4.2\\ \hline\end{array}$	14. $\begin{array}{r}527\\ \times .26\\ \hline\end{array}$	15. $\begin{array}{r}39.5\\ \times 1.8\\ \hline\end{array}$
16. $\begin{array}{r}86.4\\ \times .25\\ \hline\end{array}$	17. $\begin{array}{r}29.1\\ \times 3.8\\ \hline\end{array}$	18. $\begin{array}{r}74.3\\ \times 14.2\\ \hline\end{array}$	19. $\begin{array}{r}651\\ \times 1.56\\ \hline\end{array}$	20. $\begin{array}{r}507\\ \times 35.4\\ \hline\end{array}$

Use shortcuts to find these products.

21. 3.82×10	22. 70.8×10	23. 56.3×10
24. 4.26×10	25. $.915 \times 10$	26. 35.9×10
27. 2.63×100	28. 3.952×100	29. 35.48×100
30. 46.17×100	31. 6.18×100	32. 394.5×100
33. 7.826×1000	34. 5.37×1000	35. $.653 \times 1000$
36. 8.291×1000	37. 742.83×1000	38. 561.94×1000

306

Complete.

39. To change kilometers to meters, multiply by _?_.

40. To change meters to centimeters, multiply by _?_.

41. To change liters to milliliters, multiply by _?_.

42. To change kilograms to grams, multiply by _?_.

Complete.

43. Longest Bicycle

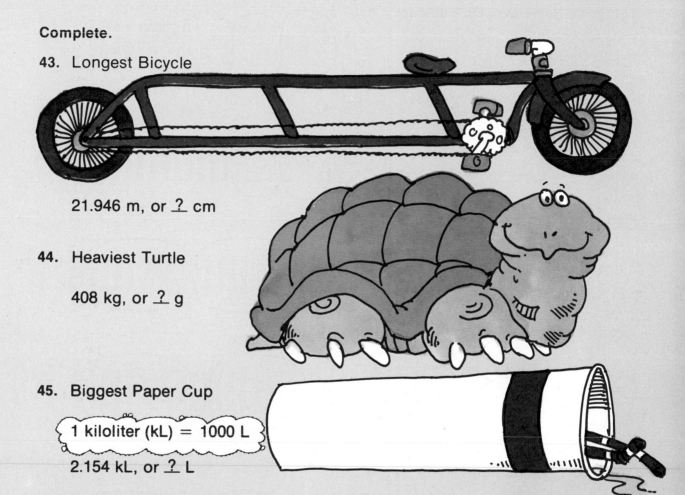

21.946 m, or _?_ cm

44. Heaviest Turtle

408 kg, or _?_ g

45. Biggest Paper Cup

1 kiloliter (kL) = 1000 L

2.154 kL, or _?_ L

Can you make up a story to fit?

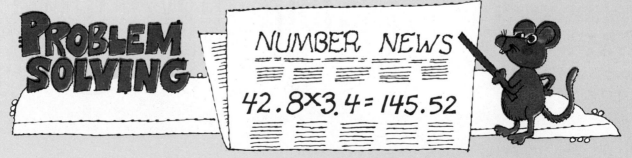

PROBLEM SOLVING

NUMBER NEWS

42.8 × 3.4 = 145.52

Dividing a decimal

You divide a decimal the same way you divide a
whole number.

EXAMPLE. $3\overline{)4.47}$

Step 1. Divide ones. Subtract.

$$\begin{array}{r} 1 \\ 3\overline{)4.47} \\ \underline{-3} \\ 1 \end{array}$$

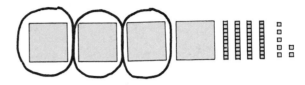

Step 2. Regroup 1 one for 10 tenths.

$$\begin{array}{r} 1 \\ 3\overline{)4.47} \\ \underline{-3} \\ 14 \end{array}$$

Step 3. Divide tenths. Subtract.

$$\begin{array}{r} 1.4 \\ 3\overline{)4.47} \\ \underline{-3} \\ 14 \\ \underline{-12} \\ 2 \end{array}$$

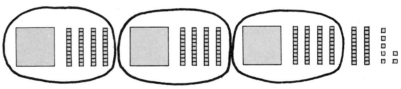

Step 4. Regroup 2 tenths for 20 hundredths.

$$\begin{array}{r} 1.4 \\ 3\overline{)4.47} \\ \underline{-3} \\ 14 \\ \underline{-12} \\ 27 \end{array}$$

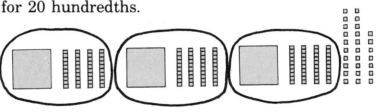

Step 5. Divide hundredths. Subtract.

$$\begin{array}{r} 1.49 \\ 3\overline{)4.47} \\ \underline{-3} \\ 14 \\ \underline{-12} \\ 27 \\ \underline{-27} \\ 0 \end{array}$$

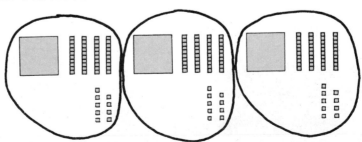

Study these examples.

```
        5.34                    .461
  12 ) 64.08          243 ) 112.023
      ⁻60                    ⁻972
       40                    1482
      ⁻36                   ⁻1458
        48                     243
       ⁻48                    ⁻243
         0                      0
```

EXERCISES
Divide.

1. 3) 52.2   2. 5) 6.85   3. 7) 3.92   4. 8) .360   5. 2) 76.4

6. 4) 5.96   7. 6) 29.4   8. 9) .783   9. 4) 70.8   10. 8) .896

11. 7) 7.56   12. 3) 92.1   13. 5) 8.55   14. 9) .666   15. 6) 92.4

16. 14) 33.74   17. 25) 975.5   18. 39) 95.94   19. 56) 565.6   20. 45) 5.670

Solve.

21.

Weight: 2 kilograms
Price: $12.58
What is the price per kilogram?

22.

What is the total cost? (Give the answer to the nearest cent.)

23. Mr. Johnson drove his car 283.6 kilometers in 4 hours. How many kilometers per hour did he average?

24. Barbara earned $25.90 for working 14 hours. How much did she earn per hour?

25. Find the end number.

26. Find the starting number.

More about dividing decimals

Study the example. Notice the zeros written in the dividend.

EXAMPLE. $4\overline{)3.1}$

Step 1. Divide.

$$\begin{array}{r} .7 \\ 4\overline{)3.1} \\ \underline{-28} \\ 3 \end{array}$$

Write 0 here.

Step 2. Regroup 3 tenths for 30 hundredths.

$$\begin{array}{r} .7 \\ 4\overline{)3.10} \\ \underline{-28} \\ 30 \end{array}$$

Step 3. Divide.

$$\begin{array}{r} .77 \\ 4\overline{)3.10} \\ \underline{-28} \\ 30 \\ \underline{-28} \\ 2 \end{array}$$

Write 0 here.

Step 4. Regroup 2 hundredths for 20 thousandths.

$$\begin{array}{r} .77 \\ 4\overline{)3.100} \\ \underline{-28} \\ 30 \\ \underline{-28} \\ 20 \end{array}$$

Step 5. Divide.

$$\begin{array}{r} .775 \\ 4\overline{)3.100} \\ \underline{-28} \\ 30 \\ \underline{-28} \\ 20 \\ \underline{-20} \\ 0 \end{array}$$

Other examples.

$$\begin{array}{r} .125 \\ 8\overline{)1.000} \\ \underline{-8} \\ 20 \\ \underline{-16} \\ 40 \\ \underline{-40} \\ 0 \end{array}$$

$$\begin{array}{r} 1.375 \\ 16\overline{)22.000} \\ \underline{-16} \\ 60 \\ \underline{-48} \\ 120 \\ \underline{-112} \\ 80 \\ \underline{-80} \\ 0 \end{array}$$

EXERCISES

Divide.

1. $5\overline{)2.7}$ 2. $4\overline{)3.5}$ 3. $2\overline{)9.1}$ 4. $8\overline{)5.2}$ 5. $4\overline{)9.6}$

6. $8\overline{)19}$ 7. $5\overline{)24}$ 8. $2\overline{)27}$ 9. $4\overline{)19}$ 10. $8\overline{)23}$

11. $24\overline{)9}$ 12. $24\overline{)15}$ 13. $10\overline{)62.4}$ 14. $14\overline{)2.8}$ 15. $32\overline{)20}$

16. $84\overline{)39.48}$ 17. $48\overline{)3.408}$ 18. $92\overline{)7.636}$ 19. $65\overline{)2.47}$ 20. $38\overline{)1311}$

You can divide a decimal by 10 by moving the decimal point 1 place to the left.

$$10\overline{)6.380} \quad .638$$

Use the shortcut to find these quotients.

21. $62.4 \div 10$ 22. $345 \div 10$

23. $8.95 \div 10$ 24. $.6 \div 10$

See if you can find a shortcut for dividing by 100.

25. $42.8 \div 100$ 26. $725 \div 100$

27. $5.9 \div 100$ 28. $.8 \div 100$

Keeping Skills Sharp

Give each difference in lowest terms.

1. $\dfrac{5}{9} - \dfrac{1}{9}$ 2. $\dfrac{5}{8} - \dfrac{3}{8}$ 3. $\dfrac{1}{2} - \dfrac{1}{4}$ 4. $\dfrac{3}{4} - \dfrac{1}{2}$ 5. $\dfrac{7}{8} - \dfrac{1}{4}$ 6. $\dfrac{3}{2} - \dfrac{3}{8}$

7. $\dfrac{7}{8} - \dfrac{5}{6}$ 8. $\dfrac{5}{4} - \dfrac{5}{8}$ 9. $\dfrac{7}{6} - \dfrac{2}{3}$ 10. $\dfrac{3}{2} - \dfrac{5}{4}$ 11. $\dfrac{2}{3} - \dfrac{5}{8}$ 12. $\dfrac{7}{4} - \dfrac{5}{6}$

311

Estimating

If you learn to estimate before you calculate, you will know whether you answer makes sense.

Remember to work inside the grouping symbols first.

EXERCISES
First estimate, then calculate.

1. (5.8 + 4.2) − 3.9

2. 5.8 + (4.2 − 3.9)

3. (3.9 × 2.8) + 4.2

4. 3.9 × (2.8 + 4.2)

5. (19.7 − 3.1) × 2.8

6. 19.7 − (3.1 × 2.8)

7. (6.24 ÷ 3) × 2

8. 6.24 ÷ (3 × 2)

9. (16.8 − 8.1) − 2.9

10. 16.8 − (8.1 − 2.9)

11. (4.1 × 20.2) ÷ 2

12. 4.1 × (20.2 ÷ 2)

13. (25.2 × 3.9) − 2.03

14. 25.2 × (3.9 − 2.03)

15. (43.6 + 18.9) × 4.17

16. 43.6 + (18.9 × 4.17)

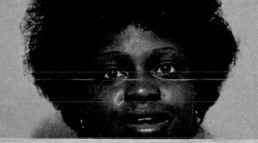

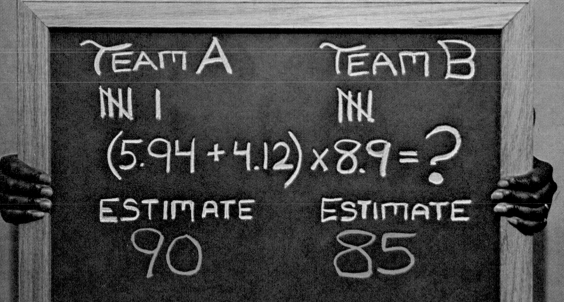

1. Calculate the problem shown above.

2. How close was Team A's estimate?
   How close was Team B's estimate?

3. Which estimate was closer?

Play the game.

1. Divide the class into two teams.

2. A player from each team goes to the chalkboard and faces the class.

3. The teacher writes a decimal problem on the chalkboard.

4. On a signal, the two players look at the problem and have 15 seconds to write their estimates on the chalkboard.

5. The player with the closer estimate earns 1 point for his/her team.

6. Continue to play until each player has had at least 1 turn.

7. The team with the greater score wins.

313

Problem solving

1. Hal had $53.72. He bought a backpack for $25.20 and a sleeping bag for $22.89 before going on the hike. How much money did he have left?

2. The 6 backpackers took enough water so that they could each drink 1.75 liters of water each day. How much water did they take for the 2-day hike?

3. The total food bill for the 6 backpackers was $52.73. What was each backpacker's share of the food cost? Give your answer to the nearest penny.

4. The leader and the 5 backpackers carried a total of 64 kg of food and equipment. The leader carried 16 kg and the rest was divided among the other backpackers. How much did each carry?

5. The group had a map that used a scale of 1 cm on the map for 2.5 km on the hiking trail. On the map they found that it was 3.5 cm from the starting point to where they were to have lunch. How far did they have to hike before lunch?

6. After lunch they hiked 8.25 km before taking a break. If it took them 3 hours, how many km did they average each hour?

7. By looking at their map, they could see that the elevation of the mountain was 2856.4 m. While hiking on the trail, they saw an elevation marker of 1793.8 m. How much higher was the mountain top?

8. The next day, they averaged 4.25 km per hour hiking down the mountain. If it took them 4.5 hours, how far was it down the mountain?

CHAPTER CHECKUP

Multiply. [pages 302–307]

1.	.8 ×.3	2.	1.4 ×.5	3.	37 ×.8	4.	19.6 ×4	5.	2.14 ×.7

6.	4.2 ×1.2	7.	53 ×.32	8.	7.8 ×6.1	9.	42.6 ×.48	10.	5.37 ×5.6

11.	52.3 ×10.3	12.	60.4 ×251	13.	49.3 ×3.25	14.	8.26 ×472	15.	7.14 ×56.8

Divide. [pages 308–311]

16. 2)43.6   17. 4)9.12   18. 6)5.88   19. 9)2.52   20. 7)38.5

21. 8)3   22. 4)3   23. 8)15   24. 5)31   25. 4)53

26. 19)124.07   27. 28)229.88   28. 32)203.2   29. 57)62.13   30. 75)126

Solve. [pages 314–315]

31.

bananas $.68 a kg

What is the price of 3.5 kilograms?

32.

oranges   weight: 4kg $3.96

How much for 1 kg of oranges?

33. A rectangular lawn is 52.4 m by 30.5 m. What is the area of the lawn?

34. An airplane flew 2619 km in 4 hours. How many km did it average each hour?

316

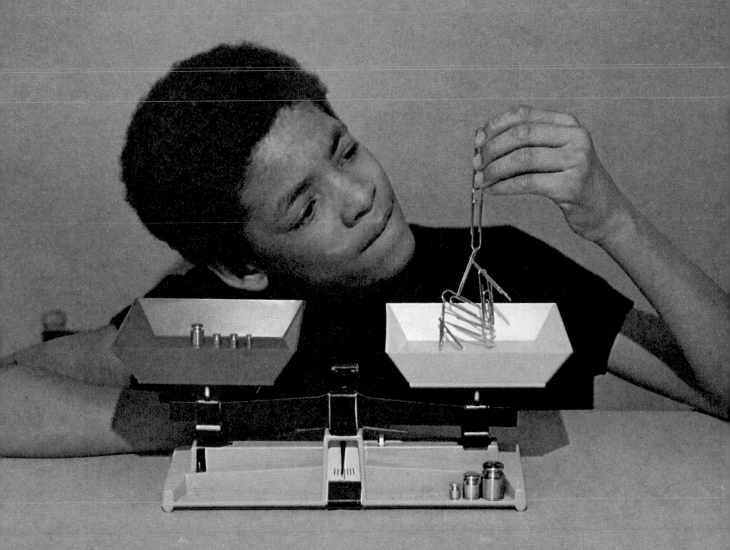

To find out how much one paper clip weighs, you can first weigh 10 paper clips to the nearest gram and then divide by 10.

Use this method to "weigh" these objects.
1. a larger paper clip
2. a straight pin
3. a thumbtack
4. a small paper clip

CHAPTER REVIEW

Multiply.

```
 28.6  ← 1 digit
× .24  ← 2 digits
─────
 1144      3 digits
5720
─────
6.864  ←
```

1. 3.5
   × .7

2. 7.48
   × .6

3. 52.6
   × 4.3

4. 82.5
   × .47

```
.02  ← 2 digits
× .3  ← 1 digit
─────
.006  ← 3 digits
```

5. .4
   × .2

6. .03
   × .3

7. 1.2
   × .04

8. .21
   × .2

Divide.

```
     .59
  4 )2.36
    -20
    ───
     36
    -36
    ───
      0
```

9. 6)16.2

10. 8)34.88

11. 24)84.48

12. 63)17.829

```
      .375
  16 )6.000
     -48
     ───
      120
     -112
     ────
       80
      -80
      ───
        0
```

13. 4)3

14. 8)5

15. 16)46

16. 12)57

CHAPTER CHALLENGE

Copy and complete.

1. ➡⊕➡

3.64	?	8.52
4.18	?	7.09
?	?	?

⬇⊕

2. ➡⊗➡

3	1.51	?
1.2	.8	?
?	?	?

⬇⊗

3. ➡⊕➡

9.34	3.86	?
?	?	?
5.16	2.05	?

⬇⊖

4. ➡⊗➡

3	1	?
4	2	?
?	?	?

⬇÷

5. ➡⊗➡

6.4	1.5	?
2	?	6
?	?	?

⬇÷

6. ➡⊕➡

?	6.23	?
?	?	5.14
?	2.26	4.45

⬇⊖

Form

14 ¦ ¦ ¦ ¦ ¦ ¦
    a   b   c   d
15 ¦ ¦ ¦ ¦ ¦ ¦

34 ¦ ¦
      a   b   c

14 ¦ ¦ ¦ ¦ ¦ ¦

4 ¦ ¦
      c   d
30 ¦ ¦ ¦ ¦ ¦ ¦
      a   b   c   d
31 ¦ ¦ ¦ ¦ ¦ ¦
      a   b   c   d

MAJOR CHECKUP
Standardized Format

Choose the correct letter.

1. Which way is *not* a way to write about the angle shown?

   a. ∠ABC
   b. ∠B
   c. ∠CBA
   d. ∠BCA

2. $\overleftrightarrow{AB}$ is parallel to:

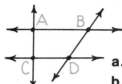

   a. $\overleftrightarrow{CD}$
   b. $\overleftrightarrow{DB}$
   c. $\overleftrightarrow{CA}$
   d. none of these

3. $4 + \frac{2}{3} =$

   a. $\frac{14}{3}$
   b. $\frac{8}{3}$
   c. 2
   d. none of these

---

4. $\frac{5}{6} - \frac{1}{4} =$

   a. 2
   b. $\frac{7}{12}$
   c. $\frac{1}{3}$
   d. none of these

5. $\frac{5}{9} \times \frac{3}{2} =$

   a. $\frac{5}{6}$
   b. $\frac{4}{9}$
   c. $\frac{15}{9}$
   d. none of these

6. $\frac{5}{6} \div \frac{2}{3} =$

   a. $\frac{4}{5}$
   b. $\frac{2}{5}$
   c. $\frac{5}{2}$
   d. none of these

---

7. $15.6 + 7.5 =$

   a. 90.6
   b. 9.06
   c. 23.1
   d. none of these

8. $49.6 - 3.82 =$

   a. 45.78
   b. 11.4
   c. 1.14
   d. none of these

9. The perimeter of this triangle is

   a. 48 cm
   b. 24 cm
   c. 14 cm
   d. none of these

---

10. What is the price of 1?

   a. 22¢
   b. 23¢
   c. 24¢
   d. none of these

11. Add.

$$4\frac{1}{2}$$
$$+3\frac{5}{8}$$

   a. $7\frac{1}{8}$
   b. $8\frac{1}{8}$
   c. $7\frac{7}{8}$
   d. none of these

12. Subtract.

$$6\frac{1}{3}$$
$$-2\frac{3}{4}$$

   a. $4\frac{5}{12}$
   b. $4\frac{7}{12}$
   c. $3\frac{7}{12}$
   d. none of these

1	Basic addition facts, sums through 18	3 +4	9 +0	6 +7	9 +8	8 +7
2	Addition without or with regrouping	42 +23	32 +48	37 +26		58 +79
3	Addition with regrouping	528 +146	359 +670	546 +278		945 +697
4	Addition with regrouping	3789 +1546		84962 +57698		348716 +655029
5	Addition with regrouping	74 29 +63	185 76 640 + 57	3921 1823 4765 +5283		86945 6913 7428 + 5317
6	Basic subtraction facts, sums through 18	8 – 8	12 – 5	18 – 9		16 – 7
7	Subtraction without or with regrouping	58 – 12	70 – 35	93 – 27		64 – 56
8	Subtraction with regrouping	750 – 429	621 – 385	803 – 256		900 – 664
9	Subtraction with regrouping	4218 – 1072		68102 – 34529		726300 – 459275

10	Basic multiplication facts, products through 9 × 9	8 ×0	3 ×7	9 ×4	6 ×8	7 ×9
11	Multiplication without and with regrouping	32 ×2	24 ×4	65 ×8	89 ×7
12	Multiplication with regrouping	151 ×5	278 ×3	578 ×6	758 ×9
13	Multiplication with regrouping	7283 ×4	5096 ×6		4179 ×8
14	Multiplying by 10 and 100	258 ×10	3192 ×10	764 ×100	5978 ×100
15	Multiplying by 10s and 100s	78 ×30	526 ×60	885 ×400	942 ×700
16	Multiplication with or without regrouping	42 ×21	68 ×16	325 ×48	674 ×53
17	Multiplication with regrouping	328 ×142	536 ×240	755 ×526	889 ×703
18	Division facts, quotients through 81 ÷ 9	9)36	5)0	6)42	9)54
19	Division with or without regrouping	2)86	6)72	4)68	3)87

20	Division with remainder	$5\overline{)73}$	$4\overline{)91}$	$3\overline{)74}$	$6\overline{)99}$

21	Division with regrouping	$7\overline{)945}$	$5\overline{)745}$	$8\overline{)289}$	$9\overline{)593}$

22	Division with regrouping	$16\overline{)688}$	$28\overline{)952}$	$42\overline{)978}$	$33\overline{)809}$

23	Division with regrouping	$68\overline{)2516}$	$74\overline{)95634}$	$53\overline{)72974}$

24	Reducing to lowest terms	$\frac{5}{10} = \underline{?}$	$\frac{6}{8} = \underline{?}$	$\frac{9}{6} = \underline{?}$	$\frac{8}{12} = \underline{?}$

25	Adding fractions	$\frac{4}{9}$ $+\frac{1}{9}$	$\frac{3}{8}$ $+\frac{1}{8}$	$\frac{1}{2}$ $+\frac{1}{4}$	$\frac{3}{2}$ $+\frac{5}{8}$	$\frac{2}{3}$ $+\frac{3}{4}$

26	Subtracting fractions	$\frac{8}{9}$ $-\frac{3}{9}$	$\frac{5}{6}$ $-\frac{1}{6}$	$\frac{3}{4}$ $-\frac{1}{2}$	$\frac{7}{2}$ $-\frac{7}{4}$	$\frac{5}{6}$ $-\frac{3}{4}$

27	Changing a mixed number to a fraction	$1\frac{1}{2} = \underline{?}$	$3\frac{1}{4} = \underline{?}$	$2\frac{2}{3} = \underline{?}$	$3\frac{4}{5} = \underline{?}$

28	Changing a fraction to a mixed number	$\frac{4}{3} = \underline{?}$	$\frac{5}{2} = \underline{?}$	$\frac{10}{3} = \underline{?}$	$\frac{15}{4} = \underline{?}$

29	Fraction of a number	$\frac{1}{4}$ of 20 = ?	$\frac{3}{4}$ of 24 = ?	$\frac{2}{3}$ of 18 = ?

30	Multiplying fractions	$\frac{2}{3} \times \frac{4}{5}$	$\frac{5}{8} \times \frac{4}{3}$	$\frac{5}{6} \times \frac{6}{5}$

31	Dividing fractions	$\frac{3}{8} \div \frac{1}{8}$	$\frac{3}{4} \div \frac{1}{2}$	$\frac{4}{5} \div \frac{2}{3}$

32	Adding decimals	$\begin{array}{r} 3.9 \\ +2.6 \end{array}$	$\begin{array}{r} 7.85 \\ +3.96 \end{array}$	$\begin{array}{r} 2.786 \\ +9.374 \end{array}$	$\begin{array}{r} 69.78 \\ +56.95 \end{array}$

33	Subtracting decimals	$\begin{array}{r} 3.4 \\ -2.6 \end{array}$	$\begin{array}{r} 7.03 \\ -2.56 \end{array}$	$\begin{array}{r} 5.078 \\ -2.193 \end{array}$	$\begin{array}{r} 82.14 \\ -19.57 \end{array}$

34	Adding mixed numbers	$\begin{array}{r} 5\frac{4}{9} \\ +2\frac{1}{9} \end{array}$	$\begin{array}{r} 3\frac{5}{8} \\ +6\frac{1}{4} \end{array}$	$\begin{array}{r} 6\frac{1}{2} \\ +5\frac{3}{4} \end{array}$	$\begin{array}{r} 8\frac{2}{3} \\ +6\frac{3}{4} \end{array}$

35	Subtracting mixed numbers	$\begin{array}{r} 9\frac{3}{5} \\ -4\frac{1}{5} \end{array}$	$\begin{array}{r} 8\frac{2}{3} \\ -1\frac{1}{6} \end{array}$	$\begin{array}{r} 6\frac{1}{4} \\ -2\frac{1}{2} \end{array}$	$\begin{array}{r} 7\frac{2}{9} \\ -3\frac{5}{6} \end{array}$

36	Multiplying decimals	$\begin{array}{r} 1.3 \\ \times .2 \end{array}$	$\begin{array}{r} 4.2 \\ \times 3.4 \end{array}$	$\begin{array}{r} 6.05 \\ \times 5.3 \end{array}$	$\begin{array}{r} 68.5 \\ \times 5.37 \end{array}$

37	Dividing decimals	$8\overline{)7.92}$	$42\overline{)235.2}$	$38\overline{)28.12}$

EXTRA PRACTICE

Set 1   What does the red digit stand for?

1. 395

2. 742

3. 826

4. 935

5. 3642

6. 7891

7. 2539

8. 6428

9. 8888

10. 8888

11. 8888

12. 8888

Set 2   In 569,714, what digit is in the

1. hundreds place?

2. ten thousands place?

3. ones place?

4. hundred thousands place?

5. tens place?

6. thousands place?

Set 3   < or >?

1. 642 ● 644

2. 570 ● 569

3. 900 ● 899

4. 5913 ● 5842

5. 7563 ● 7581

6. 6534 ● 6487

7. 35,291 ● 36,384

8. 82,917 ● 85,389

9. 78,126 ● 521,384

10. 396,421 ● 43,897

11. 158,296 ● 159,295

12. 743,815 ● 735,000

Set 4   Round to the nearest thousand.

1. 7926

2. 8034

3. 2799

4. 6500

5. 74,824

6. 52,009

7. 82,643

8. 18,500

9. 365,294

10. 381,666

11. 592,500

12. 763,004

13. 859,600

14. 537,499

15. 399,832

16. 799,500

Set 5　Give the standard numeral.

1. sixteen million
2. one hundred forty-six million
3. thirty-two million, three hundred two thousand, two hundred sixty-five
4. five hundred thirty-nine million, eight hundred ninety-seven thousand, four hundred two
5. eight hundred fifty-one million, three hundred thirty-five
6. ninety-five million, fifty-two thousand

Set 6

1. 3	2. 9	3. 4	4. 4	5. 6	6. 5	7. 9
+5	+0	+8	+6	+6	+7	+4

8. 6	9. 3	10. 8	11. 5	12. 9	13. 3	14. 6
+8	+8	+8	+6	+9	+9	+7

15. 5	16. 9	17. 7	18. 9	19. 9	20. 9	21. 9
+8	+8	+7	+6	+7	+5	+8

Set 7

1. 5	2. 3	3. 5	4. 3	5. 2	6. 4	7. 5
2	7	6	6	8	1	5
+5	+4	+4	+7	+8	+9	+6

8. 3	9. 7	10. 5	11. 4	12. 7	13. 9	14. 3
6	8	3	3	4	4	4
5	3	6	6	5	1	6
+4	+2	+5	+1	+3	+6	+8

Set 8

1. 23	2. 32	3. 62	4. 28	5. 46	6. 58
+41	+27	+51	+37	+38	+19

7. 58	8. 86	9. 65	10. 94	11. 44	12. 37
+36	+53	+87	+93	+50	+93

13. 98	14. 75	15. 85	16. 97	17. 84	18. 89
+36	+39	+15	+74	+75	+56

Set 9

1. 221 +436	2. 275 +105	3. 645 +428	4. 736 +319	5. 827 +216
6. 506 +709	7. 721 +192	8. 365 +294	9. 638 +270	10. 376 +898

Set 10

1. 5298 +2486	2. 3174 +5834	3. 2653 +1789	4. 8521 +6524
5. 72538 +29164	6. 93825 +61943	7. 42351 +16089	8. 51783 +29468
9. 321748 +596317	10. 629634 +789519	11. 639768 +417956	12. 399999 +427835

Set 11

1. 335 558 +219	2. 315 218 +476	3. 598 421 +782	4. 495 342 +687	5. 627 258 +846
6. 3088 7809 +2546	7. 5005 9637 +2824	8. 9057 4706 +3958	9. 6787 2953 +3069	10. 4308 7295 +6578
11. 238 567 429 +531	12. 698 42 385 +756	13. 8276 3755 9284 +3615	14. 4038 192 78 +5964	15. 36175 8930 65274 +5971

Set 12

1. 9 − 4	2. 10 − 7	3. 12 − 9	4. 14 − 5	5. 11 − 8	6. 13 − 5	7. 15 − 6
8. 16 − 8	9. 13 − 6	10. 11 − 9	11. 18 − 9	12. 12 − 8	13. 11 − 4	14. 12 − 7
15. 12 − 6	16. 14 − 6	17. 17 − 9	18. 13 − 4	19. 15 − 7	20. 14 − 7	21. 16 − 9

Set 13

1. 58 − 36	2. 68 − 13	3. 82 − 55	4. 54 − 29	5. 90 − 38	6. 64 − 38
7. 62 − 58	8. 56 − 49	9. 87 − 48	10. 62 − 46	11. 55 − 35	12. 87 − 87
13. 50 − 42	14. 92 − 43	15. 81 − 27	16. 73 − 16	17. 64 − 48	18. 76 − 39

Set 14

1. 784 − 198	2. 328 − 136	3. 334 − 77	4. 963 − 479	5. 946 − 268
6. 587 − 398	7. 458 − 157	8. 970 − 375	9. 452 − 175	10. 715 − 149
11. 701 − 346	12. 604 − 429	13. 803 − 275	14. 700 − 358	15. 900 − 736

Set 15

1. 5287 − 2158	2. 3964 − 1479	3. 5203 − 3425	4. 7812 − 1699
5. 78134 − 12965	6. 92514 − 30427	7. 63810 − 26593	8. 52004 − 24685
9. 365128 − 159675	10. 965437 − 374882	11. 805604 − 527607	12. 920653 − 819299

Set 16

1. 5 ×5	2. 6 ×8	3. 7 ×4	4. 6 ×5	5. 7 ×7	6. 8 ×5	7. 8 ×3
8. 9 ×5	9. 9 ×3	10. 8 ×8	11. 4 ×9	12. 4 ×8	13. 5 ×7	14. 6 ×9
15. 7 ×9	16. 6 ×6	17. 7 ×8	18. 9 ×9	19. 6 ×7	20. 8 ×9	21. 5 ×9

Set 17

1. 52
×5

2. 76
×5

3. 45
×8

4. 29
×6

5. 53
×6

6. 63
×7

7. 28
×9

8. 36
×6

9. 47
×9

10. 44
×8

11. 78
×5

12. 86
×9

13. 57
×6

14. 48
×8

15. 93
×5

16. 65
×9

17. 74
×7

18. 83
×4

Set 18

1. 342
×2

2. 620
×4

3. 456
×3

4. 578
×9

5. 956
×6

6. 827
×9

7. 578
×7

8. 742
×5

9. 609
×5

10. 693
×2

11. 827
×4

12. 755
×8

13. 819
×7

14. 990
×6

15. 748
×5

Set 19

1. 5216
×2

2. 3805
×3

3. 9174
×5

4. 2636
×8

5. 52813
×6

6. 74159
×5

7. 63820
×4

8. 50073
×7

9. 491432
×8

10. 381764
×6

11. 928314
×9

12. 743448
×7

Set 20

1. 248
×10

2. 326
×10

3. 534
×100

4. 291
×100

5. 753
×100

6. 819
×10

7. 650
×100

8. 748
×10

9. 847
×100

10. 950
×10

11. 966
×10

12. 300
×10

13. 853
×10

14. 700
×100

15. 542
×100

329

Set 21

1. 142
×20

2. 453
×300

3. 836
×70

4. 742
×400

5. 558
×60

6. 945
×90

7. 627
×500

8. 234
×30

9. 915
×700

10. 747
×80

11. 412
×600

12. 900
×50

13. 640
×800

14. 823
×900

15. 370
×40

Set 22

1. 63
×27

2. 62
×45

3. 86
×19

4. 67
×56

5. 99
×18

6. 76
×32

7. 605
×26

8. 567
×33

9. 558
×72

10. 288
×34

11. 693
×40

12. 873
×54

13. 475
×35

14. 320
×62

15. 781
×58

16. 625
×73

17. 914
×86

18. 846
×91

Set 23

1. 572
×121

2. 384
×235

3. 754
×352

4. 848
×218

5. 369
×205

6. 621
×243

7. 519
×309

8. 832
×642

9. 950
×538

10. 783
×436

11. 257
×103

12. 846
×208

13. 435
×236

14. 364
×316

15. 818
×514

Set 24

1. $4\overline{)16}$

2. $6\overline{)24}$

3. $3\overline{)21}$

4. $6\overline{)18}$

5. $3\overline{)27}$

6. $4\overline{)20}$

7. $8\overline{)32}$

8. $4\overline{)36}$

9. $6\overline{)48}$

10. $6\overline{)36}$

11. $5\overline{)40}$

12. $7\overline{)56}$

13. $5\overline{)45}$

14. $4\overline{)28}$

15. $8\overline{)72}$

16. $9\overline{)54}$

17. $6\overline{)42}$

18. $9\overline{)81}$

19. $7\overline{)49}$

20. $8\overline{)64}$

Set 25

1. $4\overline{)48}$
2. $3\overline{)39}$
3. $2\overline{)48}$
4. $5\overline{)55}$
5. $2\overline{)68}$

6. $6\overline{)60}$
7. $2\overline{)84}$
8. $4\overline{)44}$
9. $2\overline{)44}$
10. $3\overline{)93}$

11. $3\overline{)69}$
12. $4\overline{)40}$
13. $5\overline{)50}$
14. $3\overline{)90}$
15. $4\overline{)84}$

Set 26

1. $5\overline{)60}$
2. $2\overline{)74}$
3. $3\overline{)87}$
4. $8\overline{)96}$
5. $5\overline{)75}$

6. $3\overline{)54}$
7. $5\overline{)65}$
8. $6\overline{)84}$
9. $3\overline{)57}$
10. $6\overline{)96}$

11. $4\overline{)92}$
12. $3\overline{)51}$
13. $7\overline{)91}$
14. $2\overline{)64}$
15. $6\overline{)90}$

Set 27

1. $4\overline{)97}$
2. $3\overline{)59}$
3. $5\overline{)78}$
4. $6\overline{)62}$
5. $7\overline{)94}$

6. $6\overline{)79}$
7. $5\overline{)83}$
8. $8\overline{)99}$
9. $3\overline{)44}$
10. $4\overline{)95}$

11. $3\overline{)80}$
12. $7\overline{)87}$
13. $4\overline{)89}$
14. $5\overline{)94}$
15. $6\overline{)94}$

Set 28

1. $2\overline{)784}$
2. $3\overline{)168}$
3. $4\overline{)396}$
4. $2\overline{)840}$
5. $6\overline{)364}$

6. $5\overline{)405}$
7. $3\overline{)748}$
8. $8\overline{)836}$
9. $9\overline{)528}$
10. $4\overline{)848}$

11. $7\overline{)318}$
12. $6\overline{)370}$
13. $4\overline{)409}$
14. $5\overline{)519}$
15. $7\overline{)683}$

Set 29

1. $13\overline{)846}$
2. $23\overline{)690}$
3. $15\overline{)542}$
4. $28\overline{)943}$
5. $16\overline{)706}$

6. $25\overline{)929}$
7. $34\overline{)756}$
8. $23\overline{)758}$
9. $42\overline{)653}$
10. $39\overline{)802}$

11. $43\overline{)829}$
12. $26\overline{)693}$
13. $37\overline{)874}$
14. $30\overline{)658}$
15. $44\overline{)942}$

Set 30

1. 23$\overline{)7821}$ 2. 42$\overline{)5906}$ 3. 18$\overline{)3748}$ 4. 29$\overline{)9261}$ 5. 46$\overline{)7403}$

6. 65$\overline{)8005}$ 7. 37$\overline{)8916}$ 8. 49$\overline{)6413}$ 9. 58$\overline{)5921}$ 10. 70$\overline{)6508}$

11. 83$\overline{)32164}$ 12. 92$\overline{)59708}$ 13. 84$\overline{)35214}$ 14. 76$\overline{)60058}$ 15. 95$\overline{)93774}$

Set 31 **What fraction of the marbles are red?**

1.   2.   3.   4.

5.   6.   7.    8.

Set 32 **Give the "next" three equivalent fractions.**

1. $\frac{1}{2}, \frac{2}{4}, \underline{?}, \underline{?}, \underline{?}$

2. $\frac{1}{6}, \frac{2}{12}, \underline{?}, \underline{?}, \underline{?}$

3. $\frac{2}{5}, \frac{4}{10}, \underline{?}, \underline{?}, \underline{?}$

4. $\frac{5}{4}, \underline{?}, \underline{?}, \underline{?}$

5. $\frac{3}{8}, \underline{?}, \underline{?}, \underline{?}$

6. $\frac{5}{2}, \underline{?}, \underline{?}, \underline{?}$

Set 33 **Reduce to lowest terms.**

1. $\frac{2}{4}$ 2. $\frac{3}{9}$ 3. $\frac{6}{8}$ 4. $\frac{16}{6}$ 5. $\frac{2}{8}$ 6. $\frac{15}{10}$ 7. $\frac{4}{6}$

8. $\frac{3}{12}$ 9. $\frac{6}{4}$ 10. $\frac{2}{6}$ 11. $\frac{3}{6}$ 12. $\frac{6}{9}$ 13. $\frac{8}{6}$ 14. $\frac{4}{12}$

15. $\frac{5}{10}$ 16. $\frac{8}{12}$ 17. $\frac{10}{16}$ 18. $\frac{5}{15}$ 19. $\frac{9}{6}$ 20. $\frac{4}{8}$ 21. $\frac{9}{12}$

Set 34 **< or >?**

1. $\frac{3}{5}$ ⬤ $\frac{2}{5}$ 2. $\frac{4}{9}$ ⬤ $\frac{5}{9}$ 3. $\frac{3}{2}$ ⬤ $\frac{1}{2}$ 4. $\frac{5}{6}$ ⬤ $\frac{1}{6}$

5. $\frac{1}{2}$ ⬤ $\frac{1}{4}$ 6. $\frac{3}{4}$ ⬤ $\frac{1}{2}$ 7. $\frac{5}{8}$ ⬤ $\frac{3}{4}$ 8. $\frac{3}{4}$ ⬤ $\frac{7}{8}$

9. $\frac{1}{2}$ ⬤ $\frac{1}{3}$ 10. $\frac{2}{3}$ ⬤ $\frac{3}{4}$ 11. $\frac{3}{2}$ ⬤ $\frac{2}{3}$ 12. $\frac{4}{3}$ ⬤ $\frac{3}{2}$

Set 35 Add. Give answers in lowest terms.

1. $\frac{3}{5} + \frac{1}{5}$
2. $\frac{1}{6} + \frac{1}{6}$
3. $\frac{3}{8} + \frac{1}{8}$
4. $\frac{4}{9} + \frac{2}{9}$

5. $\frac{1}{4} + \frac{1}{4}$
6. $\frac{5}{8} + \frac{1}{8}$
7. $\frac{5}{6} + \frac{0}{6}$
8. $\frac{5}{9} + \frac{2}{9}$

9. $\frac{2}{3} + \frac{1}{3}$
10. $\frac{5}{6} + \frac{5}{6}$
11. $\frac{3}{2} + \frac{0}{2}$
12. $\frac{3}{8} + \frac{3}{8}$

Set 36 Add. Give answers in lowest terms.

1. $\frac{1}{4} + \frac{3}{4}$
2. $\frac{4}{5} + \frac{3}{5}$
3. $\frac{5}{8} + \frac{1}{8}$
4. $\frac{1}{2} + \frac{0}{4}$

5. $\frac{3}{10} + \frac{3}{5}$
6. $\frac{5}{8} + \frac{1}{4}$
7. $\frac{1}{2} + \frac{7}{8}$
8. $\frac{5}{6} + \frac{5}{6}$

9. $\frac{1}{8} + \frac{3}{4}$
10. $\frac{5}{8} + \frac{3}{4}$
11. $\frac{5}{6} + \frac{1}{3}$
12. $\frac{1}{6} + \frac{2}{3}$

13. $\frac{5}{6} + \frac{4}{3}$
14. $\frac{7}{4} + \frac{5}{8}$
15. $\frac{3}{2} + \frac{3}{8}$
16. $\frac{5}{9} + \frac{5}{3}$

Set 37 Add. Give answers in lowest terms.

1. $\frac{1}{3} + \frac{1}{2}$
2. $\frac{1}{4} + \frac{1}{3}$
3. $\frac{1}{4} + \frac{1}{5}$
4. $\frac{3}{2} + \frac{2}{3}$

5. $\frac{2}{3} + \frac{5}{8}$
6. $\frac{5}{6} + \frac{3}{4}$
7. $\frac{1}{2} + \frac{2}{3}$
8. $\frac{5}{6} + \frac{1}{4}$

9. $\frac{2}{3} + \frac{3}{4}$
10. $\frac{3}{8} + \frac{1}{3}$
11. $\frac{2}{9} + \frac{5}{6}$
12. $\frac{3}{4} + \frac{1}{3}$

13. $\frac{5}{9} + \frac{5}{6}$
14. $\frac{3}{4} + \frac{1}{5}$
15. $\frac{3}{4} + \frac{4}{3}$
16. $\frac{1}{4} + \frac{3}{5}$

Set 38 Subtract. Give answers in lowest terms.

1. $\frac{3}{4} - \frac{1}{4}$
2. $\frac{2}{3} - \frac{1}{3}$
3. $\frac{5}{8} - \frac{1}{8}$
4. $\frac{9}{10} - \frac{1}{10}$

5. $\frac{5}{6} - \frac{1}{6}$
6. $\frac{8}{9} - \frac{2}{9}$
7. $\frac{3}{5} - \frac{1}{5}$
8. $\frac{5}{3} - \frac{1}{3}$

9. $\frac{3}{8} - \frac{1}{8}$
10. $\frac{9}{5} - \frac{4}{5}$
11. $\frac{5}{4} - \frac{3}{4}$
12. $\frac{5}{9} - \frac{2}{9}$

13. $\frac{4}{5} - \frac{4}{5}$
14. $\frac{7}{4} - \frac{1}{4}$
15. $\frac{7}{10} - \frac{3}{10}$
16. $\frac{4}{3} - \frac{2}{3}$

Set 39 Subtract. Give answers in lowest terms.

1. $\frac{1}{2} - \frac{1}{4}$ 2. $\frac{1}{4} - \frac{1}{8}$ 3. $\frac{2}{3} - \frac{1}{6}$ 4. $\frac{2}{5} - \frac{1}{10}$

5. $\frac{3}{8} - \frac{1}{4}$ 6. $\frac{5}{6} - \frac{1}{3}$ 7. $\frac{2}{3} - \frac{5}{9}$ 8. $\frac{5}{6} - \frac{2}{3}$

9. $\frac{7}{8} - \frac{0}{2}$ 10. $\frac{9}{10} - \frac{3}{10}$ 11. $\frac{3}{4} - \frac{5}{8}$ 12. $\frac{7}{10} - \frac{2}{10}$

13. $\frac{4}{3} - \frac{1}{6}$ 14. $\frac{5}{8} - \frac{1}{2}$ 15. $\frac{8}{9} - \frac{2}{3}$ 16. $\frac{3}{2} - \frac{5}{8}$

Set 40 Subtract. Give answers in lowest terms.

1. $\frac{1}{2} - \frac{1}{3}$ 2. $\frac{1}{4} - \frac{1}{6}$ 3. $\frac{3}{4} - \frac{1}{3}$ 4. $\frac{4}{5} - \frac{1}{2}$

5. $\frac{7}{8} - \frac{0}{3}$ 6. $\frac{2}{5} - \frac{1}{6}$ 7. $\frac{3}{2} - \frac{3}{5}$ 8. $\frac{2}{3} - \frac{1}{2}$

9. $\frac{3}{2} - \frac{2}{3}$ 10. $\frac{3}{4} - \frac{2}{3}$ 11. $\frac{7}{8} - \frac{2}{3}$ 12. $\frac{5}{6} - \frac{3}{4}$

13. $\frac{9}{8} - \frac{1}{3}$ 14. $\frac{2}{3} - \frac{3}{10}$ 15. $\frac{3}{2} - \frac{4}{3}$ 16. $\frac{4}{3} - \frac{5}{4}$

Set 41 Change to a fraction.

1. $1\frac{1}{2}$ 2. $2\frac{1}{2}$ 3. $3\frac{2}{3}$ 4. $1\frac{1}{3}$ 5. $3\frac{1}{4}$ 6. $1\frac{2}{3}$ 7. $4\frac{1}{3}$

8. $2\frac{7}{8}$ 9. $1\frac{3}{4}$ 10. $4\frac{2}{3}$ 11. $3\frac{5}{6}$ 12. $1\frac{7}{8}$ 13. $6\frac{1}{2}$ 14. $3\frac{2}{5}$

15. $4\frac{2}{9}$ 16. $3\frac{4}{5}$ 17. $2\frac{3}{5}$ 18. $2\frac{1}{3}$ 19. $4\frac{3}{4}$ 20. $2\frac{5}{8}$ 21. $5\frac{3}{8}$

Set 42 Change to a mixed number.

1. $\frac{4}{3}$ 2. $\frac{5}{4}$ 3. $\frac{11}{8}$ 4. $\frac{3}{2}$ 5. $\frac{9}{8}$ 6. $\frac{5}{3}$ 7. $\frac{6}{5}$

8. $\frac{9}{2}$ 9. $\frac{11}{6}$ 10. $\frac{5}{2}$ 11. $\frac{9}{5}$ 12. $\frac{6}{4}$ 13. $\frac{7}{6}$ 14. $\frac{8}{5}$

15. $\frac{10}{4}$ 16. $\frac{8}{3}$ 17. $\frac{7}{4}$ 18. $\frac{7}{3}$ 19. $\frac{10}{3}$ 20. $\frac{7}{2}$ 21. $\frac{9}{4}$

Set 43

1. $\frac{1}{2}$ of 8 = ?   2. $\frac{1}{3}$ of 18 = ?   3. $\frac{1}{5}$ of 20 = ?   4. $\frac{1}{2}$ of 12 = ?

5. $\frac{1}{4}$ of 16 = ?   6. $\frac{1}{6}$ of 18 = ?   7. $\frac{1}{8}$ of 24 = ?   8. $\frac{1}{4}$ of 24 = ?

9. $\frac{1}{3}$ of 9 = ?   10. $\frac{1}{3}$ of 15 = ?   11. $\frac{1}{2}$ of 6 = ?   12. $\frac{1}{6}$ of 12 = ?

13. $\frac{1}{8}$ of 32 = ?   14. $\frac{1}{5}$ of 30 = ?   15. $\frac{1}{6}$ of 24 = ?   16. $\frac{1}{4}$ of 20 = ?

Set 44

1. $\frac{2}{3}$ of 15 = ?   2. $\frac{5}{8}$ of 40 = ?   3. $\frac{3}{5}$ of 15 = ?   4. $\frac{2}{3}$ of 30 = ?

5. $\frac{5}{3}$ of 21 = ?   6. $\frac{4}{3}$ of 12 = ?   7. $\frac{3}{4}$ of 36 = ?   8. $\frac{5}{6}$ of 36 = ?

9. $\frac{3}{4}$ of 12 = ?   10. $\frac{3}{2}$ of 16 = ?   11. $\frac{2}{3}$ of 24 = ?   12. $\frac{5}{9}$ of 18 = ?

13. $\frac{4}{5}$ of 20 = ?   14. $\frac{4}{3}$ of 18 = ?   15. $\frac{3}{8}$ of 24 = ?   16. $\frac{3}{4}$ of 24 = ?

Set 45   Multiply. Give answers in lowest terms.

1. $\frac{1}{4} \times \frac{1}{2}$ = ?   2. $\frac{1}{3} \times \frac{3}{4}$ = ?   3. $\frac{5}{8} \times \frac{4}{5}$ = ?   4. $\frac{2}{9} \times \frac{3}{4}$ = ?

5. $\frac{5}{8} \times \frac{3}{4}$ = ?   6. $\frac{2}{3} \times \frac{2}{3}$ = ?   7. $\frac{5}{6} \times \frac{3}{5}$ = ?   8. $\frac{7}{8} \times \frac{4}{7}$ = ?

9. $\frac{3}{10} \times \frac{5}{2}$ = ?   10. $3 \times \frac{1}{2}$ = ?   11. $\frac{4}{3} \times \frac{7}{10}$ = ?   12. $\frac{4}{3} \times \frac{4}{3}$ = ?

13. $\frac{4}{5} \times 3$ = ?   14. $\frac{3}{4} \times \frac{4}{3}$ = ?   15. $\frac{2}{3} \times \frac{3}{2}$ = ?   16. $2 \times \frac{3}{8}$ = ?

Set 46   Divide. Give answers in lowest terms.

1. $\frac{3}{8} \div \frac{1}{8}$ = ?   2. $\frac{4}{5} \div \frac{2}{5}$ = ?   3. $\frac{1}{6} \div \frac{4}{5}$ = ?   4. $\frac{5}{8} \div \frac{3}{4}$ = ?

5. $\frac{2}{5} \div \frac{4}{5}$ = ?   6. $\frac{5}{4} \div \frac{1}{2}$ = ?   7. $\frac{5}{6} \div \frac{5}{3}$ = ?   8. $\frac{3}{8} \div \frac{3}{2}$ = ?

9. $\frac{4}{9} \div \frac{2}{3}$ = ?   10. $\frac{5}{9} \div \frac{4}{3}$ = ?   11. $\frac{3}{8} \div \frac{1}{2}$ = ?   12. $\frac{2}{3} \div \frac{3}{5}$ = ?

13. $\frac{5}{9} \div \frac{2}{3}$ = ?   14. $\frac{4}{5} \div \frac{1}{2}$ = ?   15. $\frac{3}{2} \div \frac{5}{4}$ = ?   16. $\frac{7}{8} \div \frac{3}{4}$ = ?

Set 47 Give a decimal for the number of shaded squares.

1.   2.   3.

4.   5. ... ...   6.   ...

Set 48   In 821.946, what digit is in the

1. hundreds place?   2. tens place?

3. ones place?   4. hundredths place?

5. thousandths place?   6. tenths place?

Set 49   <, =, or >?

1. 7.28 ⬤ 7.36   2. 52.8 ⬤ 51.9   3. 35.6 ⬤ 3.52

4. 6.080 ⬤ 6.08   5. 93.74 ⬤ 93.7   6. 5.3 ⬤ 5.30

7. 18.394 ⬤ 18.4   8. 63.41 ⬤ 6.341   9. 17.281 ⬤ 17.29

10. 16.04 ⬤ 16.040   11. 5.964 ⬤ 5.963   12. 36.04 ⬤ 36.40

13. 43.61 ⬤ 4.4   14. 7.528 ⬤ 7.582   15. .367 ⬤ 1.0

Set 50

1. 4.6 +7.8	2. .49 +.76	3. 2.04 +1.67	4. 2.35 +9.93	5. 82.3 +79.9	6. .237 +.994
7. 5.75 +9.39	8. 6.78 +4.56	9. 3.76 +9.88	10. 83.8 +51.9	11. 20.3 +50.8	12. 99.9 +99.9
13. .275 +.396	14. .582 +.491	15. 6.84 +4.75	16. 8.94 +3.67	17. 9.74 +3.62	18. .358 +.297

Set 51

1. 9.6
− 4.3

2. 4.9
− 2.4

3. 6.09
− 4.04

4. 46.0
− 39.5

5. 84.6
− 23.9

6. .463
− .397

7. 4.60
− 1.39

8. 95.8
− 23.9

9. 6.04
− 4.87

10. 56.3
− 21.8

11. .835
− .598

12. 6.00
− 3.95

13. .342
− .168

14. 92.3
− 25.8

15. .205
− .096

16. 8.61
− 3.95

17. .431
− .278

18. .520
− .274

Set 52 Add or subtract.

1. 3.64
+2.5

2. 3.64
− 2.5

3. 4.78
+1.9

4. 4.78
− 1.9

5. .881
+.69

6. .881
− .69

7. 4.3
+2.65

8. 4.3
− 2.65

9. .835
+.67

10. .835
− .67

11. .9
+.354

12. .9
− .354

13. 5
+3.42

14. 5
− 3.42

15. 2.64
+.8

16. 2.64
− .8

17. 28
+5.9

18. 28
− 5.9

Set 53

1. 3 wk = ? da

2. 12 wk = ? da

3. 63 da = ? wk

4. 48 da = ? wk ? da

5. 10 da = ? h

6. 28 h = ? da ? h

7. 200 h = ? da ? h

8. 15 h = ? min

9. 420 min = ? h

10. 500 min = ? h ? min

11. 7 min = ? s

12. 250 s = ? min ? s

Set 54 How much time?

1. 9:15 to 9:30

2. 8:10 to 8:50

3. 6:20 to 7:00

4. 3:00 to 4:25

5. 6:00 to 7:50

6. 5:25 to 7:00

7. 10:45 to 12:30

8. 9:20 to 11:00

9. 8:50 to 10:00

10. 2:15 to 3:50

11. 4:24 to 6:35

12. 7:55 to 9:45

Set 55

1. 20 mm = _?_ cm
2. 40 mm = _?_ cm
3. 70 mm = _?_ cm
4. 100 mm = _?_ cm
5. 24 mm = _?_ cm
6. 52 mm = _?_ cm
7. 83 mm = _?_ cm
8. 125 mm = _?_ cm
9. 6 cm = _?_ mm
10. 5 cm = _?_ mm
11. 8 cm = _?_ mm
12. 13 cm = _?_ mm
13. 5.1 cm = _?_ mm
14. 4.6 cm = _?_ mm
15. 3.4 cm = _?_ mm

Set 56

1. 3 m = _?_ cm
2. 8 m = _?_ cm
3. 15 m = _?_ cm
4. 28 m = _?_ cm
5. 1.5 m = _?_ cm
6. 2.4 m = _?_ cm
7. 13.6 m = _?_ cm
8. 34.3 m = _?_ cm
9. 500 cm = _?_ m
10. 350 cm = _?_ m
11. 442 cm = _?_ m
12. 625 cm = _?_ m
13. 4 km = _?_ m
14. 12 km = _?_ m
15. 1100 m = _?_ km

Set 57

1. 3000 mL = _?_ L
2. 2500 mL = _?_ L
3. 3400 mL = _?_ L
4. 2560 mL = _?_ L
5. 2 L = _?_ mL
6. 5 L = _?_ mL
7. 5.2 L = _?_ mL
8. 8.4 L = _?_ mL
9. 4000 g = _?_ kg
10. 7000 g = _?_ kg
11. 6800 g = _?_ kg
12. 800 g = _?_ kg
13. 5 kg = _?_ g
14. 6.2 kg = _?_ g
15. .782 kg = _?_ g

Set 58 Add or subtract.

1. 3 ft 5 in.
   +1 ft 2 in.

2. 6 ft 8 in.
   +3 ft 9 in.

3. 25 ft 9 in.
   +12 ft 3 in.

4. 30 ft 11 in.
   +26 ft 9 in.

5. 4 yd 1 ft
   +3 yd 1 ft

6. 8 yd 2 ft
   +5 yd 1 ft

7. 9 yd 2 ft
   +7 yd 2 ft

8. 22 yd 1 ft
   +18 yd 2 ft

9. 9 ft 7 in.
   − 2 ft 3 in.

10. 7 ft 4 in.
   − 3 ft 6 in.

11. 12 ft 1 in.
   − 4 ft 9 in.

12. 20 ft
   − 8 ft 4 in.

13. 5 yd 2 ft
   − 1 yd 1 ft

14. 8 yd 1 ft
   − 5 yd 1 ft

15. 16 yd 1 ft
   − 7 yd 2 ft

16. 24 yd
   − 13 yd 1 ft

Set 59

1. 8 c = _?_ pt
2. 4 qt = _?_ gal
3. 6 qt = _?_ half-gal
4. 14 pt = _?_ qt
5. 5 qt = _?_ pt
6. 3 gal = _?_ qt
7. $5\frac{1}{2}$ gal = _?_ qt
8. 18 pt = _?_ c
9. $4\frac{1}{2}$ qt = _?_ pt
10. $5\frac{1}{2}$ pt = _?_ c
11. $2\frac{1}{2}$ gal = _?_ qt
12. $1\frac{3}{4}$ gal = _?_ qt
13. 5 lb = _?_ oz
14. 9 lb = _?_ oz
15. 150 oz = _?_ lb _?_ oz

Set 60

1. $\boxed{3 \text{ for } 49\text{¢}}$
How much for 1?

2. $\boxed{4 \text{ for } 69\text{¢}}$
How much for 1?

3. $\boxed{3 \text{ for } \$2.00}$
How much for 2?

4. $\boxed{5 \text{ for } \$1.19}$
How much for 2?

5. $\boxed{3 \text{ for } 89\text{¢}}$
How much for 2?

6. $\boxed{4 \text{ for } 85\text{¢}}$
How much for 3?

Set 61 Compute the sale price.

1. $\$1.50$ $\frac{1}{3}$ off
2. $\$2.80$ $\frac{1}{4}$ off
3. $\$4.56$ $\frac{1}{2}$ off
4. $\$5.25$ $\frac{1}{4}$ off
5. $\$4.89$ $\frac{1}{3}$ off
6. $\$6.00$ $\frac{1}{5}$ off
7. $\$8.20$ $\frac{1}{6}$ off
8. $\$7.75$ $\frac{2}{3}$ off
9. $\$8.20$ $\frac{3}{4}$ off

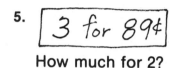
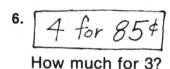

Set 62 Add. Give answers in lowest terms.

1. $3\frac{1}{3}$
$+2\frac{1}{3}$

2. $4\frac{1}{4}$
$+3\frac{1}{8}$

3. $4\frac{1}{4}$
$+2\frac{1}{4}$

4. $5\frac{1}{2}$
$+2\frac{3}{8}$

5. $3\frac{1}{3}$
$+4\frac{1}{3}$

6. $5\frac{3}{8}$
$+3\frac{3}{8}$

7. $6\frac{2}{5}$
$+3\frac{1}{10}$

8. $5\frac{4}{9}$
$+2\frac{1}{3}$

9. $9\frac{1}{2}$
$+8\frac{1}{3}$

10. $7\frac{1}{9}$
$+5\frac{2}{3}$

11. $6\frac{1}{3}$
$+6\frac{1}{2}$

12. $8\frac{2}{5}$
$+4\frac{1}{2}$

339

Set 63 Add. Give answers in lowest terms.

1. $5\frac{1}{2}$ $+2\frac{3}{4}$

2. $5\frac{1}{4}$ $+3\frac{3}{4}$

3. $5\frac{1}{2}$ $+3\frac{1}{4}$

4. $8\frac{3}{8}$ $+9\frac{3}{4}$

5. $6\frac{1}{3}$ $+4\frac{7}{9}$

6. $7\frac{3}{8}$ $+9\frac{5}{8}$

7. $7\frac{3}{4}$ $+1\frac{5}{8}$

8. $8\frac{2}{3}$ $+6\frac{1}{2}$

9. $9\frac{1}{4}$ $+6\frac{1}{2}$

10. $7\frac{5}{9}$ $+4\frac{2}{3}$

11. $4\frac{3}{4}$ $+7\frac{2}{3}$

12. $7\frac{2}{3}$ $+3\frac{5}{6}$

Set 64 Subtract. Give answers in lowest terms.

1. $8\frac{7}{8}$ $-2\frac{3}{8}$

2. $5\frac{3}{4}$ $-3\frac{1}{2}$

3. $9\frac{5}{8}$ $-2\frac{1}{4}$

4. $9\frac{5}{6}$ $-4\frac{1}{3}$

5. $6\frac{3}{4}$ $-3\frac{3}{8}$

6. $8\frac{1}{3}$ $-4\frac{2}{9}$

7. $7\frac{1}{2}$ $-4\frac{1}{4}$

8. $8\frac{1}{3}$ $-3\frac{1}{6}$

9. $3\frac{5}{6}$ $-1\frac{1}{3}$

10. $6\frac{5}{8}$ $-3\frac{1}{4}$

11. $4\frac{1}{2}$ $-1\frac{1}{3}$

12. $5\frac{5}{8}$ $-1\frac{3}{8}$

Set 65 Subtract. Give answers in lowest terms.

1. $8\frac{1}{5}$ $-2\frac{4}{5}$

2. $3\frac{1}{6}$ $-1\frac{5}{6}$

3. $7\frac{1}{3}$ $-3\frac{2}{3}$

4. $10\frac{1}{4}$ $-5\frac{3}{4}$

5. $9\frac{3}{8}$ $-\frac{5}{8}$

6. $7\frac{1}{3}$ $-\frac{2}{3}$

7. $5\frac{1}{4}$ $-2\frac{1}{2}$

8. $9\frac{2}{3}$ $-6\frac{3}{4}$

9. $8\frac{1}{3}$ $-4\frac{5}{9}$

10. $5\frac{2}{5}$ $-3\frac{9}{10}$

11. $7\frac{1}{3}$ $-6\frac{5}{9}$

12. $9\frac{1}{6}$ $-3\frac{3}{4}$

Set 66

1. 5.29 $\times.5$

2. 35.8 $\times.4$

3. 71.5 $\times.6$

4. 42.7 $\times.3$

5. .826 $\times.7$

6. 6.66 $\times.2$

7. 81.1 $\times.8$

8. 74.2 $\times.6$

9. 8.56 $\times.9$

10. .674 $\times.3$

Set 67

1. .3 ×.2	2. .4 ×.2	3. .3 ×.3	4. .03 ×.2	5. .04 ×.2

6. 1.04 ×2.5	7. 34.6 ×3.7	8. 7.81 ×5.8	9. 50.3 ×63	10. 605 ×4.3

11. 71.7 ×1.58	12. 82.9 ×20.9	13. 6.48 ×534	14. 83.5 ×3.21	15. 96.3 ×2.76

Set 68

1. 3)52.5   2. 5)3.045   3. 4)27.36   4. 8)4.968   5. 6)94.44

6. 9)7.533   7. 7)25.34   8. 2)4.798   9. 8)579.2   10. 9)3.951

11. 23)14.72   12. 15)1.875   13. 42)348.6   14. 68)29.24   15. 74)466.2

Set 69

1. 8)3   2. 4)3   3. 8)9   4. 4)5   5. 8)11

6. 2)1.7   7. 4)1.5   8. 4)29   9. 8)47   10. 2)4.5

11. 34)7.82   12. 43)98.9   13. 65).78   14. 78)2.652   15. 54)1.998

Set 70   Multiply or divide.

1. 52.6 × 10   2. .391 × 100   3. .748 × 1000
4. 6.352 × 1000   5. 7.419 × 100   6. 3.006 × 10
7. 82.7 ÷ 10   8. 94.3 ÷ 100   9. 658 ÷ 1000
10. 7215 ÷ 1000   11. 396.8 ÷ 100   12. 44.06 ÷ 10

EXTRA PROBLEM SOLVING

Set 1

Use the chart to find the total number of calories in each meal.

Food	Calories
apple, medium	100
beans, green, 1 cup	30
blueberry muffin	150
bun, hamburger	100
butter, pat	50
coleslaw, 1 cup	110
corn flakes, 1 cup	50
egg, boiled	100
hamburg patty	200
ice cream, 1 cup	300
lettuce	15
milk, 1 cup	150
noodle soup, 1 cup	150
oatmeal, 1 cup	100
orange juice, 1 cup	100
peas, 1 cup	75
potato, baked	90
strawberry shortcake	300
sirloin steak, 3 oz.	225
toast, 1 slice	75
tomato, 1 medium	40

1. 1 boiled egg
   1 slice of toast
   1 pat of butter
   1 cup of milk

2. 2 boiled eggs
   1 cup of orange juice
   1 blueberry muffin

3. 1 cup of oatmeal
   1 cup of milk
   2 slices of toast
   2 pats of butter

4. 1 cup of corn flakes
   1 cup of milk
   1 blueberry muffin
   2 pats of butter
   1 cup of orange juice

5. 1 hamburg patty
   1 hamburger bun
   1 cup of orange juice
   lettuce
   1 medium tomato

6. 2 cups of noodle soup
   1 cup of milk
   1 medium tomato
   1 cup of coleslaw

7. 2 hamburg patties
2 hamburger buns
1 cup of milk
1 cup of ice cream

8. 2 boiled eggs
1 medium tomato
lettuce
2 blueberry muffins

9. 1 3-oz. sirloin steak
1 cup of peas
1 baked potato
1 strawberry shortcake

10. 1 hamburg patty
2 cups of green beans
1 cup of coleslaw
2 blueberry muffins

11. 1 3-oz. sirloin steak
1 baked potato
2 medium tomatoes
1 cup of peas
1 cup of green beans

12. 2 hamburg patties
1 cup of coleslaw
1 medium tomato
2 slices of toast
2 pats of butter
1 cup of milk

Tell which meal has more calories.

13. **a.** 2 boiled eggs
2 slices of toast
2 pats of butter
1 cup of milk

 b. 2 boiled eggs
1 cup of orange juice
2 blueberry muffins
1 cup of milk

14. **a.** 1 hamburg patty
1 hamburger bun
1 cup of milk
1 cup of ice cream

 b. 2 cups of noodle soup
1 cup of milk
1 medium apple
2 blueberry muffins

15. **a.** 1 cup of noodle soup
1 hamburg patty
1 cup of peas
1 medium tomato

 b. 1 cup of orange juice
1 hamburg patty
1 cup of coleslaw
1 medium tomato

16. **a.** 1 3-oz. sirloin steak
1 medium tomato
1 baked potato
1 strawberry shortcake

 b. 1 3-oz. sirloin steak
2 medium tomatoes
2 cups of green beans
lettuce
1 cup of ice cream

Set 2

1. The Wilsons are planning a trip to Rapid River, which is 412 kilometers from their home. How far will the round trip be?

2. The Wilsons live 412 kilometers from Rapid River. During the first morning they drove 186 kilometers. How much farther did they have to drive to get to the river?

3. Vince took $7.65 and Paige took $9.00. How much more did Paige take?

4. The Wilsons arrived at 8:05 A.M. The rafts were to leave at 9:15 A.M. How many minutes did they have to wait?

5. For the 3-day float trip, the adult tickets were $32.50 and the children's tickets were $18.75. How much did 2 adult tickets and 2 children's tickets cost?

6. The total number of people that the 5 rafts could take was 205. 138 tickets had been sold. How many more could they sell?

7. Before the float trip, Vince bought some lemonade for $.75, a sandwich for $1.65, and some insect repellent for $1.79. How much did he spend?

8. Paige took with her 2 rolls of film. She could take 36 pictures on each roll. During the first day she took 29 pictures. How many more pictures could she take?

9. Vince helped serve the hot dogs at the first night's camp. He served 2 each to 118 people and 1 each to 87 people. How many hot dogs did he serve?

10. The 3-day float trip covered 121 kilometers. The first day they floated 37 kilometers and the second day 41 kilometers. How far did they float the third day?

11. All 205 people returned to the starting point in 2 large buses and 3 small buses. Each large bus took 56 people. How many people rode the smaller buses?

12. Paige bought 2 postcards for $.22 each and a *Tales of Rapid River* booklet for $3.79. How much did she spend in all?

Set 3

**Tickets Sold for
School Fun Night**

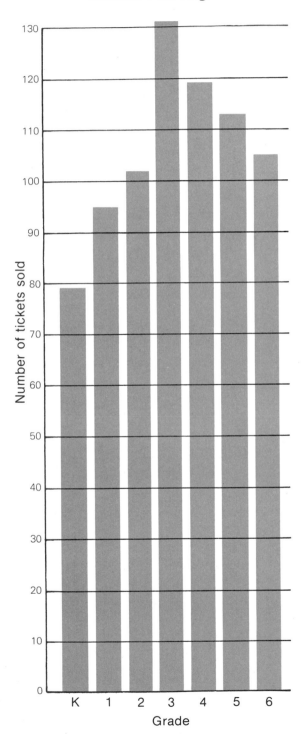

The bar graph shows the number of tickets sold by each grade for the school Fun Night.

1. How many tickets were sold by the kindergarten?

2. Which grade sold the most tickets?

3. How many grades sold more than 110 tickets?

4. How many grades sold less than 100 tickets?

5. Which grade sold exactly 102 tickets?

6. How many grades sold more than the sixth grade?

7. At the end of the first week, 397 tickets had been sold. The school's goal was to sell 450 tickets during the first week. How many tickets short of the goal were they?

8. The sixth-grade goal was to sell 120 tickets. By how many tickets were they short of their goal?

9. Find the total number of tickets sold by grades K, 1, and 2.

10. What was the total number of tickets sold?

11. The school goal was to sell 900 tickets. By how many tickets did they miss their goal?

12. The sixth grade sold how many more tickets than the kindergarten?

13. The fifth and sixth grades sold how many more tickets than the first and second grades?

14. There were 519 adult tickets sold and 225 children's tickets sold. How many more adult tickets were sold?

15. Of the 744 people who bought tickets, 658 went to Fun Night. How many did not go to Fun Night?

16. The school made $372 on tickets and $243.20 on refreshments, and spent $78.75 for door prizes. How much profit did they make?

Set 4

1. Leon wants to buy a $139.95 camera. He can trade his old camera in for $25. How much will the difference be?

2. Leon has $146.18. If he trades his old camera in on the new one, how much money will be left? (See exercise 1.)

3. Later Leon bought a roll of black-and-white film for $1.97, a roll of colored film for $2.85, and some flashbulbs for $2.59. What was the total cost?

4. The Shutter Store charges $2.85 for colored film and $4.69 for developing the film. What is the total cost?

5. Thirty-six pictures can be taken with one large roll of film. How many pictures can be taken with 4 rolls?

6. Leon wants to buy $45 worth of darkroom supplies. He has $31.19 and can earn $6.50 for mowing a lawn. How much more will he need then?

7. Before going on his summer vacation, Leon bought 3 rolls of 24 exposures and 2 rolls of 36 exposures. How many pictures is that?

8. One photo company charges 8¢ a picture for developing black-and-white film. How much would they charge for 3 rolls of 24?

9. One store charges $1.59 for developing 24 black-and-white pictures. Another charges 8¢ for each picture. How much cheaper is the first store?

10. One of Leon's albums has 64 pages. If he puts 9 pictures on a page, how many pictures will the album hold?

11. Leon bought two 48–page albums that hold 8 pictures per page. How many pictures will the albums hold?

12. The Shutter Store charged $2.85 for colored film and $4.69 for developing. During a special, they sold and developed the film for $5.95. How much would the savings be on 2 rolls?

Set 5

DIAL-DIRECT						
sample rates from Champaign, Illinois, to:	**WEEKDAY** full rate		**EVENING** 35% discount		**NIGHT & WEEKEND** 60% discount	
	First Minute	Each Additional Minute	First Minute	Each Additional Minute	First Minute	Each Additional Minute
Atlanta, Ga.	.50	.34	.32	.23	.20	.14
Boston, Mass.	.50	.34	.32	.23	.20	.14
Denver, Colo.	.50	.34	.32	.23	.20	.14
Detroit, Mich.	.48	.34	.31	.23	.19	.14
Los Angeles, Cal.	.52	.36	.33	.24	.20	.15
Miami, Fla.	.52	.36	.33	.24	.20	.15
Milwaukee, Wis.	.46	.32	.29	.21	.18	.13
Minneapolis, Minn.	.48	.34	.31	.23	.19	.14
New Orleans, La.	.50	.34	.32	.23	.20	.14
New York, N.Y.	.50	.34	.32	.23	.20	.14
Seattle, Wash.	.52	.36	.33	.24	.20	.15
Washington, D.C.	.50	.34	.32	.23	.20	.14

1. During the week, is it cheaper to call in the daytime or in the evening?

2. Which are cheaper, evening rates or night rates?

3. For a weekday call to Atlanta, what is the charge for the first minute? The second minute?

4. For an evening call to Los Angeles, what is the charge for the first minute? The second minute?

5. What is the charge for a 2-minute evening call to Los Angeles? *Hint:* See exercise 4.

6. What is the charge for a 2-minute weekday call to New York?

Use the table to find the cost of a

7. 3-minute weekday call to Atlanta.

8. 5-minute weekday call to New Orleans.

9. 15-minute evening call to Seattle.

10. 28-minute night call to Detroit.

11. 2-hour evening call to New York.

How much cheaper is it to call at night than to call during a weekday for a

12. 9-minute call to Boston?

13. 17-minute call to Miami?

14. 25-minute call to Washington, D.C.?

15. 38-minute call to Denver?

16. 1-hour call to Minneapolis?

Set 6

1. **Tickets**

   Adult: $3.25
   Child: $1.35

   How much for one child and one adult?

2. **Home Games**

   162 games in all
   79 played away

   How many are played at home?

3. **Seats in Section**

   28 seats in each row
   9 rows

   How many seats?

4. **Bat Night**

   $1.85 a bat
   258 given away

   What was the total cost?

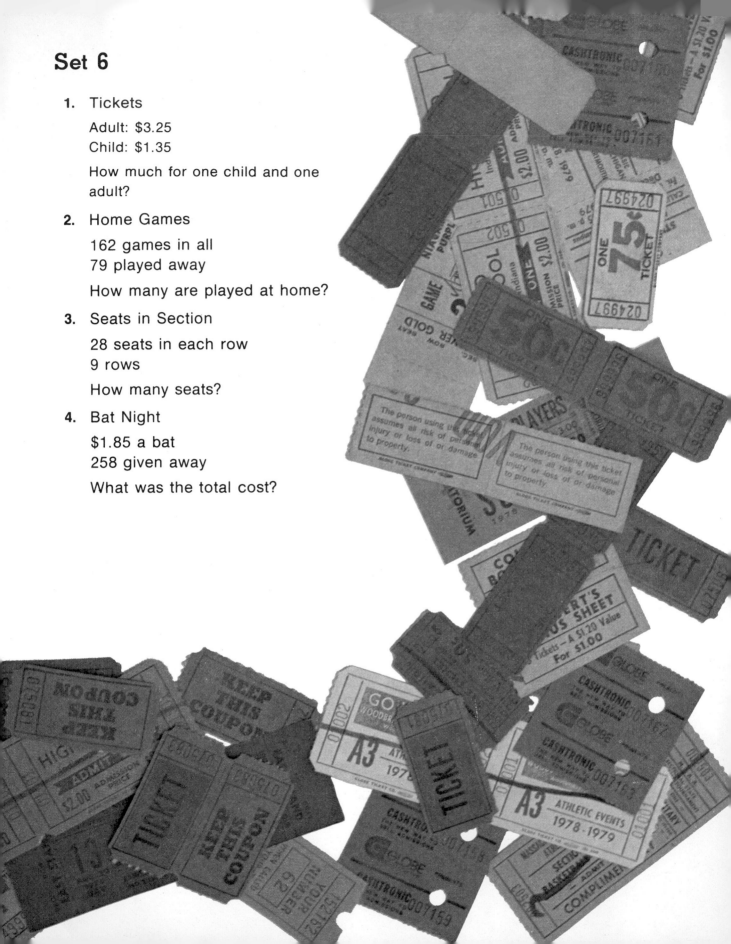

5. Day's Attendance

32,508 seats
19,759 came to game

How many empty seats?

6. Refreshments

Popcorn: $.75
Peanuts: $.60
Soft drink: $.60

What is the total?

7. Program

Cost: $1.25
Gave: $5 bill

How much change?

8. Seats in Bleachers

3,252 seats in all
6 sections the same size

How many seats in each
section?

9. Number of Games

162 games during season
95 games played

How many games left to play?

10. Home Runs

8 players
112 home runs in all

What is the average per player?

11. Attendance at Home

Total attendance: 168,840
Number of days: 9

What was the average daily
attendance?

12. Year's Attendance

Average per game: 13,593
Games: 95

What was the attendance for
the 95 games?

Set 7

1. One hundred eighteen fifth-graders and ninety-eight sixth-graders went on a field trip to visit a bicycle factory. How many students went on the field trip?

2. Each bus could take 24 students. How many buses were needed for the field trip? (See exercise 1.)

3. The buses left the school at 9:25. They arrived at the factory at 10:15. How long did it take to get to the bicycle factory?

4. Each tour guide could take 27 students. How many guides were needed for the 216 students?

5. The students first saw a film on a bicycle race. The winner rode 124 kilometers in 4 hours. How many kilometers did he average per hour?

6. One tour guide said that the workers built 73,819 bicycles last year and expect to build 85,000 this year. How many more will be built this year?

7. After seeing a safety film, the students toured the factory. One worker could build a frame in 48 minutes. How long would it take her to build 18 frames?

8. A certain frame takes 3 meters of large tubing. How much tubing is needed for an order of 739 such frames?

9. Another worker put 4 reflectors on each bicycle. He finished 6 bicycles an hour. How many reflectors could he install in an 8-hour day?

10. Some workers built wheels. Each wheel took 36 spokes. How many wheels could be built with 10,000 spokes? How many spokes would be left over?

11. The average hourly wage was $6.32. At that rate, how much would a worker receive for a 40-hour week?

12. After the tour, each of the 216 students was given an $.85 reflector and a $.40 decal. What was the total value of the gifts?

Better Burgers

Sonic Burger	$1.59
Better Burger	1.29
Better Burger with cheese	.95
Double Burger	1.15
Ham and Cheese	1.75
Fish Sandwich	1.35
French Fries	.49
Onion Rings	.65
Apple Pie	.45

Drinks

Cola, Orange	
Small	.30
Medium	.45
Large	.60
Shakes	
Small	.75
Medium	.90
Large	1.15
Coffee	.25
Milk	.30

Give the total price of

1. 1 Sonic Burger
   1 French Fries
   1 Medium Cola

2. 2 Better Burgers
   1 Onion Rings
   2 Large Orange

3. 3 Double Burgers
   2 French Fries
   2 Small Shakes
   1 Large Cola

4. 4 Fish Sandwiches
   2 French Fries
   2 Onion Rings
   3 Large Shakes
   1 Medium Orange

Solve.

5. Alan bought a large shake and a burger for $2.44. Which burger did he buy?

6. At Better Burgers, Alan spent $2.44, Rick spent $1.84, and David spent $2.50. What was the average amount spent?

7. John had $5. He bought a Sonic Burger, an apple pie, and 2 milks. How much money did he have left?

8. Sara and a friend had $3.65. They each wanted to buy a Double Burger, French fries, and a small shake. How much more money did they need?

9. Alice wants to treat some friends to a small cola. She has $2. How many colas can she? How much would she have left over?

10. One week Sonic Burgers were on special for $1.25 each. How much would the savings be on 18 Sonic Burgers?

11. A Little League coach treated her 15 players at Better Burgers. She spent $29.25. What was the average spent per player?

12. The same team saved Better Burgers coupons for a year. They saved 509 coupons. If it takes 12 coupons for a Sonic Burger, how many can they get? How many coupons will be left?

Set 9

The circle graph shows the results of a school survey. For example, it shows that baseball was the favorite sport of $\frac{1}{4}$ of the students surveyed.

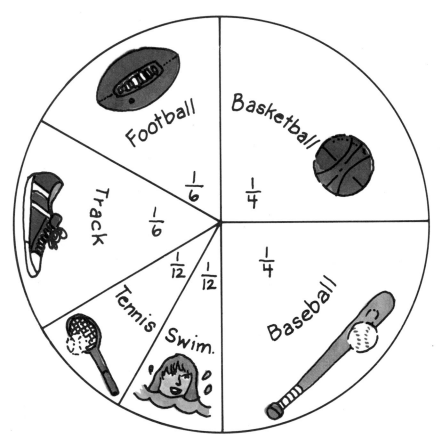

1. There were 624 students in the school. Only 208 were in the survey. How many were not in the survey?

2. What fraction of the students were surveyed? (See exercise 1.)

3. During lunch hour, 13 people each surveyed 9 students. How many students were surveyed during lunch hour?

4. Thirteen students conducted the survey of the 208 students. What was the average number of students surveyed by each?

5. Did more students choose baseball or swimming?

6. What fraction of the students did not choose baseball?

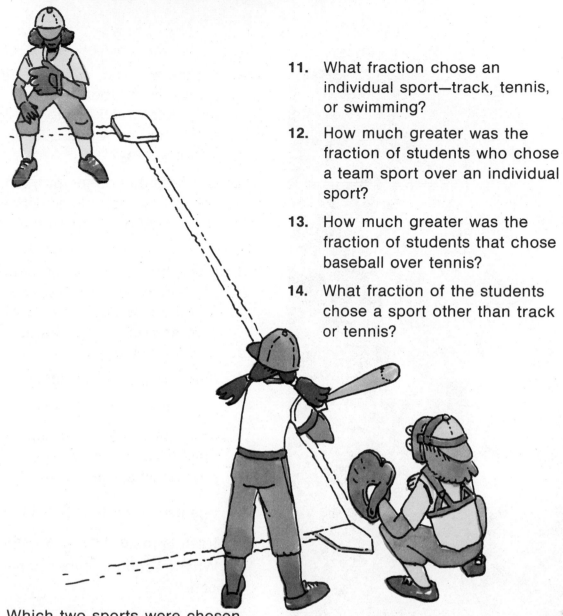

11. What fraction chose an individual sport—track, tennis, or swimming?

12. How much greater was the fraction of students who chose a team sport over an individual sport?

13. How much greater was the fraction of students that chose baseball over tennis?

14. What fraction of the students chose a sport other than track or tennis?

7. Which two sports were chosen by half of the students?

8. What fraction of the students liked either football or baseball?

9. What fraction liked either tennis or track?

10. What fraction chose a team sport—baseball, basketball, or football?

Set 10

1. On the average, each American throws away about 2000 pounds of trash each year. How many pounds would a family of 4 throw away?

2. Of the 2000 pounds of trash, about 1200 pounds are paper. How many pounds are not paper?

3. If you throw away 2000 pounds of trash in a year, how much would you average per week? Give answer as the nearest whole number.

4. If you throw away 2000 pounds of trash a year and $\frac{1}{6}$ is cans, how many pounds of cans is that? Give answer as the nearest whole number.

5. It is estimated that $\frac{3}{5}$ of the trash is paper and $\frac{1}{6}$ is cans. What fraction is either paper or cans?

6. About $\frac{1}{6}$ of the trash is cans and $\frac{1}{16}$ is bottles. How much greater is the fraction for cans?

7. One-eighth of the trash is bottles and plastic products. What fraction of the trash is not bottles or plastic?

8. Of the 1200 pounds of paper that each person throws away, only $\frac{1}{5}$ is recycled. How many pounds is that?

9. Suppose that you throw away 40 pounds of trash per week. If $\frac{3}{5}$ of it is paper, how many pounds of paper is that?

10. Suppose that you throw away 40 pounds of trash per week. If $\frac{1}{16}$ is bottles and $\frac{1}{16}$ is plastic products, how many pounds of bottles and plastic products do you throw away?

11. An elementary school raised money by collecting 6000 pounds of aluminum cans. They were paid $34.75 a ton (2000 pounds). How much money did they get?

12. A merchant will pay 7¢ each for returnable soft-drink bottles. How much refund will there be for 2 cases of bottles? (There are 24 bottles in a case.)

Set 11

1. Mrs. Rogers' class could make 9 small valentines from 1 piece of construction paper. How many could be made from 36 pieces of construction paper?

2. The class had $13.50 to buy materials for making valentines. They spent $4.75 for paper, $3.15 for paste, $2.50 for glitter, and $2.65 for ribbon. How much money did they have left?

3. Mrs. Rogers bought 14 yards of ribbon for $4.48. What was the average price per yard?

4. They got 9 jars of paste for $3.15. What was the price of one jar?

5. They got $\frac{3}{4}$ yard of red ribbon and $\frac{2}{3}$ yard of white ribbon. How many yards was that?

6. The class had $\frac{3}{4}$ yard of red ribbon and used $\frac{2}{3}$ of a yard. How much red ribbon was left?

7. One kind of valentine called for $\frac{2}{3}$ foot of lace. How much lace would be needed for 6 such valentines?

8. The class had 3 packages of glitter. One-fourth package was needed for each valentine. How many glitter valentines could they make?

9. Alfredo had $\frac{3}{4}$ of a yard of pink ribbon. If he used $\frac{1}{4}$ yard per valentine, how many valentines could he make?

10. Allison made 36 valentines. She gave $\frac{2}{3}$ of them to her classmates. How many was that?

11. Eight class members each brought 2 dozen cookies to the valentine party. How many cookies were brought to the party?

12. Three class members made 10 quarts of punch. If there are 32 ounces in a quart, how many ounces should each of the 28 children get? Round your answer to the nearest ounce.

Set 12

1. This year 834 people watched the all-city track meet. This was an increase of 106 people over last year. How many people watched the meet last year?

2. The bleachers had 16 rows with 64 seats in a row. How many people would they hold?

3. If 834 people watched the track meet, how many empty seats were there? (See exercise 2.)

4. There were 352 adult tickets and 482 student tickets sold for the track meet. Adult tickets sold for $.75 and student tickets sold for $.35. What was the total?

5. Members of the swimming team sold lemonade at the track meet. They sold 92 lemonades for $.45 each. How much money did they get?

6. The total sales from cold drinks were $82.65, and the popcorn sales totaled $72.50. The total expenses were $37.52. How much profit was made?

7. Of the 75 students who competed in the track meet, $\frac{2}{5}$ were girls. How many girls is that?

8. The times for the 100-meter dash were: Jones, 12.24 seconds; Davis, 12.42 seconds; Weaver, 11.94 seconds; Montez, 11.09 seconds. Who had the best (least) time?

9. In the 100-meter dash, Montez (11.09 seconds) set a new all-city record by .18 second. What was the old record?

10. The relay team ran the 4 laps in the 1600-meter relay in 59.3, 60.1, 59.5, and 58.9 seconds. What was the total time?

11. The first- and last-place times in the 200-meter dash were 26.03 seconds and 29.58 seconds. What was the difference in the times?

12. A year ago, Grace ran the 400-meter race in 62.23 seconds. This year she bettered her time by 2.47 seconds. What was her time this year?

Set 13

1. **Supplies**

   Had $45
   Spent $38.53

   How much money was left?

2. **Packing Supplies**

   336 pounds
   12 hikers

   How many pounds for each?

3. **Height of Mountain**

   Base: 1,309 feet
   Peak: 6,159 feet

   How high is the mountain?

4. **Rest Stops**

   First stop: $\frac{1}{2}$ hour

   Second stop: $\frac{3}{4}$ hour

   How long did they rest?

5. Drinking Water

12 hikers

$\frac{3}{4}$ quart per hiker

How many quarts in all?

7. Ate Soup

Made $1\frac{1}{2}$ gallons

Ate $1\frac{1}{4}$ gallons

How much was left?

8. Distance Hiked

First day: $6\frac{1}{2}$ miles

Second day: $8\frac{2}{3}$ miles

How many miles in all?

9. Making Chili

8 packages

$\frac{3}{4}$ quart of water
  for each package

How much water?

10. Sleep

Went to bed at 10:30 P.M.
Got up at 6:00 A.M.

How many hours of sleep?

11. Fishing Stream

Caught 34 trout
Average weight: 14 ounces

How many pounds of fish?
Round your answer to the
nearest whole number.

6. Hiking Time

Before lunch: $3\frac{1}{2}$ hours

After lunch: $2\frac{3}{4}$ hours

How many hours in all?

12. Returning Home

Trail up: $15\frac{1}{6}$ miles

Trail back: $18\frac{3}{4}$ miles

How much longer was the trail
back?

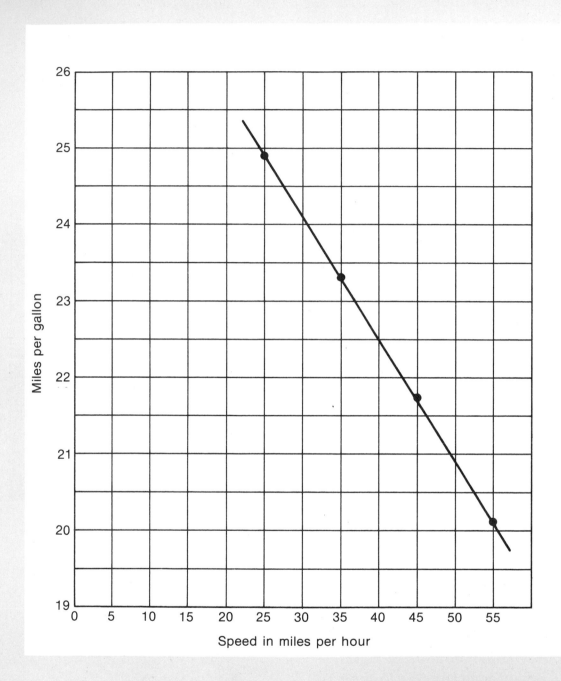

The line graph shows the number of miles per gallon that a certain car averages at different speeds. Use the graph to solve the following problems.

How many miles per gallon can be averaged at

1. 25 miles per hour?
2. 35 miles per hour?
3. 45 miles per hour?
4. 55 miles per hour?

At about what speed do you get

5. 20 miles per gallon?
6. 22 miles per gallon?

What is the difference in miles per gallon at 55 miles per hour and

7. 45 miles per hour?
8. 25 miles per hour?

At 55 miles per hour, how far should you travel on

9. 10 gallons?
10. 15.5 gallons?
11. 12.8 gallons?

Suppose that the tank holds 18.5 gallons. How much farther could you drive on a full tank of gas at 25 miles per hour than at

12. 35 miles per hour?
13. 45 miles per hour?
14. 55 miles per hour?

Suppose that the tank holds 18 gallons and is half full. About how far could you drive at

15. 25 miles per hour?
16. 40 miles per hour?

Set 15

1. It is 683 miles from Chicago to Tulsa and 1452 miles from Tulsa to Los Angeles. How far is the entire route?

2. It is 1067 miles from Milwaukee to Jacksonville. A trucker had driven 679 miles. How many miles did he have left to go?

3. A certain truck could haul 15 tons (30,000 pounds). How many 345-pound crates could it haul? Round your answer down to the nearest whole number.

4. The tanks of a certain truck hold 82.5 gallons. It took 57.6 gallons of fuel to fill the tanks. How much fuel was in the tanks before they were filled?

5. The trucker paid $1.15 per gallon for 57.6 gallons of fuel. What was the total cost? Round your answer to the nearest cent.

6. During the next 235.8 miles the truck used 52 gallons of fuel. How many miles per gallon did it average? Round your answer to the nearest tenth.

7. The Kellys have a truck payment of $683.45 a month. How much is that per year?

8. During 12 hours, Mr. and Mrs. Kelly drove their truck 625.2 miles. How many miles per hour did they average?

9. A certain toll road charged them 6.74¢ per mile. How much did they pay for 87.5 miles? Round your answer to the nearest cent.

10. On the return trip they hope to average 6.3 miles per gallon. If so, could they travel 500 miles after filling their tanks (82.5 gallons)?

11. The license plates cost $13.84 per year and the insurance costs $87.35 a month. How much do they spend for license and insurance each year?

12. One year they drove their truck 117,507 miles. How many miles did they average per month?

Toll Roads		
Name	*Length (miles)*	*Price per Mile*
Atlantic City Expressway	44	2.85¢
H. E. Bailey Turnpike	86.4	1.97¢
Bluegrass Parkway	72	1.81¢
Connecticut Turnpike	129	1.55¢
Garden State Parkway	173	1.59¢
Hutchinson River Parkway	14.5	1.67¢
Indiana National Turnpike	105.2	2.14¢
Indiana Toll Road	157	1.78¢

1. What is the combined length of the Atlantic City Expressway and the Garden State Parkway?

2. How much longer is the Indiana National Turnpike than the H. E. Bailey Turnpike?

3. How many of the toll roads are more than $1\frac{1}{2}$ ¢ a mile?

4. Which toll road is about 6 times as long as the Hutchinson River Parkway?

5. Which toll road is 42.6 miles longer than the H. E. Bailey Turnpike?

6. What is the difference in price per mile of the Atlantic City Expressway and the Garden State Parkway?

7. How much would it cost to travel 9 miles on the Bluegrass Parkway? Round your answer up to the next cent.

8. The Gomez family paid $1.24 (124¢) to drive 80 miles on one of the toll roads listed above. Which toll road did they drive?

9. How much more would it cost to drive 50 miles on the Atlantic City Expressway than on the Indiana Toll Road? Round your answer up to the next cent.

10. Suppose that you drove the entire length of the Connecticut Turnpike. What would be the cost? Round your answer to the next cent.

11. Mr. Austin drove 34.5 miles on the Indiana National Turnpike. How much did it cost? Round your answer up to the next cent.

12. Ms. Lindstrom drives the entire Hutchinson River Parkway to and from school. How much does she pay each way? Round your answer up to the next cent. How much would she spend in a week (5 days)?

Glossary

acute angle An angle whose measure is less than 90°.

addend A number used in an addition problem.

$$9 \leftarrow \text{addend}$$
$$+4 \leftarrow \text{addend}$$
$$13 \leftarrow \text{sum}$$

angle A figure formed by two rays with the same endpoint.

area The number of unit squares that cover a figure. The area of this figure is 5 square centimeters.

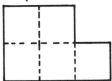

average The average of 4, 5, 5, 7, and 9 is 6. To find the average, add the numbers and divide by the number of numbers.

bisect To cut into halves.

The segment is bisected.

The angle is bisected.

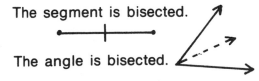

Celsius temperature (°C) The metric temperature scale in which 0°C is the freezing point of water and 100°C is the boiling point of water.

centimeter A metric unit of length. One centimeter is one hundredth of a meter.

circle A curved figure with all points a given distance from the center.

circumference The distance around a circle.

common denominator A common denominator for $\frac{1}{2}$ and $\frac{1}{3}$ is 6, because $\frac{1}{2} = \frac{3}{6}$ and $\frac{1}{3} = \frac{2}{6}$. A common denominator is a common multiple of the denominators of the two fractions.

common factor 2 is a common factor of 4 and 6, because 2 is a factor of 4 and a factor of 6.

common multiple 30 is a common multiple of 5 and 6, because it is a multiple of 5 and a multiple of 6.

congruent figures Figures that have the same size and shape.

corresponding parts In congruent figures, the parts that fit are called corresponding parts.

cube A rectangular solid with all edges the same length.

decimal In a decimal a dot (decimal point) is written between the ones place and tenths place.

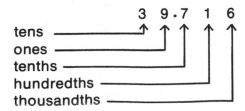

degree A unit for measuring angles. This is a 1° (1 degree) angle.

denominator In $\frac{2}{3}$, the denominator is 3.

diameter The distance across a circle through its center.

2 cm

difference The answer to a subtraction problem.

$$\begin{array}{r} 7 \\ -3 \\ \hline 4 \end{array} \leftarrow \text{difference}$$

discount An amount subtracted from the regular price of an item.

equation A sentence with an equals sign, such as

$$3 \times 9 = 27$$

equilateral triangle A triangle with all sides congruent.

equivalent fractions Fractions for the same number. $\frac{1}{2}$, $\frac{2}{4}$, and $\frac{3}{6}$ are equivalent fractions.

even number A multiple of 2.

factors Numbers used in a multiplication problem.

$$\begin{array}{r} 8 \leftarrow \text{factor} \\ \times 6 \leftarrow \text{factor} \\ \hline 48 \leftarrow \text{product} \end{array}$$

fraction A number such as $\frac{1}{2}$, $\frac{3}{4}$, and $\frac{4}{6}$.

gram A unit of weight (mass) in the metric system. One gram is one thousandth of a kilogram.

graph A picture used to show numerical information.

greater than A comparison of two numbers that are not the same. The symbol is >. For example, 7 > 2. (Another comparison is *less than*.)

greatest common factor The greatest common factor of 8 and 12 is 4. The other common factors are 2 and 1.

grouping property of addition Changing the grouping of the addends does not change the sum. Also called the associative property of addition.

$$(7 + 3) + 2 = 7 + (2 + 3)$$

hexagon A plane figure with six sides.

interest A payment for the use of money.

isosceles triangle A triangle with two congruent sides.

kilogram A unit of weight (mass) in the metric system. A kilogram is 1000 grams.

kilometer A unit of length in the metric system. A kilometer is 1000 meters.

least common multiple The least (smallest) common multiple of 2 and 3 is 6. Other common multiples are 12, 18, 24, 30, and so on.

less than A comparison of two numbers that are not the same. The symbol is <. For example, 3 < 8. (Another comparison is *greater than*.)

line of symmetry If a figure can be folded along a line so the two parts of the figure match, the fold line is a line of symmetry.

line of symmetry

liter A unit of volume in the metric system.

meter A unit of length in the metric system. A meter is 100 centimeters.

metric system An international system of measurement that uses meter, liter, gram, and Celsius temperature.

milliliter A unit of volume in the metric system. One milliliter is one thousandth of a liter.

millimeter A unit of length in the metric system. One millimeter is one thousandth of a meter.

mixed number A number that has a whole-number part and a fraction part. $2\frac{3}{4}$ is a mixed number.

multiple A product. 0, 4, 8, 12, 16, 20, and so on, are multiples of 4.

numerator In $\frac{2}{3}$, the numerator is 2.

obtuse angle An angle whose measure is greater than 90°.

odd number A whole number that is not divisible by 2. The numbers 1, 3, 5, 7, 9, 11, and so on, are odd.

order property of addition The order in which two numbers are added does not change the sum. Also called the commutative property of addition.

$$7 + 9 = 9 + 7$$

order property of multiplication The order in which two numbers are multiplied does not change the product. Also called the commutative property of multiplication.

$$7 \times 9 = 9 \times 7$$

ordinal number The numbers *first*, *second*, *third*, *fourth*, *fifth*, and so on, are ordinal numbers. They tell the order of objects.

parallel lines Lines in a plane that do not cross.

percent (%) Percent means per hundred. 5% is a percent. It equals $\frac{5}{100}$.

perimeter The distance around a figure. The sum of the lengths of the sides.

2 cm   3 cm   4 cm

The perimeter is 9 cm.

perpendicular lines Lines that intersect to form right angles.

place value A system for writing numbers in which the value of a digit is determined by its position.

prime number 2, 3, 5, 7, 11, 13, and so on, are prime numbers. They cannot be obtained by multiplying smaller whole numbers.

protractor A "ruler" for measuring angles.

quadrilateral A plane figure with four sides.

quotient The answer to a division problem.

radius The distance from the center of a circle to the circle.

ratio A comparison of two quantities by division. In a quadrilateral, the ratio of sides to diagonals is 4 to 2, 4:2, or $\frac{4}{2}$.

ray A part of a line that has one endpoint. This is ray AB.

$$A \bullet\!\!-\!\!\bullet\!\!-\!\!-\!\!\to$$
$$\quad\quad B$$

reciprocal Two numbers are reciprocals if their product is 1.

$$\frac{3}{4} \times \frac{4}{3} = 1$$
$$\text{reciprocals}$$

rectangle A figure with four sides and four square corners.

rectangular solid A box whose flat surfaces are all rectangles. A rectangular solid has length, width, and height.

remainder The number "left over" after a division.

$$\begin{array}{r} 5 \\ 3\overline{)16} \\ -15 \\ \hline 1 \end{array} \leftarrow \text{remainder}$$

right angle An angle whose measure is 90°.

round To replace a number by another one that is easier to use. You round a number to the nearest ten by choosing the nearest multiple of ten. (5 is rounded up.)

$$13 \to 10 \quad\quad 27 \to 30 \quad\quad 45 \to 50$$

You round a number to the nearest hundred by choosing the nearest multiple of one hundred.

$$487 \to 500 \quad 1238 \to 1200 \quad 550 \to 600$$

sales tax A tax paid when you make a purchase.

scalene triangle A triangle with no congruent sides.

segment Part of a line that has two endpoints. This is segment AB, segment BA, $\overline{AB}$, or $\overline{BA}$.

square A rectangle with all four sides congruent.

symmetry A figure has symmetry if it can be folded so the two parts of the figure match.

triangle A figure with three sides.

vertex The point at the "corner" of an angle, plane figure, or solid figure.

vertex   vertex   vertex

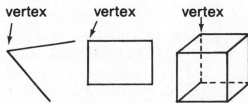

whole number Any of the numbers 0, 1, 2, 3, 4, and so on.

Index

1 2 3 4 5 6 7 8 9 0